D0883635

TWO RENAISSANCE MYTHMAKERS

Two Renaissance Mythmakers

CHRISTOPHER MARLOWE AND BEN JONSON

Selected Papers
from the English Institute, 1975–76

New Series, no. 1

Edited, with a Foreword, by Alvin Kernan

WITHDRAWI

THE JOHNS HOPKINS UNIVERSITY PRESS
BALTIMORE AND LONDON

Manufactured in the United States of America

The Johns Hopkins University Press, Baltimore, Maryland 21218
The Johns Hopkins Press Ltd., London

Library of Congress Catalog Number 77-3518
ISBN 0-8018-1971-7

Library of Congress Cataloging in Publication data
will be found on the last printed page of this book.

Contents

Foreword

In his essay "Ben Jonson" (1919), T. S. Eliot noted the close similarities in the plays of Marlowe and Jonson and went on to remark that "if Jonson's comedy is a comedy of humours, then Marlowe's tragedy, a large part of it, is a tragedy of humours." Eliot's suggestion that these two seemingly very different writers resemble one another in very basic ways has by now been accepted and critically elaborated. Marlowe and Jonson stand as the mythmakers whose works express in direct, relatively undisguised, even grotesque images the fundamental energies and conflicts that drove the English drama forward and made a great theater out of what was before then, for all its vitality and attractiveness, a folk tradition of popular entertainment. Jonson, of course, thought of himself as no rough progenitor but as a remarkably sophisticated dramatist, perhaps the only one writing for the English theater, and Marlowe believed that his sophisticated "tragic glass" would replace the scorned older drama, the "jigging veins of rhyming mother wits." But in the light of history, the works of both are the basic myths underlying the main body of Elizabethan and Jacobean drama.

It is therefore very fitting that the English Institute arranged a panel on Ben Jonson in 1975, chaired by Professor Jonas Barish, and followed it in the succeeding year with papers on Christopher Marlowe. With one exception (Professor Snow's essay on Marlowe) the papers given on those occasions make up this volume. Taken together, they constitute a remarkably coherent exploration, despite the instructively wide variety of critical methods used, of the dramatic energy that Marlowe handles in a heroic and Jonson in a comic fashion.

Marlowe created, of course, the heroic and tragic archetypes of the drama, the "overreachers" as Harry Levin has called them: the great warrior who conquers all the world, the merchant and politician who accumulate all wealth and power, the sensualist who pursues pleasure into death, the great scholar-scientist who sells his soul for knowledge. Jonson gives us the other, the comic, side of the coin, and in his plays the same energies take shape as the great trickster and pretender, Volpone; a pair of swindler scientists, the alchemists Face and Subtle; fools on the heroic scale, like Justice Overdo and Sir Epicure Mammon; or zealous hypocrites, like Zeal-of-the-land Busy. Heroic or comic, the figures are all outsize, grotesque images of the major directions in which the men of the Renaissance sought power, knowledge, and control over the world. And all threaten to destroy the still essentially medieval order of contemporary society by refusing to accept limit, control, or hierarchy.

The appearance, first, of a great tragic mythmaker, and then at some later time of a comic mythmaker who parodies the tragic figures seems to be a characteristic pattern in our few great dramatic periods. Aeschylus and Aristophanes, Corneille and Molière, Strindberg and Bernard Shaw, all present in direct, almost crude forms, the titanic and the ludicrous aspects of the great energies disrupting the traditional orders of society in search of fulfillment. It remained for their more subtle, more skeptical and comparatively more realistic fellows, those dramatists who were the centers of their dramatic traditions—Sophocles, Shakespeare, Racine, Ibsen, and Chekhov—to give these great energies and the figures who voiced them full dramatic existence by turning monologue into a dialogue that gives conflicting values full expression, by transforming rhetoric into a dramatic poetry that opens up the complex depths of character and the strange conflicts of motivation, and by extending episode into a plot that reveals the steady change that life endures in the course of time.

To take up Marlowe first because he was chronologically first, the four essays on this playwright all center on trying to identify and define the nature of the reaching for transcendence that, though always finally unsatisfied, is central to Marlowe's plays. Majorie Garber uses a formalistic critical method to define the basic Marlovian pattern "closure in inclosure," the paths by which the thrust for the infinite arrives at last at a literal and a psychological confinement, Barabas in his cauldron, Faustus in the hellmouth, and all the heroes in the aspiring words they have so grandly uttered. For Professor Garber, the essential Marlovian myth is that of Dedalus, which Michael Goldman translates as "ravishment," the condition of being "aroused by a single source to the possibility of entire bliss." Goldman's approach is from the direction of the actor and stage performance, and he sees the actor, mirroring the Marlovian character, giving himself totally, from the very outset of the play, to some object or idea: beauty, conquest, wealth, knowledge. But once achieved, the object sought is soon scorned as mere "trash," and the character is left with a desire of even greater intensity that can never seem to find a satisfactory object. The Marlovian character and actor play their part to the hilt from the start, commit themselves totally to desire, where, as Goldman points out most interestingly, the Shakespearean character—Hamlet, Othello, Brutus—is always unwilling to play at the outset of his play and is only brought gradually and reluctantly to full commitment.

Stephen Greenblatt looks at the Marlovian energy, at least initially, from a social and historical point of view: "it is his own countrymen that [Marlowe] broods upon and depicts." Marlowe's heroes, like the Renaissance philosophers and explorers, are, in Greenblatt's view, increasingly "homeless," lost in a boundless space and time, an endless number of possible social structures and identities, and desperately committing titanic and savage acts, endlessly repeated, "as a means of marking boundaries, effecting transformations, signalling closure." But the results, as all of our essayists note, are ironic, and no matter how desperate the acts, how frequently repeated, the consciousness of longing cannot be quelled or "all intimations of unreality silenced." Edward Snow, concentrating on *Doctor Faustus*, uses a phenomenological method to take an even more radical view of the nature of the Marlovian desire or energy and to show with great subtlety "how complex the relationship between subjective and objective experience is" in this play. For Snow, the most revealing elements of the play are not characters or patterns of action but words like "end," "terminate," "conclusion," etc., and he traces the ironic use of these terms—ironic from the viewpoint of author and audience— as Faustus keeps trying to create a self and construct his own identity out of emptiness by positing "ends" towards which he futilely moves. All of this makes of Marlowe a very modern consciousness, and very little of a Renaissance moralist, but all our essayists agree in finding this quality of desperate and ultimately defeated effort at self-definition or "character making" to be the central energy of the plays, the essential element of the myth.

Gabriele Jackson defines the connection between Marlowe and Jonson, arguing that the "basic Renaissance fantasy" is "the fantasy of self-sufficiency," which holds sway in the drama from *Doctor Faustus* to *The Duchess of Malfi*, and in the real world captures "the minds of absolute monarchs, of lone explorers, of merchants seeking patents for monopolies." Marlowe's and Jonson's characters share this fantasy, in Professor Jackson's view, and the very different effects achieved by the two dramatists are those appropriate to tragedy and comedy. In Marlovian, and in all, tragedy, the fantasy takes terrifying form because there is no "authoritative social reality" that controls or limits it; while in Jonsonian comedy, "reality prevails" and the fantasy is deflated and revealed as an impossible dream.

Hermaphroditism is a prime image of a characteristic Jonsonian "fantasy of self-sufficiency," and the essay follows through the ways in which this and other dreams of being a world unto the self are exploded and the dreamers brought into some necessary, if temporary, relationship with others and with the social order of a community.

Comedy such as this depends very much on the firmness with which the controlling "reality" is presented and supported, and some part of the special tone of Jonson comes from the fact that despite his pronounced and frequently self-claimed reputation as a moralist, his plays are not always unambiguous and rock-solid in their depiction of moral and social authority. This is Ian Donaldson's subject, and he remarks that "To read Jonson's work as a whole is to be made . . . acutely aware of the dynamic, shifting, and various nature of Jonson's moral thought." Jonson may always ultimately bring his characters, in poems and in plays, to the bar of justice and administer to them strong doses of reality and morality, but that reality is always somewhat too shaky for much reassurance, and in Donaldson's view, Jonson has a "habit of humorously and gently questioning the propriety of being a moralist at all."

Dealing primarily with the poems, Richard Newton nevertheless still finds a Jonson with the "two differing apprehensions of the texture of our life," so central to the plays. On the one hand, there is the skeptical "Baconian" Jonson "inclined to fragments more than to wholes and to denials more than to affirmations," the reducer of life to its most basic and undeniable realities, most often expressed in aphorism, maxim, epigram:

> The Baconian aphorism and the typical Jonsonian epigram certainly strive for a similar authority. But they seek the authority while performing the multiple tasks of rejecting received and external authority, offering a new and personal observation of empirical reality, and attempting to establish a sense of authority which is not merely personal.

On the other hand, there is Jonson the follower of Sir Philip

Sidney, the poet of "lyric impulse" who "tends not to posit a Baconian world stripped to its merely brazen facts and broken into discrete pieces but rather directly to affirm instead a special world, a golden, coherent, and ornamental one." Newton is doubtless right that the Baconian realistic point of view prevailed in Jonson's poetry over the Sidnean impulse to song and expansive release, and he may even be right in going on to remark that "While one of the greatest of our poets, Jonson is the author of remarkably few of those poems which make up our anthologies. The Bacon in him seems to balance too evenly with the Sidney for single poems of his to stand comfortably alone." But if this is correct for Jonson's lyric poetry, it is not at all true for his drama, since theater as a form is better designed to express just such contradictory impulses in all their fullness, and the opposing forces that Newton finds at work in the grammar and structure of Jonsonian poetry are the same impulses and energies that our other essays have shown to be at work in the drama.

While using a wide variety of critical terms and methods, these essays center in trying to define some kind of dramatic aspiration, some violent commitment found in both Marlowe and Jonson that seems determined to hammer out new realities in a world where the old boundaries and limitations have lost definition and certainty. At the same time, the essays all agree that for all of the daring and energy voiced in these plays, neither characters nor playwrights ever quite succeed in breaking free of some kind of limits and controls, and yet these controls and limits never seem entirely solid or certain either.

Both Marlowe and Jonson are finally presented as showing with mythic directness and power the central social and psychological energies and conflicts of their own age, and of the modern world that was then coming into being. But such was the uneasy nature of the idea that the heroic myth never quite managed to escape the limits it needed to transcend to avoid appearing somewhat grotesque, bombastic, and ludicrous even to itself. As Barabas disappears into his pot and Faustus into his fire-belching hellmouth, it is difficult to avoid at least some sense of bathos. On the other hand, the comic myth never quite managed to put its energies firmly enough in their social place to eliminate entirely a certain nervous quality in the laughter as Volpone recites his litany of pleasure, Sir Epicure Mammon envisions all the world as lust and gold, and Zeal-of-the-land Busy with absolute certainty of the righteousness in his own heart tears down the gingerbread stand and the toy stalls of the fair.

ALVIN KERNAN
Princeton, 1977

CHRISTOPHER MARLOWE

Marjorie Garber

"Infinite Riches in a Little Room"

CLOSURE AND ENCLOSURE IN MARLOWE

As audiences and readers have long been aware, much of the dramatic tension in Marlowe's plays derives from the dialectic between aspiration and limitation. Barabas wants infinite riches, Tamburlaine infinite dominion, Faustus infinite knowledge; the Duke of Guise tells us "that like I best that lies beyond my reach" (2.42), and Edward II confesses that he loves Gaveston "because he loves me more than all the world" (1.4.77). Reflecting the aspirations of such characters is a rhetoric of expansiveness, shimmering with far-flung place names and exotic objects: Tamburlaine's conquests, Faustus's travels, Barabas's bags of fiery opals, sapphires, and emeralds. In fact, so consistent is this common impulse toward the infinite—the unbounded, unclosed and unenclosed—that it is personified by Marlowe throughout all the plays in a single figure who is repeatedly evoked as the emblem of perfection—the figure, of course, of Helen of Troy.

Helen makes her only physical appearance in *Doctor Faustus*, the archetypal exposition of the Marlovian fable, and even there she remains unattainable: she will not speak, and we learn that she is a succuba, not really Helen at all. Elsewhere in the plays, we hear of her repeatedly as the paragon of beauty—and the quintessence of destruction. Tamburlaine argues that had Zenocrate "liv'd before the siege of Troy" (*2 Tam.* 2.4.86), it would be she, not Helen, who was the "argument / Of every epigram" (94–95), the ultimate Muse. In *Edward II*, Lancaster angrily draws a comparison between Helen and Gaveston, "That like the Greekish strumpet, train'd to arms / And bloody wars so many valiant knights" (2.4.14–16). Edward's single-minded quest for perfection in love, like that of Paris before him, brings down in ruins an entire world. *Dido, Queen of Carthage*, of

3

course, takes place against the background of the Trojan War, and Dido herself draws the comparison:

> All the world calls me a second Helen
> For being entangled by a stranger's looks . . .
> Would, as fair Troy was, Carthage might be sack'd,
> And I be called a second Helena!
>
> (5.1.144–45, 147–48)

But Dido's Trojan prince chooses duty over love, and it is she, and not her city, who dies in flames.

One pole of the Marlovian universe is thus demarcated by Helen, the unattainable woman and Muse for whose love the walls of Troy were breached and burned. At the other pole stand a number of closely linked figures—Icarus, Phaeton, and Lucifer—who attempt to breach forbidden barriers and are brought to grief for their presumption. Each of these figures has an unattainable object of his own: Icarus,[1] son of Daedalus, attempts to fly too near the sun; Phaeton, Apollo's child, foolishly tries to guide his father's chariot; Lucifer, once an angel "most dearly loved of God" (*Faustus* 1.3.65), rises against Him "in aspiring pride and insolence" (67) and is cast down into the pit. Thus Warwick calls Gaveston an "Ignoble vassal, that like Phaeton / Aspir'st unto the guidance of the sun" (*Edw.* 1.4.16–17), and Lancaster's emblematic device pictures him as a flying fish, devoured by a fowl of the air. Edward, as king, is conventionally associated with the sun, but he is nonetheless no Apollo, rather another Phaeton, pulled down by passions he cannot control. Likewise, Tamburlaine cautions his son against the fate of Phaeton in guiding the royal chariot of state ("As precious is the charge thou undertak'st / As that which Clymene's brain-sick son did guise . . . Be warned by him, then" [*2 Tam.* 5.3.230–31, 234]). Yet, even as he hands over the reins of his chariot, grotesquely drawn by yoked and bitted kings, Tamburlaine resembles not only the father, immortal Apollo, but also the son, Phaeton, striving against his own mortality.

Other Marlovian heroes are more aware of the inevitable trajectory of aspiration and limit. Dido, for example, herself proposes to become an Icarus, that she might fall upon Aeneas's ship and into his arms (5.1.243–46); Mortimer speaks of the "point, to which when men aspire, / They tumble headlong down" (*Edw.* 5.6.60–61), and the Duke of Guise pledges to "mount the top with my aspiring wings, / Although my downfall be the deepest hell" (*Massacre*, 2.46–47). Once again, the most explicit indication of the pattern is to be found in *Doctor Faustus*, where not only are we told in the prologue that Faustus's "waxen wings did mount above his reach" (*Prol.* 21), but we are also confronted in the body of the play with a literal emblem of "aspiring pride and insolence": the personage of Lucifer himself.

The fate of all such aspirants, as the Guise and Mephastophilis agree, is a kind of hell; those who would transcend limits are remanded to a place that "hath no limits, nor is circumscrib'd" (*Faustus* 2.1.120). It is noteworthy that in virtually every play, there is such a descent, and such an enclosure. To give this downward trajectory additional emphasis, Marlowe as dramatist appears to reverse the Augustinian adage that the Lord throws down that He may raise; by contrast Marlowe raises, that he may throw down. In *Faustus* itself, the hell is of course a literal one, "discovered" to audience and actor alike as the Good Angel ascends on a celestial throne. This physically upward movement, which places salvation tantalizingly beyond Faustus's reach, is balanced by his own despairing cry: "O I'll leap up to my God! Who pulls me down?" (5.2.138), as a moment of aspiration again comes too little, too late. In a number of other plays, the hell, the ultimate enclosure, is only slightly masked. Dido immolates herself upon a funeral pyre that is the metaphorical counterpart of her own despair, moments after she has imagined herself like Icarus high above the earth. In Part 1 of *Tamburlaine*, the unfortunate Bajazet, imprisoned in his cage, likens it to the "nooks of hell" (5.1.256), and, sending Zabina away for water to cool his "burning breast" (275), seizes the chance to brain himself against the bars. In Part 2, Tamburlaine himself builds a bonfire in which he burns the holy books of the Mohammedans, declaring that "Mahomet remains in hell; / He cannot hear the voice of Tamburlaine" (5.1.197); fewer than twenty lines later, he finds himself "distemper'd suddenly" (216) with a mortal sickness, and dies, as I have said, with the cautionary tale of Phaeton upon his lips. At the close of *The Jew of Malta*, we see Barabas high in spirit, gloating over the invention of a "dainty gallery" whose floor falls through to catapult the unsuspecting "into a deep pit past recovery" (5.5.35, 38). He begins the scene literally high upon the upper stage, entering "With a hammer, above, very busy" (SD), only to fall into the boiling cauldron, where "the extremity of heat," he says, pinches him "with intolerable pangs" (5.5.89–90). Edward II, once the sun of England and seated high on its throne with Gaveston at his side, dies in a noisome dungeon where all the filth of the castle falls.[2] Harry Levin has pointed out that the name of Lightborn, his executioner, "is nothing more or less than an Anglicization of 'Lucifer,' "[3] and Lightborn ministers to the king with deceptive words, raising Edward for a moment to futile hope. "One jewel have I left," he says (5.5.83), casting his pearls before swine—and the swine then, literally, turn and rend him. Even in *The Massacre at Paris*, King Henry exults at the death of the Duke of Guise, "Monsieur of Lorraine, sink away to hell!" (22.92). In short, play after play finds its closure in enclosure; the inner stage, or discovery space, becomes a version of hell, and a place of final entrapment.

Moreover, when we come to look more comprehensively at the nature of stage properties and the texture of metaphor in the plays, we can, I think, begin to see that enclosure poses a constant threat both to Marlowe's protagonists and to those who get in their way. A glance at the inventory of the Admiral's Company for 1598 found in the Henslowe *Papers* reveals, among

other suggestive properties, the following of particular significance for Marlowe's plays: one cage, one tomb, one hellmouth;
one tomb of Dido; Tamburlaine's bridle; one dragon in *Faustus;*
and of course the notorious "cauldron for the Jew." With the
exception of Faustus's dragon, all of these are enclosing and
restraining artifacts, emblems of the constant attempt by
characters within the plays to control, imprison, and wall
up one another, while maintaining to themselves the fiction
of breaking boundaries down. A brief look at some dominant
patterns in the plays will make the use of such props and stays
clearer.

We may begin, perhaps, with Dido, who from the first
attempts to close off Aeneas from his destiny in Italy. Her
means are frankly sexual; she meets him in a cave, a refuge
from the storm that seems a counterpart of her own passions,
and there they consummate their love. Her question to him,
and his answer, suggest the irony of her situation, the binder
bound:

> *Dido:* Tell me, dear love, how found you out this cave?
> *Aeneas:* By chance, sweet Queen, as Mars and Venus met.
> *Dido:* Why, that was in a net, where we are loose;
>   And yet I am not free—O would I were!
>
> (3.4.3–6)

In her innocence, Dido thinks her lack of freedom comes from
the need to tell her love; in fact, the net of passion holds her,
and cannot hold Aeneas. Not only the cave and the net, but the
very walls of Carthage are emblems of her attempt to encircle
and enclose; Aeneas promises "never to leave these new-
upreared walls, / Whiles Dido lives" (49–50), but again there is a
hidden irony, and the ominous qualification of this promise
leads directly to the funeral pyre. As early as their first meeting,
in Act 2, Aeneas has told a tale that will be the paradigm of
Dido's, the story of Priam's eagerness to welcome the Trojan

horse. "Impatient of delay," he tells her (2.1.173), the king himself became the traitor within his city, and

> Enforc'd a wide breach in the rampir'd wall
> Which thousand battering-rams could never pierce.

(174–75)

Aeneas is Dido's Trojan horse; she welcomes him into her city walls, and into the cave of love, and like "rich Ilion" (264) Dido ends in flames. Tragically, she believes that she has the power to enclose. She seeks the cave, and fails to see the net. "O," she cries, naively, "that I had a charm to keep the winds / Within the closure of a golden ball" (4.4.99–100). But Aeneas, avoiding "her silver arms which coll [i.e., hug, encircle] me round about" (4.3.51), sails for Italy, and leaves her to the ultimate enclosure of the funeral pyre.

In *Tamburlaine*, the equation of enclosure and power is equally marked, and, of course, considerably more successful. Tamburlaine himself seems determined to destroy all enclosures and barriers that stand in his way, from the monumental—the sacking of city walls—to the laughable—the plucking of Mycetes' crown from the ignominious hole where he has hidden it. The remarkably vivid image of Bajazet imprisoned in a cage, and used for a footstool, expresses the essential captivity of humanity, from which Tamburlaine feels himself exempt; the incident, of course, is present in the sources, but clearly its impression on the playwright was so great that he conceived, for Part 2, the even more bizarre spectacle of the chariot of eastern kings. In fact, by Part 2, Tamburlaine's definition of kingship, as told to his sons, is simply "Keeping in iron cages emperors" (1.3.49). The visually spectacular entrance of the chariot in 4.3 makes metaphor into reality, reducing the subject kings to less than human status, while literalizing Tamburlaine's self-chosen role as the scourge of God. But the ultimate barrier he attempts to break is not that of man and beast, but of man and God, and in Part 2 the most quietly startling enclosure of all is the hearse of the unburied Zenocrate that accompanies Tamburlaine everywhere he goes. The play's final stage property, the map of the world, becomes also its final icon of limitation, as the re-frain to his last speeches makes clear: "And shall I die, and this unconquered?" (5.3.150, 158). But even in this play of super-human conquest the encloser is himself enclosed. His mortal body is the final and inescapable enclosure, though death finds him still incredulous: "Shall sickness prove me now to be a man?" (5.3.44).

Though in some ways antithetical in personality, the Jew of Malta is closely congruent to Tamburlaine in his response to enclosure. The "little room," which is his countinghouse, filled with the metals of the Indian mines and the jewels of "the wealthy Moor" (1.1.37; 21) is his equivalent to Tamburlaine's map—the emblem of ultimate conquest. Characteristically, his desires there are expressed in images of compression, enclosing wealth into the smallest possible unit, diamonds and wedges of gold: "And as their wealth increaseth, so inclose / Infinite riches in a little room" (1.1.37–38). Moreover, he has further enclosed a portion of his wealth, "closely hid[den]" (1.2.247) against the search of the Christians, a cache within a cache. He seeks to enclose not only money, but also other people. When his house becomes a nunnery, a socially valued enclosure that paradoxically promises spiritual freedom, he sends his daughter Abigail to violate it. The "nunnery, where none but their own sect / Must enter in" (1.2.253), is ironically a double limitation, enclosing the nuns and excluding all others. Barabas promises Abigail "enlargement" from its confines, as later he offers "enlargement" to Ferneze, but both kinds of escape are actually devices to recapture and reuse these prisoners for his "policy." Twice he lures victims into his house with the promise of a jewel, bait he himself could not resist. Lodowick is offered a diamond, which he understands to mean Abigail, and, coming to the house, quickly meets his death. Barabas pictures him as a violator and lock-picker, in a slyly sexual taunt to his rival Mathias: "And when he comes, she locks herself up fast, / Yet through the key-hole will he talk to her" (2.3.260–61). "O treacherous Lodowick," cries Mathias, and the deed is as good as done. The second jewel, a pearl, is offered to Calymath, the Turkish general, as a way of enticing him and his men into Malta's walls. The soldiers are lured to a monastery, Calymath to the Jew's own house, and all are destined for captivity and death.

As for Barabas himself, he tells us in a famous passage that he walks abroad a-nights, and kills sick people groaning under walls. Averse alike to captivity and sociability, he seems always to be outside walls rather than within them. Appropriately, when the Maltese think him dead, they throw him over the city walls, and characteristically, he makes his triumphal return by tunneling under them through the sewers, at the head of a band of Turks. We have already noticed the series of false rises, or elevations, that precede his final fall into the steaming cauldron; here is yet another:

> Now, whilst you give assault unto the walls,
> I'll lead five hundred soldiers through the vault,
> And rise with them in the middle of the town.

> (5.5.187–89)

The cauldron itself is, of course, the play's final and fitting enclosure; it is also the oversized counterpart of that poisoned pot of porridge Barabas has dispatched, with such glee, as alms to the nunnery. In an ironical parody of Genesis, Ithamore steals, or thinks he steals, Abigail's birthright for a mess of pottage, and reaps her legacy of death. The almost dreamlike enlargement of the pot seems to parallel the transformation of Bajazet's cage into the chariot of kings; if this is to some extent a matter of eleven buckram men grown out of two, it is also a striking visual emblem on the stage, and an appropriate counterpart to the increasing broadness with which Barabas himself is painted.

Interestingly, the pattern of stage enclosure in *Doctor Faustus* offers a close analogy to that in *The Jew*. Here the trajectory leads not from countinghouse to cauldron, but from Faustus's study to hell, from an admirable and chosen enclosure to an enforced and deadly one. Faustus, like Tamburlaine, feels enclosed by his humanity: "Yet art thou still but Faustus, and a man" (1.1.23). His ambitions include not only raising the wind and rending the clouds, but also such enclosing actions as walling Germany with brass and circling "fair Wittenberg" with the "swift Rhine" (1.1.86–87). He rejects the very idea of his own limitation on earth, traversing the globe, reaching back in time for the figures of Helen and Alexander, even liberating the Saxon Bruno from Pope Adrian's order to "bear him . . . to Ponte Angelo, / And in the strongest tower enclose him fast" (3.1.186–87). Curiously, though, when Mephastophilis informs him that "Hell hath no limits" (2.2.12), he rejoins brusquely that "hell's a fable" (136), circumscribing it in a literary category, and thereby attempting to control even the concept of damnation. The most evident visual emblem of his wish to dominate by enclosure is the protective conjuring circle he draws on the floor. But though Mephastophilis dutifully appears to him, it is quickly plain that he has come, as he says, of his own accord, in search of a vulnerable soul, and not in response to Faustus's commands. Like Barabas, Faustus becomes in time his own encloser, trapped by his need to do away with limits. Too late, he comprehends the consequence of this for the mortal soul, and pleads with God to

> Impose some end to my incessant pain:
> Let Faustus live in hell a thousand years,
> A hundred thousand, and at last be sav'd.
>
> (5.3.162–64)

But "no end is limited to damned souls" (165), and the man who sought to transcend limits finds himself forever enclosed by a hell that has none.

A striking contrast to this Faustian pattern is offered, finally, by Edward II, whose attitude towards enclosure more closely resembles that of Dido than that of Marlowe's other protagonists. Edward, in fact, is eager to be enclosed, both in imagery and in action. He is willing to dismantle his entire kingdom and give it to the barons,

> So I may have some nook or corner left
> To frolic with my dearest Gaveston.

> (1.4.72–73)

(Without belaboring the point, I would call this a sexual metaphor, quite like Dido's cave.) At Tynemouth castle he expresses the same sentiment:

> Do what they can, we'll live in Tynemouth here,
> And so I walk with him about the walls,
> What care I though the earls begirt us round?

> (2.2.220–22)

Where Tamburlaine has a chariot drawn by kings, Edward has a wall made of earls. His only impulse toward the realization of excess is the offer to Gaveston of limitless gifts and power, but to this Gaveston replies

> It shall suffice me to enjoy your love,
> Which, whiles I have, I think myself as great
> As Caesar riding in the Roman street
> With captive kings at his triumphant car.

> (1.1.170–73)

Here is the chariot of Tamburlaine yet again, now driven by Gaveston, the Phaeton out of control—and the captive king, now glorying in his captivity, is Edward. As Edward loses power, he progresses from figurative enclosures, like the "nook or corner" in which he dreams of frolicking, toward literal ones:

Tynemouth, Killingworth, Berkeley, even the Welsh monastery where he seeks, unsuccessfully, to renounce the world. Toward the end, he is shunted continually from castle to castle under guard. The whole country has become his prison, because he is a captive to the self, and the final hellish dungeon, with its instruments of torture, is a quintessential version of all the prisons that have gone before. Because he is a king, there *is* no nook or corner for him. He and Gaveston cannot away to prison to sing like birds in the cage; they are caged only to die.

Mortimer, Edward's antithesis as well as his nemesis, is, by contrast, inimical to enclosures of all kinds. "What, Mortimer!" he exclaims,

> Can ragged stony walls
> Immure thy virtue that aspires to heaven?

(3.3.71–72)

In fact, he succeeds in escaping from the Tower of London, appearing to answer his own question, but his Icarian language foreshadows his recapture and subsequent death.

Cave, wall, nunnery, monastery, cage, chariot, countinghouse, study, circle, cauldron—the list of literal enclosures is striking and consistent. There is, however, another kind of enclosure that is repeatedly stressed in the plays, one equally germane to the nature and possibility of power. I refer to the limit represented by language—by the powers of silence and speech. Manifestly, however great its power, language is ultimately an enclosure. Once uttered, a phrase is unalterable and unrecapturable, and may convey the speaker into the power of his hearers, whether they are on or off the stage. A concrete example of this is the fate of letters in Marlowe, which seem always to form an enclosed system that traps the sender. Barabas's feigned challenge to Lodowick returns to accuse him, and so, more vividly, do both the love letter of the Duchess of Guise—which she claims was written to a lady friend—and Mortimer's deliberately "unpointed" letter commanding Edward's death. Spoken words, too, are sometimes dangerous, especially when they are not matched with action. A constant concern of strong protagonists in Marlowe's plays is to limit both their own speech and that of others. Barabas enjoins Abigail to silence when she would plead with Ferneze, and sets the suitors against one another by trusting to the misleading powers of a dumb show: "Here must no speeches pass" (2.3.337). His own language is closely guarded by "policy," and it is only at the moment of his death that he yields to impolitic and unlimited speech: "Tongue, curse thy fill, and die!" (5.5.91). Faustus cautions his spectators not to speak during the presentation of the spirits of Helen and Alexander, nor do the specters speak to him; thus, in the midst of this demonstration of his power as a conjuror, the audiences both on and off the stage are forcibly reminded of its limits.

Tamburlaine praises his confederate's choice of the hortatory mode, which suits with his own degree of power:

> Well said, Theridimas. Speak in that mood,
> For *will* and *shall* best fitteth Tamburlaine.
>
> (3.3.41–42)

Edward, encountering the same rhetorical mode, is its helpless victim:

> Must! 'Tis somewhat hard when kings must go.
>
> (4.6.82)

Tamburlaine has "working words" (2.3.25), "persuasions more pathetical" (1.2.211), but he can do without them; silently he condemns Agydas to death with a wrathful glance, and seals the fate of Damascus and its eloquent virgins with his silent tents of white, red, and black. Even his battle against the "powers of heaven" (*2 Tam.* 5.3.48), which sap his strength, is to be declared with "black streamers in the firmament, / To signify the slaughter of the gods" (49–50). By contrast, Edward, like Mycetes, cannot manage the language of command, and depends instead upon "speaking fair"—that is, upon flattery. He fails to grasp the essential truth that Mortimer shares with Tamburlaine—that language has its limits. Mortimer tells the queen he will not fight "if words will serve; if not, I must" (1.2.83), and advises her to avoid passionate speeches if she aspires to be a warrior. The young king, Edward III, comes of age when he learns the language of command, and is no longer "frighted with words" (5.6.27). He sends his mother to the Tower lest he "pity her if she speak again" (86). Of all the reminders of the limits of language in the plays, however, none is more arresting than Edward's grotesque fantasy of a reward for his queen, who has, at his request, championed the cause of Gaveston:

> I'll hang a golden tongue about thy neck,
> Seeing thou hast pleaded with such good success.
>
> (1.4.327–28)

Here we have perhaps the quintessential example of the false enclosure, which traps the encloser; it is Isabella's success in pleading that ensures the deaths of both Gaveston and Edward himself, keeping them in England rather than permitting them to escape and live.

All these enclosures, physical and verbal, correspond, as we should expect, and in ways I need not specify, to the pattern of meaning generated by the plays that contain them. In each play, however, there is one enclosure that is set apart, and becomes, substantially, a metaphor for the entire action of the play. These enclosures take the form of encapsulated artifacts, literal works of art, that sum up the argument of the play and its intrinsic ambiguities in a single, striking visual gesture. In *Edward II*, this artifact is the letter Mortimer sends to Matrevis and Gurney, artfully insinuating Edward's death. You will remember that the letter is "unpointed"—unpunctuated—and that its message can be variously read "Fear not the king, 'tis good he die," or "Kill not the king, 'tis good to fear the worst"

(5.4.9, 12). Such are the capacities of the Latin tongue. In fact the letter reflects the essential ambiguity of the play—*is* it good to kill the king, either politically or morally? Is the appropriate audience viewpoint one of realpolitik, or of Christian forgiveness? Should we deplore regicide—and if we do, can we yet countenance the reign of an impotent king? Mortimer clearly regards his letter as an open, which is to say ambiguous, device, that will have its intended effect and yet protect him from the consequences. In the event, of course, the letter proves to be yet another enclosure, sealing Mortimer's death when it comes to the new king's hand, and the play's close presents the head of Mortimer and the hearse of Edward simultaneously upon the stage. With its mutually concealing and seemingly contradictory instructions, the letter sums up the conflict at the center of the play, for both of its statements are true.

For *The Jew of Malta*, the symbolic artifact is manifestly the cauldron. We see Barabas like a studious artisan building the "dainty gallery" from which it will hang, busily designing the cranes and pulleys that will hurl its victim below. "Leave nothing loose," he admonishes the carpenters, once more in the language of enclosure. "Why, now I see that you have art indeed" (5.5.4–5). Once again, the artifact is ambiguous, like the apparently benign pot of rice porridge, and once again the artisan becomes the enclosed, not the encloser.

The encapsulated artifact in *Tamburlaine*, as I suggested earlier, is the projected tomb of Tamburlaine and Zenocrate, which he describes at the moment of her death. Throughout his lifetime, he says, he will keep her body with him, unburied, as a deliberate self-deception, a balm to his mind.

> Though she be dead, yet let me think she lives,
> And feed my mind that dies for want of her.
> Where'er her soul be, thou shalt stay with me,
> Embalm'd with cassia, ambergris, and myrrh,

> Not lapp'd in lead, but in a sheet of gold,
> And till I die thou shalt not be interr'd.
>
> (2 Tam. 2.4.127–32)

What Tamburlaine does here is to make Zenocrate's coffin, not into a *memento mori*, but instead into a *memento vitae*, a reminder of life—an emblem, deliberately fictive, of the eternity he somehow imagines will be his. Once again, the emblem is highly ambiguous; the audience may well read the omnipresent coffin as a reminder of death, ironically misconceived by its maker. But Tamburlaine's gesture is superbly myopic, and oddly, if temporarily, successful. In a remarkable dramatic moment in the play's last scene, we see him exchange the chariot of kings for the hearse in which he intends to join his dead queen. Stage manager of his court in life, Tamburlaine plays the same role on his deathbed, commanding first the installation of his son in the chariot, and then the fetching of the hearse. One conveyance, one enclosure, replaces the other, and finally, his mind preoccupied with the story of Phaeton, Tamburlaine enters upon a yet unconquered world.

As for Faustus, his encapsulating artifact is the conjuring circle he lays out in 1.3, which is meant to protect him from dangerous spirits:

> Within this circle is Jehovah's name
> Forward and backward anagrammatiz'd;
> Th' abbreviated names of holy saints,
> Figures of every adjunct to the heavens,
> And characters of signs and erring stars
> By which the spirits are enforc'd to rise.
>
> (1.3.8–13)

The "anagrammatiz'd" name was a staple of necromantic practice, but it also provides, like Mortimer's letter, an additional hint of verbal ambiguity; the words can literally go either way. On the stage, this scene is considerably more striking than it is in the written text, and the circle more vividly perceptible as an enclosing artifact. Unfortunately for Faustus, however, he, too, has misconstrued the nature of his artwork. Though Mephastophilis does appear to him, it is at his own accord and for his own reasons, and the conjuring circle, mistakenly conceived as an island of safety, becomes the final entrapping enclosure for Faustus himself.

The radical error made by each of these Icarian figures is to imagine that they are not Icaruses, but Daedaluses, not Phaetons, but Apollos. It was of course just such a misconception that brought grief to their mythological forebears; in Marlowe, it produces enclosure and tragedy. Daedalus, the master craftsman of myth, was celebrated not only for the waxen wings, but also for the maze he built to hold the minotaur—a maze that is the prototype of all enclosing artifacts. And the maze of Daedalus is an icon of human society, a walling off of the sub- or partly-human from the confines of civilization, the id encircled by the ego and the superego, man half-god confronting and containing man half-beast. In each of Marlowe's mature plays, there is, I think an artifact similarly designed to be its craftsman's masterwork, in order to bring human nature and the human condition under his control. Fittingly, these encapsulated and encapsulating artifacts usually appear near the closure of the play; in each case, the enclosure victimizes its maker, and becomes, not a Daedalian maze, but a Pandora's box.

In fact, the story of Daedalus is one that comes close to the heart of the Renaissance, as close perhaps as that of Faustian man—though the Daedalus story was not to find its perfect embodiment until Prospero stied Caliban in a rock. In Marlowe's plays, the story is omnipresent beneath the surface, and points ultimately to the true identities of Daedalus and Apollo, the master craftsman and the god of poetry. *Terminat hora diem, terminat Author opus*, wrote Marlowe at the close of *Doctor Faustus*. The hour ends the day, the author ends the work. The author himself is the final encloser, the one figure whose control over the realm of imagination and the world of the stage is complete. His is the language that encloses, as his is the mind that invents. Some years before, Sidney had made a similar observation:

> Only the poet, disdaining to be tied to any such subjection, lifted up with the vigour of his own invention, doth grow, in effect, into another nature, in making things either better than nature bringeth forth, or, quite anew, forms such as never were in nature, as the heroes, demi-gods, cyclops, chimeras, furies, and such like; so as he goeth hand in hand with Nature, not enclosed within the narrow warrant of her gifts, but freely ranging only within the zodiac of his own wit.[4]

Even when the poetry seems to be disavowing its own power, as in Tamburlaine's speech on "all the pens that ever poets held" (*1 Tam*. 1.5.161), the inexpressibility topos is employed as a suitably Marlovian way of expressing the inexpressible, containing the uncontainable.

In Marlowe's language, itself, and particularly in his use of the blank verse form, we find striking evidence of this authorial closure. A number of his most memorable lines employ what could perhaps be described as an "aspiring foot," which seeks to break the boundary imposed on it by the pentameter line. Thus we discover, for example, in Tamburlaine's famous praise of an earthly crown,

That perfect bliss and sole felicity,

(1 Tam. 2.7.29)

that the caesura emphasizes the internal rhyme between "bliss" and "felic-." The remaining foot, "-ity," breaks through the enclosure of rhyme, but is itself enclosed by the unseen but inexorable domination of the author's chosen verse form. Similarly, in the well known lines from *The Jew of Malta*,

> And as their wealth increaseth, so inclose
> Infinite riches in a little room
>
> (1.1.37)

the word "room" differs markedly in aural tone from the rest of
the line, which is again internally balanced, this time by the con-
gruence of the two "in"s and the short *i* sounds in "-finite," and
"riches" and "little." The "in"s are carried over from the previous
line, "And as their wealth *in*creaseth, so *in*close / *In*finite riches *in*
a little room," giving a further impetus of energy and escape.
But "room," the aspiring foot, is again captured, this time not
only by the pentameter line, but also by the syntactic close of
the phrase. The effect is here doubly emphasized by the fact
that the subject, as well as the form, of these lines is closure
itself.

In an even more elegant example from the same passage,
Barabas declares that

> This is the ware wherein consists my wealth.
>
> (1.1.33)

Here the first four feet of the line take an extreme and emblematic
form of closure, chiasmus: "this"-"consists," "ware"-"where."
The short *is* of "this"-"consists" seem to enclose the "wares"
successfully, but the aspiring foot, "my wealth," slips out from
this verbal noose, only to be caught and halted by the poet and
his pentameter line. Finally, there is discoverable in *Faustus* yet
another literal version of a gesture metaphorically expressed in
the other plays. In Faustus's despairing cry, "O I'll leap up to
my God! Who pulls me down?" (5.2.138), we can count not ten
but eleven syllables; at the very moment that he aspires most
fervently to escape damnation, his language aspires to escape
the formal strictures of the verse.

Yet the answer to Faustus's question is clear: once again it is
the author who succeeds in enclosing, where his characters fail.
Behind the Icaruses and Phaetons who dominate his drama,

striving to enclose others, themselves enclosed at last, looms the Daedalian figure of the dramatist, whose maze is his art, whose enclosure is the only one that is timeless. For as Marlowe encloses, he discloses; as he cages and entraps his characters, so he opens up meaning to his audience. As the author ends the work, as he *terminat*, he sets limits, so he is able, working within the confines of the tiny Elizabethan stage, to "inclose / Infinite riches in a little room."

NOTES

1. For the fortunes of Icarus in the Renaissance, see Douglas Cole, *Suffering and Evil in the Plays of Christopher Marlowe* (Princeton: Princeton University Press, 1962), p. 196 & n. The presence of Icarus and Phaeton in the plays has also been noted, among others, by Harry Levin, *The Overreacher: A Study of Christopher Marlowe* (Cambridge, Mass.: Harvard University Press, 1952), pp. 52, 112, and by A. Bartlett Giamatti, "Marlowe: The Arts of Illusion," *The Yale Review* 2, no. 62 (Summer, 1972): 530–43.

2. Cole, pp. 180 ff., notes the resemblance of Edward's dungeon to hell.

3. Levin, p. 101.

4. Philip Sidney, *Defence of Poesy*, ed. Dorothy M. Macardle (London: Macmillan and Co., 1962), p. 7.

Michael Goldman

Marlowe and the Histrionics of Ravishment

I want to begin by considering a histrionic pattern, a system by means of which a particular emotion gets acted out in most of Marlowe's plays. The pattern links the leading actor to certain objects in the world of the play, and the exact terms of this relation seem to me of some importance for understanding Marlowe's art. The emotion or state of mind in question is what I shall call "ravishment," a perhaps not very silver-tongued term, but one at least reasonably close to Marlowe's vocabulary. For in Faustus's sense of the word, Marlowe's heroes are all ravished men. That is the state of mind in which we find them, and the first acting opportunity Marlowe gives to Tamburlaine, Barabas, Faustus, Edward, and Gaveston is to express their ravishment, that is, to act it out for us.

What is it to be ravished? The condition is not easily defined, but let me offer a few approximations as a guide to what follows. To be ravished is to have been aroused by a single source to the possibility of entire bliss. It is neither obsession nor infatuation, though it may exhibit characteristics of both. It promotes passionate attachment to particular aims and achievements, yet what ravishes the Marlovian actor can never be contained within what a method actor would call an "objective." It is not *this* victory, *this* accumulation of wealth, not even this magic power—though, as we shall see, the notion of magic itself helps bring us closer to it. The ravished man's desire swells beyond any specific goal, though all the time seeming to promise a surfeit of pleasure if broadly enough achieved. To be ravished is not to be in love as, say, Romeo is, with either Juliet or Rosaline. Indeed, something of the peculiarity of dramatic impression Zenocrate creates comes from the fact that, while Tamburlaine is undoubtedly in love with her, that emotion does not seem quite in the center of his motivation. Zenocrate is a kind of sign for Tamburlaine, the Queen who will be crowned at the right time. She is not his bliss, but the emblem of it. Tamburlaine is in love with Zenocrate, but he is ravished by empery.

Ravishment is impatient, scornful. It involves, as we shall see, an impulse to escape the world. Edward is ravished not simply by a limited desire—to have Gaveston—but to have Gaveston to the exclusion of everything else. Only that will be bliss, a satisfaction that can erase all the limitations and irritations caused by the existence of everything that is not Gaveston.

Finally, however, ravishment is best defined in its histrionic context. Like everything in drama, it is something we experience through acting. Its meaning is to be found in the means Marlowe uses to have it acted out. So I will now first look at those opening expressions of ravishment to see how they are achieved, and then try to trace the connection between this process and some larger patterns of the Marlovian imagination.

Initially, Marlowe's heroes present themselves to us as ravished by referring to an object, a prop, to which they transmit their energy of impersonation and from which, in turn, they receive further energy. We are urged to perceive the prop in its particularity—this book, this heap of money—and to enjoy its particular, practical power in a world whose physics and politics are well understood and briskly evoked. At the same time, however, the hero further defines himself by in some sense rejecting the prop. The prop is a source of bliss, but it is also—in some part or aspect—trash. Out of this double-valued attack on the prop emerges the audience's sense of character as definite, and definite in a way we usually think of as Marlovian—intensely appetitive, restlessly in motion, both in love with, and curiously out of, this world.

In three plays—*Faustus, The Jew of Malta,* and *Edward II*—the definition I have described is accomplished in an opening soliloquy. In each case, there is a survey of promised power through reference to an object that is displayed, handled, cherished, and extensively discussed; a rejection of trash; and a declaration of intense excitement over a special version or possibility of the prop. This is accompanied by a vivid evocation of exotic riches and sensations, all of which the prop can somehow bring to bear. Faustus surveys his books. They have ravished him, but he is also dissatisfied with them; he is looking for a meaning in his texts that will lead him deeper than the mere show of his profession. He will be a divine in show, yet level at the end of every art; he will sound the depths of what he professes. Like Hamlet in *his* first scene, Faustus is restlessly suspicious of externals, troubled by that most theatrical of paradoxes, being and not being (*on kai me on*), to which he is eager to bid farewell. And so he rejects what at one point he calls "external trash," and turns to magic instead.

Like Faustus, Barabas first appears to us surrounded by a heap of objects that he scrutinizes with professional care and that seem to claim his delighted attention. He finds money, it would seem, as sweet as Faustus found the *Analytics*. He counts his gold precisely and with relish—but suddenly bursts out:

Fie, what a trouble 'tis to count this trash![1]

(1.1.7)

Like Faustus with his books, Barabas uses his wealth histrionically, to express a restless desire for a more significant wealth, and, like Faustus, he evokes it in terms of far-flung realms and fabulous goods. He wants a world of profit and delight not diffusely present in paltry silverlings that take so long to count, but concentrated into a gold wedge of purest mold or a superb jewel, so he may hold infinite wealth before him in his counting-house. We misunderstand Barabas and the design of his play if we neglect what he is talking about here, if we treat "infinite riches in a little room" as mere hyperbolic avarice, a touching grace note that makes greed for a moment poetical. Not wealth itself, but a magical concentration of power has ravished Barabas.

A world of profit and delight is promised to Gaveston by the letter he enters reading. Like Faustus and Barabas, he sees the letter as bringing a wide, splendid, sensually defined kingdom under his control. He, too, is almost overcome by the prospect of bliss:

> "My father is deceased. Come, Gaveston,
> And share the kingdom with thy dearest friend."
> Ah, words that make me surfeit with delight!
> What greater bliss can hap to Gaveston. . .
>
> (1.1.1–4)

Instead of Hell, it is London he confounds in Elysium (1.1.10–11). But once more the contrast of bliss with trash is insisted on, and it is an essential premise of the action of the play that follows. London may be Elysium, but Gaveston is quick to tell us he loves neither the city nor its men. He vows to continue at enmity with the world. Neither the people nor the land nor the power of England interests him—those possibilities he rejects, though they are certainly there in the letter with its invitation to "share the kingdom" with Edward. It is the rejection of political reality, of the very kingdom Edward has to offer, that dooms both lovers.

Once again, the desire that ravishes the character has been enacted in a way that deprecates vigorously, even violently, one version of the desire in favor of another that is described with a marshalling of sensual images and a scorn for the ordinary commerce of life. Like Faustus and Barabas, Gaveston concludes his self-defining statement by imagining exotic riches in a little space, the mythological pageants he will devise for Edward. Edward is the main character, of course, but Gaveston's opening statement introduces us to Edward's passion as well as his own; they are equally and similarly ravished with each other. Like Gaveston, and like Marlowe's other major heroes, Edward's fate and actions will flow from the consequences of his ravishment and constitute a working out of the exaltation and rejection it entails.

While Tamburlaine is not on stage at the beginning of his play, a very similar histrionic process is worked out over the first two scenes. In the opening scene, though we become instantly aware of the power of a crown and the fascination it exercises, we are made equally aware of the crown as a mere external. Even in Mycetes' hands, the crown has magical power. As a king, he could kill Cosroe with a word. Now, verbal style and political power have been provocatively equated both in the prologue and the opening lines of the first scene, and one trouble with Mycetes' verbal style is that his pentameters have an awkward habit of landing flatly on some trivial or embarrassing feature:

> Then hear thy charge, valiant Theridamas,
> The chiefest captain of Mycetes' host,
> The hope of Persia, and the very legs
> Whereon our state doth lean, as on a staff.

> (1.1.57–60)

or

> Well, here I swear by this my royal seat . . .
> Embossed with silk as best beseems my state.

> (1.1.97–99)

We associate Mycetes' way with a crown with silly externals. As with his language, he cannot draw power from it or use it to transform his desires into power. The investiture of Cosroe evokes some of the imagery of shining wealth and expansive geography that will be associated with crowns later in the play, but it is only with the appearance of Tamburlaine in the second scene that we get the fully exalted sense of empery, and once more it comes from an actor who defines himself by infusing objects with his energy and drawing new energy from them.

There are two objects to watch: the first is visible, the gold

Tamburlaine has seized from Zenocrate's caravan. The second, the crown, is present only as an idea. Tamburlaine puts a double value on both. In this case, the meaning is not made through soliloquy. It rises from the deft and subtle play Tamburlaine makes between himself, the objects, and the other characters on stage. Dealing with his prisoners, he is able to treat the gold casually, almost contemptuously, as of secondary value and at the same time as an emblem of the highest profit and delight. His prisoners ask for their treasure back and Tamburlaine first plays against them through the wealth on stage to define himself in terms of the symbol of the crown:

> But since I love to live at liberty,
> As easily may you get the Soldan's crown
> As any prizes out of my precinct.

> (1.2.26–28)

Later, however, when the travelers agree to give up their treasure and ask only for their freedom, Tamburlaine puts the treasure in its place as mere wealth, though still evoking its associations with limitless power. It is a passage of characteristic hyperbole, which we can now see as the linguistic equivalent of the Marlovian process of self-definition through double-valued symbols:

> Think you I weigh this treasure more than you?
> Not all the gold in India's wealthy arms
> Shall buy the meanest soldier in my train.
> Zenocrate, lovelier than the love of Jove,
> Brighter than is the silver Rhodope,
> Fairer than whitest snow on Scythian hills,
> Thy person is worth more to Tamburlaine
> Than the possession of the Persian crown.

> (84–91)

Gold is merely gold. The crown is simply a particular crown. Once more the object has been valued downward for its mere instrumentality, its connection with limit, yet at the same time drawn upon for its promise of transcendent value, here identified with Zenocrate.

The suggestion of magic is not far off. When Theridamas arrives moments later, Tamburlaine uses the booty, in both its valuations, to win over his enemies. The gold is displayed for reasons of sound policy, but also for magical effect. Like Barabas, Tamburlaine talks now not of money but of wedges of gold:

> Lay out our golden wedges to the view,
> That their reflections may amaze the Persians.
>
> (139–40)

or, again

> See how [Jove] rains down heaps of gold in showers,
> As if he meant to give my soldiers pay;
> And as a sure and grounded argument
> That I shall be the monarch of the East,
> He sends this Soldan's daughter, rich and brave,
> To be my Queen and portly emperess.
>
> (181–86)

There is a humor in this that is characteristic of the man and deserves more analysis than I can attempt here. But the ground of the amusement is Tamburlaine's enjoyment of his resources, his awareness that wealth, military ability, force majeure, virtù make a very nice kind of magic and that, personally, he does have rather a hypnotic effect on his listeners.

The pattern I have been discussing provides an initiating figure of action in Marlowe's major plays. Further, in each, the particulars of the pattern—the double-valued object, the precise terms of the valuation, the hero's method of addressing himself to the objects—carry over significantly into the action and structure of the play. Tamburlaine, for example, not only defines himself by projecting energy into objects and gathering it up again with interest. He treats people the same way. He bounces

energy off them, as with Theridamas in their first encounter, or
seems magically to draw the power out of their bodies into his
own. He stands above Cosroe and Bajazet as they writhe in
agony and shame, and we watch him take on their power. He
insists on the posture and on the mounting strength, the crown-
ing glory, that seems to flow into him from the man he steps on
or bestrides. Now, there is a very interesting passage, toward the
end of Part 1, in which Tamburlaine appears to sum up the
emblematic significance of such scenes. It is very like his speech
about the gold wedges, and it illuminates the method of the
play—both as to the way in which the main character is enacted
and the way spectacle in the play accompanies and grows out of
the process:

> And see, my lord, a sight of strange import,
> Emperors and kings lie breathless at my feet.
> The Turk and his great empress, as it seems,
> Left to themselves while we were at the fight,
> Have desperately dispatched their slavish lives;
> With them Arabia too hath left his life;
> All sights of power to grace my victory.
> And such are objects fit for Tamburlaine,
> Wherein, as in a mirror, may be seen
> His honor, that consists in shedding blood
> When men presume to manage arms with him.
>
> (5.2.405–15)

The method of both parts of the play is to construct what
Tamburlaine here calls "sights of power," tableaux that express
and reflect his power—and generate it by reflecting it. They
are reflectors for the audience, too, intricate emblems of the
complex emotion the figure of Tamburlaine arouses. The effect
is cumulative, many of the sights recurring or continuing and
being added to, until, in both parts, they form a large concluding pageant, whose progress from the stage is a final sight of
power, a final visual chord in which the complex definition of

Tamburlaine—which we but weakly reflect with words like "terror" and "fascination"—is sustained for us to contemplate and absorb.

Zenocrate's coronation is the climax of the first part, and it certainly is an immensely lucid joining of Tamburlaine's two greatest aspirations, completing his announced design of conquest. We should recall, however, the elements that compose the marriage procession that clears the stage after Tamburlaine has placed the crown on Zenocrate's head. For it is also a procession of men in arms, fresh from strenuous battle and bloody massacre. It is, moreover, a grisly funeral procession, including the bodies of Bajazet, Zabina, and Arabia.

Similarly, Part 2 ends with a funeral procession that gathers up the main motifs of the play and that has, in effect, been gradually built up as the action has unfolded. Death cuts short the progress of Tamburlaine's pomp, as the Prologue says, but dramatically it completes it. Again we have a spectacular procession bristling with sights that invite intensely divergent responses: the bodies of Tamburlaine and Zenocrate borne in state; his mourning followers; the triumphal chariot drawn by a brace of sadistically tortured kings, bits in their mouths, harrowed at each step, the whip now cracked by the youth Amyras whose heart, he tells us, is broken. We watch him with trepidation, remembering Tamburlaine's warning, uttered moments before, that now mingles with and extends the meaning of the procession's triumph, sorrow, and barbarity, adding to it a suggestion of potential monstrous violence:

> For if thy body thrive not full of thoughts
> As pure and fiery as Phyteus' beams,
> The nature of these proud rebelling jades
> Will take occasion by the slenderest hair
> And draw thee piecemeal, like Hippolytus,
> Through rocks more steep and sharp than Caspian cliffs.
>
> (5.3.236–41)

The mixed feelings of the two endings are very different, but the technique of mixture through spectacle is the same, a trick of composition Marlowe also uses elsewhere in both plays on a smaller scale, as when he accompanies Tamburlaine's great ode on the aspiring mind with the loud, long, and painfully specific death of Cosroe at his feet, a passage we all too often discuss as if Tamburlaine's speech were a soliloquy. And yet it almost is. Tamburlaine's relation to Cosroe is that of actor to prop—always remembering Tamburlaine's special way with objects. Cosroe's body is a sight of power—the trash above which, from which, Tamburlaine's bliss is rising.

The *Tamburlaine* processions suggest that, in the course of at least two of Marlowe's plays, the emotion of ravishment spreads out to invest first one or two objects, then a set of related objects, and is in turn enriched associatively by the steady reflection of the objects back on the central character. This process is also at work in the other plays. The money, for instance, that we see at the beginning of *The Jew of Malta* keeps moving about in coins and bags throughout the play. Our analysis up to this point suggests that we should watch it as a part of a system of intensifying, widening associations initiated by the opening soliloquy. As with Tamburlaine, I would like to do this with special emphasis on the play's end.

Plot is very much the soul of *The Jew of Malta*, and Marlowe, presumably following close upon Kyd's example, energetically explores the dramatic possibilities of the revenge hero, a role that transforms an injured man into a playwright and allows intensities of rage to express themselves not merely in outcry but in ingenious theatrical contrivance. Kyd and Marlowe both find the revenge climax an irresistible symbol of the playwright overwhelmed by his creation, but where Kyd presents Hieronymo's revenge literally as a play within a play, Marlowe significantly chooses to show his plotter-hero as a carpenter, the builder of a complex mechanical trap, into which at the last moment he falls. Having tried to trap the entire Turkish army in a little room, he succeeds only in betraying himself.

Stripped of his wealth, Barabas has discovered a new obsession. From the actor's point of view, this may best be grasped as an extension into activity of the energy he has already used to express his desire for the kind of wealth that is not trash. Revenge is what ravishes him now, and he explicitly substitutes it in our formula of double valuation as early as Act 2:

> My factor sends me word a merchant's fled
> That owes me for a hundred tun of wine.
> I weigh it thus much. I have wealth enough.
> For now by this has he kissed Abigail,
> And she vows love to him and he to her.
> As sure as heaven rained manna for the Jews,
> So sure shall he and Don Mathias die.

(2.3.240–46)

The formulaic contrast is now between paltry wealth and the transcendent sustenance of revenge, which he compares to manna. And, similarly, where others in the play quest for principality, an inheritance, a wife, we feel a contrast between the limited goals of their contriving and Barabas's more restless Marlovian commitment to revenge, his interest in a kind of infinite richness of deception.

Barabas, to use the play's vocabulary, has determined to make "policy" his "profession," that is, to become a plotter. One effect of his plots will be to show how policy is very much the profession of the local Christian population, especially policy whose source is avarice. The Jew of Malta is, among other things, a brilliant satire on the substitution of mercantile values for all others, of the subversion of the Christian profession by the professions of moneymaking. The image of Barabas hugging his bags is a perversion of his grand ambition in the counting-house—and it is echoed frequently by others in the play, as in the fight of the Friars over Barabas's money, or the calculating blandishments of the courtesan. But the most striking version of the image comes at the end.

As the plots multiply, money changes hands more visibly and rapidly. While Barabas is busy preparing the climax, dispensing gold to the workmen, hammering his trap into place, testing the cords and hinges, the governor appears with a bag containing a hundred thousand pounds. There follows an interesting visual development:

> *Ferneze:* O, excellent! Here, hold thee, Barabas.
>   I trust thy word; take what I promised thee.
> *Barabas:* No, governor. I'll satisfy thee first;
>   Thou shalt not live in doubt of anything.
>
> (5.5.42–45)

Barabas's refusal of money at any time is surprising, and the reason for it here, I think, is that Marlowe is maneuvering a prop into position. He wants the governor to bring the money onstage, but not to hand it over. The governor is thus left holding the bag at the play's end. As he utters his final pious speech, we see him clutching the money to him:

> So, march away, and let due praise be given
> Neither to fate nor fortune, but to heaven.
>
> (123–24)

This drives home the satire and lets us see the governor as a mean, paltry version of the villain Barabas. At the same time, it is the final step in a process that, by its treatment of Barabas and his desire for wealth and vengeance, has managed to impart to the satire the protagonist's own fierce energy. Barabas's search for a bliss of vengeance is felt as the very attack of the play. Through Barabas, Marlowe's plot becomes a scourge and terror to the world. That is the play's real triumph, I think. We come to feel the plot itself as vehement, and feel this vehemence savaging the mercantile world Marlowe portrays. That the creator of the plot, the surrogate

playwright, is howling from the cauldron at the end only completes the picture.

The chariot of state, the bag of money—the heroes' desires
have filled these props with energy and meaning, but at the end
of both plays the presence of the props serves to diminish the
people we see wielding them; they ironize upon the human
scene. This revenge of the ambivalent object, the dangerous
autonomy of what has both been exalted and spurned away, is
of course equally strong in *Faustus* and *Edward II*. The two
most important things we learn about Faustus's magic powers
are, first, that he acquires them, ultimately, not through the
learning in his books but through the perverted ambition of his
soul, and, second, that they are mere devil's tricks—we see
spirits, not Helen or Alexander. Faustus is granted the power he
seeks in the opening scene, but the gift mocks him and his
desires. He does succeed in bidding being farewell, but not
nonbeing. The sensual longing and theatrical trickery of the
earlier scenes issue finally in the limbs strewn about the stage—
an ending that may remind us, as does the ending of the second
part of *Tamburlaine*, of Hippolytus or Phaeton, but reminds us
even more of the low comedy of the Horse Courser. Faustus
himself has been converted into a prop, to the mere external
trash he scorned. All that is left of him is a heap of broken
tricks.

In all the plays there is a close correlation between the evocation of bliss at the beginning and the vivid spectacle of physical suffering at the end. Edward II's death is too well known an
example to need demonstration. Let me, however, point out in
passing that, in addition to the apparent turning of the object of
Edward's ravishment against him in the hideous seductiveness of
Lightborn and the actual means of murder, the very prop
Gaveston first uses to express his ravishment comes back,
transformed, at the end of the play, to torture Edward—and
some others, too. While *Edward II* begins with a letter that

expresses Edward's love, the letters and documents that run through the rest of the drama reflect the interweaving of purposes and practicalities, the life of politics, the historical reality that has no interest for Edward and that destroys him. The letters of powerful men are magical, as Gaveston knows. They carry the dangerous power of government to play with people's lives. As a letter begins the action, so letters bring it to an end. An ambiguously punctuated letter is responsible not only for Edward's death but Mortimer's, and a similar message does away with Lightborn.

One way of summing up the connection between ravishment and suffering is to say that, in the course of the play, the hero effectively transforms something he loves into a source of fear. Certainly it is true of all the major heroes except Tamburlaine that their pursuit of what has ravished them when we first see them creates a circumstance that destroys them horribly. More particularly, by the end of the play we see them moving with a kind of abandon toward some deformed version of their desire: toward Lightborn, toward the Mephistophilis of Faustus's final cry, toward the cauldron. And even in *Tamburlaine* we have seen that the triumphal chariot at the end of Part 2 is as much an emblem of cruel, rending destruction as of imperial mastery. In this, Tamburlaine joins the other heroes in transforming, through his immense efforts, a source of pleasure into a source of torture, an object of desire into an engine of cruelty. Faustus is the grandest example, of course, since he succeeds in transforming a god of love into one of fear. He opts for the Evil Angel's version of Deity, and that is what he gets.

Marlowe, as Harry Levin suggests,[2] seems to have been fond of Machiavelli's passage on love and fear. In the world of the plays, as in Machiavelli's, it is plainly better to be feared than loved, far safer at all events. This is the world whose physics and politics, as I have said, are rapidly evoked very early in each drama—the world of Persian politics, or Mediterranean commerce, or German academic careerism. And the relation of fear and love in Marlowe, like that of the trashy and magical aspects of his crucial objects, is intimately bound up with the way that the real world, the secular, physical world, both is and is not of supreme interest to the Marlovian hero.

In the real world, the power-haunted world of politics and competition Marlowe evidently knew well, fear and dominance are the only successful relations shown. To give oneself up to ravishment, to live entirely toward a bliss that is conceived as answering to all one's restlessness, is invariably to summon nightmare. The distinctive conception of Marlovian bliss is important here. In spite of significant variations in each play, a general notion of bliss runs through them all, and it strongly contrasts with the drive each of the heroes manifests. It is a state of dissolution, assuagement, an expansion beyond gravity. The sense of the body resting in embraced protective comfort, of tension ended, of melting into repose, the peace of the hug, of silk, of the feather bed, of glutted satiation, is as important in Marlowe as the strenuous excitement of aspiration. It is a sensual release exactly opposite to the straining busyness with which the major heroes pursue their goals and also to the rending physical torture that three of them experience and Tamburlaine is surrounded by. On Marlowe's stage, to seek this release is to call down this torture. More than that, it is actively to initiate it.

There is a distinctive stance toward the world here, and as far as I can tell, all of Marlowe's drama flows from it. It helps explain where the ravishment comes from and where it is going. Let me, by way of conclusion, try to examine it a little further by returning where I began, to the way Marlowe's heroes are first presented to us. I have talked about a pattern of interacting with objects, a way of getting the action started by getting the acting of a principal part started. But there is also present as a starting point in any dramatic role something that might be called a disposition toward enactment, the stance from which acting in the world of the play begins—a leaning at some angle to the business of playing a part in public. And this, too, can tell us something about a playwright's imagination. Shakespeare's heroes, for example, usually begin in a stance of withdrawal—a refusal to play a part to the hilt or at least to play the part the world urges on them. They have that within which passeth show, they withdraw from their fellows like Romeo or Antipholus of Syracuse, they hide their true visage from the world like Hal or Viola, they refuse to be drawn in like Othello. But where Shakespeare's heroes normally have something inside they wish to shield from the world, and that events force them to show and test and change in action, Marlowe's heroes begin with a different kind of rejection of role-playing. Theirs is a more or less hurried eagerness to be done with disguises, to throw off the shepherd's weeds, to forget about the necessary pretences a king or favorite must make. Where Shakespeare's heroes hold back from the action, Marlowe's heroes plunge in. They are impatient to reveal themselves. Forced even briefly to dissemble, like Edward or Barabas, they are dangerously brusque; their asides leap with impatience. It is true that Faustus, in his opening lines, reminds himself to maintain a public mask, but the patient deception implied by being a divine in show is quickly abandoned for the direct self-expression of the magician's art.

I think this is a point of some importance—that for Marlowe's characters the yearning for magical solutions and objects is allied to an impatience with pretending. They abandon themselves to what has ravished them. Indeed, the notion of *abandon* is very helpful to grasping the characteristic movement of Marlowe's drama. I think that the experience of abandon must be very much on the mind and in the muscles of the actor who sets out to investigate any of Marlowe's great parts—abandon in that word's rich sense of letting go, self-exposure, the subversive unlocking of the body, the play and display of forbidden

sensations and thoughts, wildness, headlongness. And it should
also be very much on the mind of the director who wants to
stage the plays, because abandon is what the audience must
experience, too, even while it is being provocatively reminded
of the horrors and dangers it is witnessing. That is why Guthrie
was right to strike a note of lavish, almost lascivious sadism in
his magnificent *Tamburlaine*.

The Marlovian hero confounds Elysium with the stage, the
little room where he believes sweet fruition can be found, where
eventually he will be able to take truce with all the world, that
absolute relaxation of tension that only Tamburlaine briefly
obtains. To try to pull heaven down onto the stage and to
succeed only in suffering or, at best, commanding a hell there—
that is indeed a basic process of Marlovian drama. But more
than that, the process requires that the play project a ravishment that, in the experiencing, carries us to hell. The sense of
abandon is always intense, the sense of opening up to the
overwhelming appeal of the magical source.

But the movement of abandon is very precisely colored and
complicated by the way the ravishment is acted out. Marlowe's
heroes abandon themselves to the world, but it is as if they also
wish to abandon the world. They want the world, but they
seem to want also to destroy it, or render it powerless, or make
it go away. For the bliss they seek is inseparable from their
magical reading of the world. Now, a magical object—an object
viewed as magical—is at once intensely interesting and oddly
robbed of its reality. It is everything or nothing, depending on
whether the magic works. For those who are obsessed by
magic—as indeed for the secret agent or the hunter of forbidden
sexual delights—the world is both strangely present and absent.
There is a feeling for hidden concentrations of significance, a
passionate absorption in a single pursuit, a sense that life is
realer and less real than others know. Certain objects are all
important. Bliss can be wrung from them by art. The rest is

dross. All this is equally true, of course, of those who have been ravished by the theater. For them, everything becomes theatrical; and everything in the theater is either magic or tinsel.

Such is the desperately ambivalent and volatile relation to the world in which Marlowe's heroes stand. They want to leap beyond it, to make it vanish, to bestride it and absorb its power. They want to convert its riches into a talisman they can hold in their hand, to spurn all the rest of it from their path like trash. Ravished, they construct spectacles to bring them the release they seek. And when they have finished, we see they have built the machinery of Hell.

But the dramatic excitement of the plays, the real source of whatever value or meaning they may be said to contain, does not lie primarily in our recognizing it *is* Hell, any more than it does in our admiring or detesting the heroes. It lies, like the excitement of any drama, in our participating in the play, in an experience created and sustained by acting. We are frequently reminded in Marlowe of how dangerous and enticing that experience can be; indeed, we are almost taunted at times. As when the Chorus at the end of *Faustus* modulates swiftly from classical heroic praise to morality condemnation, and then directs at us the most damagingly ironic pretense that we of course have *not* gone beyond the permitted bounds of engagement in Faustus's unholy career:

> Cut is the branch that might have grown full straight,
> And burnèd is Apollo's laurel bough
> That sometime grew within this learned man.
> Faustus is gone. Regard his hellish fall,
> Whose fiendful fortune may exhort the wise
> Only to wonder at unlawful things,
> Whose deepness doth entice such forward wits
> To practice more than heavenly power permits.
>
> (Epilogue, 1–8)

But *we* have practiced more than is permitted; we have not only wondered, we have shared. You see, the Chorus seems to be saying, where your participation has brought you. And here we may remember the contemporary legend of the extra devil unaccountably present among the cast. That devil, I would say, was an index of how far Marlowe's original audience felt they had gone in their abandon. And, as I hope I have been able to suggest, it is a very distinctive kind of abandon Marlowe makes us share, rising out of the immense instabilities of ravishment — the abandon with which his heroes plunge into a world they scorn, to seek their bliss.

NOTES

1. All citations follow *The Complete Plays of Christopher Marlowe*, ed. Irving Ribner (New York: The Odyssey Press, 1963).

2. *The Overreacher: A Study of Christopher Marlowe* (Cambridge, Mass.: Harvard University Press, 1952), pp. 89, 156.

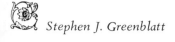
Stephen J. Greenblatt

Marlowe and Renaissance Self-Fashioning

On 26 June 1586, a small fleet, financed by the Earl of Cumberland, set out from Gravesend for the South Seas. It sailed down the West African coast, sighting Sierra Leone in October, and at this point we may let one of those on board, the merchant John Sarracoll, tell his own story:

> The fourth of November wee went on shore to a towne of the Negros, . . . which we found to be but lately built: it was of about two hundreth houses, and walled about with mightie great trees, and stakes so thicke, that a rat could hardly get in or out. But as it chanced, wee came directly upon a port which was not shut up, where wee entred with such fiercenesse, that the people fled all out of the towne, which we found to bee finely built after their fashion, and the streetes of it so intricate, that it was difficult for us to finde the way out, that we came in at. Wee found their houses and streets so finely and cleanly kept, that it was an admiration to us all, for that neither in the houses nor streets was, so much dust to bee found, as would fill an egge shell. Wee found little in their houses, except some matts, goards, and some earthen pots. Our men at their departure set the towne on fire, and it was burnt (for the most part of it) in a quarter of an houre, the houses being covered with reed and straw.[1]

This passage is atypical, for it lacks the blood bath that usually climaxes these incidents, but it will serve to remind us of what until recently was called one of the glorious achievements of Renaissance civilization, and it will serve to introduce us to the world of Christopher Marlowe.

What is most striking in Sarracoll's account, of course, is the casual, unexplained violence. Does the merchant feel that the firing of the town needs no explanation? If asked, would he have had one to give? Why does he take care to tell us why the town burned so quickly, but not why it was burned? Is there an aesthetic element in his admiration of the town, so finely built, so intricate, so cleanly kept? And does this admiration conflict with or somehow fuel the destructiveness? If he feels no uneasiness at all, why does he suddenly shift and write not *"we"* but *"our men"* set the town on fire? Was there an order or not? And, when he recalls the invasion, why does he think of rats? The questions are all met by the moral blankness that rests like thick snow on Sarracoll's sentences: "The 17 day of November wee departed from Sierra Leona, directing our course for the Straights of Magellan."

If, on returning to England in 1587, the merchant and his associates had gone to see the Lord Admiral's Men perform a new play, *Tamburlaine the Great*, they would have seen an extraordinary meditation on the roots of their own behavior. For despite all the exoticism in Marlowe—Scythian shepherds, Maltese Jews, German magicians—it is his own countrymen that he broods upon and depicts.[2] If we want to understand the historical matrix of Marlowe's achievement, the analogue to Tamburlaine's restlessness, aesthetic sensitivity, appetite, and violence, we might look not at the playwright's sources, not even at the relentless power-hunger of Tudor absolutism, but at the acquisitive energies of English merchants, entrepreneurs, and adventurers, promoters alike of trading companies and theatrical companies.

But what bearing does Marlowe actually have on a passage like the one with which I opened? He is, for a start, fascinated by the idea of the stranger in a strange land. Almost all of his heroes are aliens or wanderers, from Aeneas in Carthage to Barabas in Malta, from Tamburlaine's endless campaigns to Faustus's demonic flights. From his first play to his last, he is drawn to the idea of physical movement, to the problem of its representation within the narrow confines of the theater. Tamburlaine almost ceaselessly traverses the stage, and when he is not actually on the move, he is imagining campaigns or hearing reports of grueling marches. The obvious effect is to enact the hero's vision of a nature that "Doth teach vs all to haue aspyring minds" and of the soul that "Wils vs to weare our selues and neuer rest" (*1 Tam*. 2.6.871, 877). But as always in Marlowe, this enactment, this realization on the level of the body in time and space, complicates, qualifies, exposes, and even mocks the abstract conception. For the cumulative effect of this restlessness is not so much heroic as grotesquely comic, if we accept Bergson's classic definition of the comic as the mechanical imposed upon the living. Tamburlaine *is* a machine, a desiring machine that produces violence and death. Menaphon's admiring description begins by making him sound like Leonardo's Vitruvian Man or Michelangelo's David and ends by making him sound like an expensive mechanical device, one of those curious inventions that courtiers gave to the Queen at New Year's: a huge, straight, strongly-jointed creature with a costly pearl placed between his shoulders, the pearl inscribed with celestial symbols. Once set in motion, this *thing* cannot slow down or change course; it moves at the same frenzied pace until it finally stops.

One further effect of this unvarying movement is that, paradoxically, very little progress seems to be made, despite fervent declarations to the contrary. To be sure, the scenes change, so quickly at times that Marlowe seems to be battering against the boundaries of his own medium: at one moment the stage represents a vast space, then suddenly contracts to a bed, then turns in quick succession into an imperial camp, a burning town, a besieged fortress, a battlefield, a tent. But then all of those spaces seem curiously alike. The relevant contrast is *Antony and Cleopatra*, where the restless movement is organized around the deep structural opposition of Rome and Egypt, or *1 Henry IV*, where the tavern, the court, and the country are perceived as diversely shaped spaces, spaces that elicit and echo different tones, energies, and even realities. In *Tamburlaine*, Marlowe contrives to efface all such differences, as if to insist upon the essential meaninglessness of theatrical space, the vacancy that is the dark side of its power to imitate any place. This vacancy

—quite literally, this absence of scenery—is the equivalent in the medium of the theater to the secularization of space, the abolition of qualitative up and down, which for Cassirer is one of the greatest achievements of Renaissance philosophy, the equivalent then to the reduction of the universe to the coordinates of a map:[3]

> Giue me a Map, then let me see how much
> Is left for me to conquer all the world,
> That these my boies may finish all my wantes.
>
> (*2 Tam.* 5.3.4516–18)

Space is transformed into an abstraction, then fed to the appetitive machine. This is the voice of conquest, but it is also the voice of wants never finished and of transcendental homelessness. And though the characters and situations change, that voice is never entirely absent in Marlowe. Barabas does not leave Malta, but he is the quintessential alien: at one point, his house is seized and turned into a nunnery, at another, he is thrown over the walls of the city, only to rise with the words, "What, all alone?" Edward II should be the very opposite; he is, by his role, the embodiment of the land and its people, but without Gaveston he lives in his own country like an exile. Only in *Doctor Faustus* does there seem to be a significant difference: having signed away his soul and body, Faustus begins a course of restless wandering, but at the close of the twenty-four years, he feels a compulsion to return to Wittenberg.[4] Of course, it is ironic that when a meaningful sense of place finally emerges in Marlowe, it does so only as a place to die. But the irony runs deeper still. For nothing in the covenant or in any of the devil's speeches requires that Faustus has to pay his life where he originally contracted to sell it; the urge is apparently in Faustus, as if he felt there were a fatality in the study itself, felt it appropriate and even necessary to die there and nowhere else. "O would I had neuer seene *Wertenberge*," he despairingly tells his friends. But the play has long before this exposed such a sense of place to radical questioning. To Faustus's insistent demands to know the "where about" of hell, Mephastophilis replies,

> Hell hath no limits, nor is circumscrib'd
> In one selfe place, for where we are is hell,
> And where hell is, must we euer be.

                                                                (567–69)

By implication, Faustus's feeling about Wittenberg is an illusion, one of a network of fictions by which he constitutes his identity and his world. Typically, he refuses to accept the account of a limitless, inner hell, countering with the extraordinary, and in the circumstances, ludicrous "I thinke hell's a fable." Mephastophilis's quiet response slides from parodic agreement to devastating irony: "I, thinke so still, till experience change thy minde."[5] The experience of which the devil speaks can refer not only to torment after death but to Faustus's life in the remainder of the play: the half-trivial, half-daring exploits, the alternating states of bliss and despair, the questions that are not answered and the answers that bring no real satisfaction, the wanderings that lead nowhere. The chilling line may carry a further suggestion: "Yes, continue to think that hell's a fable, until experience *transforms* your mind." At the heart of this mental transformation is the anguished perception of time as inexorable, space as abstract. In his final soliloquy, Fautus's frenzied invocation to time to stop or slow itself gives way to horrified clarity: "The starres mooue stil, time runs, the clocke wil strike" (1460). And his appeal to nature—earth, stars, air, ocean—at once to shield him and destroy him is met by silence: space is neutral and unresponsive.

Doctor Faustus, then, does not contradict but, rather, realizes intimations about space and time in Marlowe's other plays. That man is homeless, that all places are alike, is linked to man's inner state, to the uncircumscribed hell he carries within him. And this insight returns us to the violence with which we began, the violence of Tamburlaine and of the English merchant and his men. It is not enough to say that their actions are the expression of brute power, though they are certainly that. For experiencing this limitlessness, this transformation of space and time into abstractions, men do violence as a means of marking boundaries, effecting transformations, signalling closure. To burn a town or to kill all of its inhabitants is to make an end and, in so doing, to give life a shape and a certainty that it would otherwise lack. The great fear, in Barabas's words, is "That I may vanish ore the earth in ayre, / And leaue no memory that e're I was" (I. 499–500). As the town where Zenocrate dies burns at his command, Tamburlaine proclaims his identity, fixed forever in the heavens by his acts of violence:

> Ouer my Zenith hang a blazing star,
> That may endure till heauen be dissolu'd,
> Fed with fresh supply of earthly dregs,
> Threatning a death and famine to this land.

(2 *Tam*. 3.2.3196–99)

In the charred soil and the blazing star, Tamburlaine seeks literally to make an enduring mark in the world, to stamp his image on time and space. Similarly, Faustus, by violence not on others but on himself, seeks to give his life a clear fixed shape. To be sure, he speaks of attaining "a world of profit and delight, / Of power, of honor, of omnipotence" (83–84), but perhaps the hidden core of what he seeks is the *limit* of twenty-four years to live, a limit he himself sets and reiterates. Time so marked out should have a quality different from other time, should possess its end: "Now will I make an ende immediately," he says, writing with his blood.

But in the tragic irony of Marlowe's world, these desperate attempts at boundary and closure produce the opposite effect, reinforcing the condition they are meant to efface. Tamburlaine's violence does not transform space from the abstract to the human, but rather further reduces the world to a map, the very emblem of abstraction:

> I will confute those blind Geographers
> That make a triple region in the world,
> Excluding Regions which I meane to trace,
> And with this pen reduce them to a Map,
> Calling the Prouinces, Citties and townes
> After my name and thine *Zenocrate*.

(1 Tam. 4.4.1715–20)

At Tamburlaine's death, the map still stretches out before him, and nothing bears his name save Marlowe's play (the crucial exception to which we will return).[6] Likewise at his death, pleading for "some end to my incessant paine," Faustus is haunted by eternity: "O no end is limited to damned soules" (1488).

The reasons why attempts at making a mark or an end fail are complex and vary significantly with each play, but one critical link is the feeling in almost all Marlowe's protagonists that they are *using up* experience. This feeling extends to our merchant, John Sarracoll, and his men: they not only visit Sierra Leone, they consume it. Tamburlaine exults in just this power to "Conquer, sacke, and vtterly consume / Your cities" (*2 Tam.* 4.2.3867–68). He even contrives to use up his defeated enemies, transforming Bajazet into his footstool, the kings of Trebizon and Soria into horses to be discarded, when they are broken-winded, for "fresh horse" (*2 Tam.* 5.1.4242). In a bizarrely comic moment, Tamburlaine's son suggests that the kings just captured be released to resume the fight, but Tamburlaine replies, in the language of consumption, "Cherish thy valour stil with fresh supplies: / And glut it not with stale and daunted foes" (*2 Tam.* 4.1.3761–62). Valor, like any appetite, always demands new food.

Faustus's relationship to knowledge is strikingly similar; in his opening soliloquy he bids farewell to each of his studies in turn as something he has used up. He needs to cherish his mind with fresh supplies, for nothing can be accumulated, nothing saved or savored. And as the remainder of the play makes clear, each of these farewells is an act of destruction: logic, medicine, law, and divinity are not so much rejected as violated. The violence arises not only from the desire to mark boundaries but from the feeling that what one leaves behind, turns away from, *must* no longer exist; that objects endure only for the moment of the act of attention and then are effaced; that the next moment cannot be fully grasped until the last is destroyed. Marlowe writes in the period in which European man embarked on his extraordinary career of consumption, his eager pursuit of knowledge, with one paradigm after another seized, squeezed dry, and discarded, and his frenzied exhaustion of the world's resources:[7]

> Loe here my sonnes, are all the golden Mines,
> Inestimable drugs and precious stones,
> More worth than *Asia*, and the world beside,
> And from th'Antartique Pole, Eastward behold
> As much more land, which neuer was descried,
> Wherein are rockes of Pearle, that shine as bright
> As all the Lamps that beautifie the Sky,
> And shal I die, and this vnconquered?

> (*2 Tam.* 5.3.4544–51)

So fully do we inhabit this construction of reality that most often we see beyond it only in accounts of cultures immensely distant from our own:

> The Nuer have no expression equivalent to 'time' in our language, and they cannot, therefore, as we can, speak of time as though it were something actual, which passes, can be wasted, can be saved, and so forth. I do not think that they ever experience the same feeling of fighting against time or of having to co-ordinate activities with an abstract passage of time because their points of reference are mainly the activities themselves, which are generally of a leisurely character. . . . Nuer are fortunate.[8]

Of course, such a conception of time and activity had vanished from Europe long before the sixteenth century, but English Renaissance works, and Marlowe's plays in particular, give voice to a radically intensified sense that time is abstract, uniform, and inhuman. The origins of this sense of time are difficult to locate with any certainty. Puritans in the late sixteenth century were already campaigning vigorously against the medieval doctrine of the unevenness of time, a doctrine that had survived largely intact in the Elizabethan Church Calendar. They sought, in effect, to desacramentalize time, to discredit and sweep away the dense web of saints' days, "dismal days," seasonal taboos, mystic observances, and folk festivals that gave time a distinct, irregular shape; in its place, they urged a simple, flat routine of six days work and a sabbath rest.[9] Moreover, there seem, in this period, to have been subtle changes in what we may call family time. At one end of the life cycle, traditional youth groups were suppressed or fell into neglect, customs that had allowed adolescents considerable autonomy were overturned, and children were brought under the stricter discipline of the immediate family. At the other end, the Protestant rejection of the doctrine of Purgatory eliminated the dead as an "age group," cutting off the living from ritualized communion with their deceased parents and relatives.[10] Such changes might well have contributed to a sense in Marlowe and some of his contemporaries that time is alien, profoundly indifferent to human longing and anxiety. Whatever the case, we certainly find in Marlowe's plays a powerful feeling that time is something to be resisted and a related fear that fulfillment or fruition is impossible. "Why waste you thus the time away?" an impatient Leicester asks Edward II, whose crown he has come to fetch. "Stay a while," Edward replies, "let me be king till night" (2045), whereupon, like Faustus, he struggles vainly to arrest time with incantation. At such moments, Marlowe's celebrated line is itself rich with irony: the rhythms intended to slow time only consume it, magnificent words are spoken and disappear into a void. But it is precisely this sense of the void that compels the characters to speak so powerfully, as if to struggle the more insistently against the enveloping silence.

That the moments of intensest time-consciousness all occur at or near the close of these plays has the effect of making the heroes seem to struggle against *theatrical* time. As Marlowe uses the vacancy of theatrical space to suggest his character's homelessness, so he uses the curve of theatrical time to suggest their struggle against death, in effect against the nothingness into which all characters fall at the end of a play. The pressure of the dramatic medium itself likewise underlies what we may call the *repetition compulsion* of Marlowe's heroes. Tamburlaine no sooner annihilates one army than he sets out to annihilate another, no sooner unharnesses two kings than he hitches up two more. Barabas gains and loses, regains and reloses his wealth, while pursuing a seemingly endless string of revenges and politic murders, including, characteristically, two suitors, two friars, two rulers, and, in effect, two children. In *Edward II*, the plot is less overtly episodic, yet even here, after spending the first half of the play alternately embracing and parting from Gaveston, Edward immediately replaces the slain favorite with Spencer Junior and thereby resumes the same pattern, the willful courting of disaster that is finally "rewarded" in the castle cesspool. Finally, as C. L. Barber observes, "Faustus repeatedly moves through a circular pattern, from thinking of the joys of heaven, through despairing of ever possessing them, to embracing magical dominion as a blasphemous substitute."[11] The pattern of action and the complex psychological structure embodied in it vary with each play, but at the deepest level of the medium itself the motivation is the same: the renewal of existence through repetition of the self-constituting act. The character repeats himself in order to continue to be that same character on the stage. Identity is a theatrical invention that must be reiterated if it is to endure.

To grasp the full import of this notion of repetition as self-fashioning, we must understand that it is set against the culturally dominant notion of repetition as warning or memorial. In this view, patterns exist in the history of individuals or nations in order to inculcate crucial moral lessons, passing them from generation to generation.[12] Men are notoriously slow learners, but gradually, through repetition, the paradigms may sink in. Accordingly, Tudor monarchs ordered the formal reiteration of the central tenets of the religious and social orthodoxy, carefully specifying the minimum number of times a year these tenets were to be read aloud from the pulpit.[13] Similarly, the punishment of criminals was public, so that the state's power to inflict torment and death could act upon the people as an edifying caution. The high number of such executions reflects not only judicial "massacres"[14] but the attempt to teach through reiterated terror. Each branding or hanging or disembowelling was theatrical in conception and performance, a repeatable admonitory drama enacted on a scaffold before a rapt audience. This idea of the "notable spectacle," the "theater of God's judgments," extended quite naturally to the drama itself, and, indeed, to all of literature, which thus takes its rightful place as part of a vast, interlocking system of repetitions, embracing homilies and hangings, royal progresses and rote learning.[15]

Marlowe seems to have regarded the notion of drama as admonitory fiction, and the moral order upon which this notion was based with a blend of fascination, contemptuous amusement, and loathing. *Tamburlaine* repeatedly teases its audience with the *form* of the cautionary tale, only to violate the convention. "The Gods, defenders of the innocent, / Will neuer prosper your intended driftes" (*1 Tam.* 1.2.264-65), declares Zenocrate in Act 1 and then promptly falls in love with her captor. With his dying breath, Cosroe curses Tamburlaine—a sure prelude to disaster—but the disaster never occurs. Bajazet, the King of Arabia, and even Theridamas and Zenocrate have powerful premonitions of the hero's downfall, but he passes from success to success. Tamburlaine is proud, arrogant, and blasphemous; he lusts for power, betrays his allies, overthrows legitimate authority, and threatens the gods; he rises to the top of the wheel of fortune and then steadfastly refuses to budge. Since the dominant ideology no longer insists that rise-and-decline and pride-goes-before-a-fall are unvarying, universal rhythms, we undoubtedly miss some of the shock of Tamburlaine's career, but the play itself invokes those rhythms often enough to surprise us with their failure to materialize.

Having undermined the notion of the cautionary tale in *Tamburlaine*, Part 1, Marlowe demolishes it in Part 2 in the most unexpected way—by suddenly invoking it. The slaughter of thousands, the murder of his own son, the torture of his royal captives are all without apparent consequence; then Tamburlaine falls ill, and when? When he burns the Koran! The one action that Elizabethan churchmen themselves might have applauded seems to bring down divine vengeance. The effect is not to celebrate the transcendent power of Mohammed but to challenge the habit of mind that looks to heaven for rewards and punishments, that imagines human evil as "the scourge of God." Similarly, in *Edward II*, Marlowe uses the emblematic method of admonitory drama, but uses it to such devastating effect that the audience recoils from it in disgust. Edward's grisly execution is, as orthodox interpreters of the play have correctly insisted, iconographically "appropriate," but this very appropriateness can only be established *at the expense of* every complex, sympathetic human feeling evoked by the play. The audience is forced to confront its insistence upon coherence, and the result is a profound questioning of the way audiences constitute meaning in plays and in life.[16]

This questioning is pursued as well in *The Jew of Malta* and *Doctor Faustus*. In the former, Marlowe invokes the motif of the villain-undone-by-his-villainy, but the actual fall of Barabas is brought about in his confidence in Ithamore, his desire to *avoid* the actual possession of power, and his imprudent trust in the Christian governor of Malta—in short, by the minute shreds of restraint and community that survive in him. In *Doctor Faustus*, as Max Bluestone observes in an English Institute essay, the homiletical tradition is continually introduced only to be undermined by dramatic spectacle.[17] Moreover, in these plays Marlowe questions not only the traditional value system upon which the notion of literature as a cautionary tale was based but the radical *critique* of this value system. Barabas's Machiavellianism and Faustus's skepticism are subjected to relentless probing and are exposed as themselves inadequate conceptions of reality. Marlowe's brilliant demonstration of Faustus's shallowness has long been admired; the intelligence of his analysis of Machiavellianism has been less well understood. The heart of this analysis lies not in the Prologue nor even in the fact that Barabas is outfoxed by a cleverer Machiavel than himself; it lies rather in the sketchiness of characterization that distinguishes this protagonist from Tamburlaine, Edward, and Faustus. Where the titles of Marlowe's other major plays are proper names, *The Jew of Malta* deflects the focus from the hero as fully conceived individual to the hero as embodiment of a category. Of course, the Jew has a name, but he remains curiously vague and unreal; even his account of his past—killing sick people or poisoning wells—tends to de-individualize him, accommodating him to an abstract, anti-Semitic fantasy of a Jew's past. In falling short of an existential identity, he approximates the shadowy status of Machiavelli's Prince; he is, to adapt Edward Said's characterization of Freud's Moses or Nietzsche's Dionysus, more "an idea of energy" than a man.[18] It is only as such a faceless being that the Machiavel can survive; by thrusting him in a drama and giving him a local habitation and a name, Marlowe demonstrates the inadequacy of the whole conception. Most dramatic characters—Shylock would be an appropriate example—*accumulate* identity in the course of their play; Barabas desperately tries to dispossess himself of such identity. But this steady erosion of himself is precisely what he has pledged himself to resist; his career, then, is in its very essence suicidal.

If the heart of Renaissance orthodoxy is a vast system of repetitions in which paradigms are established and men gradually learn what to desire and what to fear, the skeptics, Barabas and Faustus, remain embedded within this orthodoxy: they simply reverse the paradigms and embrace what the society brands as evil. In so doing, they imagine themselves set in diametrical opposition to their society where in fact they have already unwittingly accepted its crucial structural elements. For the issue is not man's power to disobey, but the characteristic modes of desire and fear produced by a given society, and the rebellious heroes never depart from those modes. With their passionate insistence on will, Marlowe's protagonists anticipate the perception that human history is the product of men themselves, but they fail to understand that this product is shaped, in Lukács's phrase, by forces that arise from their relations with each other and which have escaped their control.[19] As Marx writes in a famous passage in *The Eighteenth Brumaire of Louis Bonaparte*:

> Men make their own history, but they do not make it just as they please; they do not make it under circumstances chosen by themselves, but under circumstances directly found, given and transmitted from the past. The tradition of all the dead generations weighs like a nightmare on the brain of the living. And just when they seem engaged in revolutionising themselves and things, in creating something entirely new, precisely in such epochs of revolutionary crisis they anxiously conjure up the spirits of the past.[20]

Tamburlaine rebels against hierarchy, legitimacy, the whole established order of things, and to what end? To reach "The sweet fruition of an earthly crowne." His will is immeasurably stronger, but it is essentially the same as the will of Mycetes, Cosroe, Bajazet, or any of the other kings that strut around the stage. Part I ends not in an act of revolt, but in the supreme gesture of legitimacy, a proper marriage, with the Scourge of God earnestly assuring his father-in-law of Zenocrate's unblemished chastity. Similarly, the end of *The Jew of Malta* demonstrates how close Barabas has been all along to the gentile world he loathes and wishes to destroy. Barabas himself has said as much, but he somehow fails to make a connection between his perception of likeness and his violent hatred, until at the close he boils in the pot he has prepared for his enemy. Likewise, Faustus's whole career binds him ever more closely to that Christian conception of the body and the mind, that divinity, he thought he was decisively rejecting. He dreams of living "in al voluptuousnesse" (337), but his pleasures are parodic versions of Holy Communion.[21]

Marlowe stands apart, then, from both orthodoxy and skepticism; he calls into question the theory of literature and history as repeatable moral lessons, and he calls into question his age's characteristic mode of rejecting those lessons. But how does he himself understand his characters' motivation, the force that compels them to repeat the same actions again and again? The answer, as I have already suggested, lies in self-fashioning. Marlowe's heroes struggle to invent themselves; they stand, in Coriolanus's phrase, "As if a man were author of himself / And knew no other kin" (5.3.36–37). Shakespeare characteristically forces his very Marlovian hero to reach out and grasp his mother's hand; in Marlowe's plays, with the exception of *Dido Queene of Carthage*, we never see and scarcely even hear of the heroes' parents. Tamburlaine is the son of nameless "paltry" Scythians, Faustus of "parents base of stocke" (12), and Barabas, so far as we can tell, of no one at all. (Even in *Edward II*, where an emphasis on parentage would seem unavoidable, there is scant mention of Edward I). The family is at the center of most Elizabethan and Jacobean drama as it is at the center of the period's economic and social structure;[22] in Marlowe, it is something to be neglected, despised, or violated. Two of Marlowe's heroes kill their children without a trace of remorse; most prefer male friendships to marriage or kinship bonds; all insist upon free choice in determining their intimate relations. Upon his father's death, Edward immediately sends for Gaveston; Barabas adopts Ithamore in place of Abigail; Faustus cleaves to his sweet Mephastophilis; and, in a more passionate love scene than any with Zenocrate, Tamburlaine wins the ardent loyalty of Theridamas.

The effect is to dissolve the structure of sacramental and blood relations that normally determine identity in this period and to render the heroes virtually autochthonous, their names and identities given by no one but themselves. Indeed self-naming is a major enterprise in these plays, repeated over and over again as if the hero continues to exist only by virtue of constantly renewed acts of will. Augustine had written in *The City of God* that "if God were to withdraw what we may call his 'constructive power' from existing things, they would cease to exist, just as they did not exist before they were made."[23] In the neutrality of time and space that characterizes Marlowe's world, this "constructive power" must exist within the hero himself; if it should fail for an instant, he would fall into nothingness, become, in Barabas's words, "a senselesse lumpe of clay / That will with euery water wash to dirt" (I. 450–51). Hence the hero's tragic compulsion to repeat his name and his actions, a compulsion Marlowe links to the drama itself. The hero's re-presentations fade into the reiterated performances of the play.

If Marlowe's protagonists fashion themselves, they do not do so just as they please; they are, as we have seen, compelled to use only those forms and materials produced by the structure of relations in their particular, quite distinct worlds. We watch Tamburlaine construct himself out of phrases picked up or overheard: "And ride in triumph through *Persepolis*" (*1 Tam.* 2.5.754) or "I that am tearm'd the Scourge and Wrath of God" (*1 Tam.* 3.3.1142). Like the gold taken from unwary travellers or the troops lured away from other princes, Tamburlaine's identity is something *appropriated*, seized from others.[24] Similarly, Barabas is virtually composed of hard little aphorisms, cynical adages, worldly proverbs—all the neatly packaged nastiness of his society. Even Edward II, with his greater psychological complexity, can only clothe himself in the metaphors available to his station, though these metaphors—the "Imperial Lion," for example—often seem little applicable. And the most haunting instance in Marlowe of his self-fashioning by quotation or appropriation occurs in *Doctor Faustus*, when the hero concludes the signing of the fatal deed with the words "*Consummatum est*" (515).

To unfold the meaning of this repetition of Christ's dying words, we would have to trace the entire, tortuous network of Faustus's fears and desires: his blasphemy is a willful defilement of the sacred and, as such, the uncanny expression of a perverse, despairing faith; it is Faustus's appropriation to himself of the most solemn and momentous words available in his culture to mark this decisive boundary in his life; it is an ambiguous equation of himself with Christ, first as God, then as dying man; it is the culmination of his fantasies of making an end, and hence a suicide that demonically parodies Christ's self-sacrifice. And beyond all these, Faustus's use of Christ's words evokes the archetypal act of role-taking. To grasp this, we must restore the words to their context in the Gospel of John:

After this, Jesus knowing that all things were now accomplished, that the Scripture might be fulfilled, saith, I thirst. Now there was set a vessel full of vinegar: and they filled a sponge with vinegar, and put it upon hyssop, and put it to his mouth. When Jesus therefore had received the vinegar, he said, It is finished [*Consummatum est*] : and he bowed his head, and gave up the ghost. (19:28-30)[25]

As it is written in Psalm 69, "and in my thirst they gave me vinegar to drink" (21), so it is fulfilled: Christ's thirst is not identical to the body's normal longing for drink, but an *enactment* of that longing so that he may fully accomplish the role darkly prefigured in the Old Testament. The drink of vinegar is the final structural element in the realization of his identity. Faustus's blasphemy then is a demonic reenactment of the moment in which Christ acknowledges the fulfillment of his role, and the magician thereby hopes to touch upon the primal springs of identity itself.

But in the Gospel of John, as we have seen, the words "Consummatum est" are a true end; they are spoken at the moment of Christ's death. In *Doctor Faustus*, they are, rather, a beginning, spoken at the moment Faustus is embarking on his bargain. Unlike Christ, who is his own transcendent object, and whose career is precisely the realization of himself, Faustus, and all of Marlowe's self-fashioning heroes, must posit an object in order to exist. Naming oneself is not enough; one must also name and pursue a goal. The heroes do so with a splendid energy that distinguishes their words as well as their actions from the surrounding society. The Turks, friars, and Christian knights may all be driven by "The wind that bloweth all the world besides, / Desire of gold" (III. 1422-23), but only Barabas can speak of "Infinite riches in a little roome" (I. 72). Theridimas may declare that "A God is not so glorious as a King," but when he is asked if he himself would be a king, he replies, "Nay, though I praise it, I can liue without it" (*1 Tam*. 2.5. 771). Tamburlaine cannot live without it, and his reward is not only "The sweet fruition of an earthly crowne" but what Plato's rival Gorgias conceives as "the magic violence of speech."[26]

It is this Gorgian conception of rhetoric, and not the Platonic or Aristotelian, that is borne out in Marlowe's heroes. For

Gorgias, man is forever cut off from the knowledge of being, forever locked in the partial, the contradictory, and the irrational. If anything exists, he writes, it is both incomprehensible and incommunicable, for "that which we communicate is speech, and speech is not the same thing as the things that exist."[27] This tragic epistemological distance is never bridged; instead through the incantatory power of language, men construct magnificent deceptions in which and for which they live. It is precisely by means of this incantatory power that Faustus conjures up the Prince of Deceptions and that Tamburlaine makes his entire life into a project, transforming himself into an elemental, destructive force, driving irresistibly forward: "For Wil and Shall best fitteth *Tamburlain*" (*1 Tam*. 3.3.1139). He collapses all the senses of these verbs—intention, command, prophecy, resolution, and simple futurity—into his monomaniacal project.

All of Marlowe's heroes seem similarly obsessed, and the result of their passionate willing, their insistent, reiterated naming of themselves and their objects, is that they become more intensely real to us, more present, than any of the other characters. This is only to say that they are the protagonists, but once again Marlowe relates the shape of the medium itself to the central experience of the plays; his heroes seem determined to realize the Idea of themselves as dramatic heroes.[28] There is a parallel in Spenser's Malbecco, who is so completely what he is —in this case, so fanatically jealous—that he becomes the allegorical incarnation of Jealousy itself. But where this self-realization in Spenser is Platonic, in Marlowe it is Gorgian—that is, Platonism is undermined by the presence of the theater itself, the unavoidable distance between the particular actor and his role, the insistent awareness in audience and players alike of illusion.

Within the plays, this awareness is intensified by the difficulties the characters experience in sustaining their lives as projects, by that constant reiteration to which, as we have seen, they are bound. For even as no two performances or readings of a text are exactly the same, so the repeated acts of self-fashioning are never absolutely identical; indeed, as Gilles Deleuze has recently observed, we can only speak of repetition by reference to the difference or change that it causes in the mind that contemplates it.[29] The result is that the objects of desire, at first so clearly defined, so avidly pursued, gradually lose their sharp outlines and become more and more like mirages. Faustus speaks endlessly of his appetite, his desire to be glutted, ravished, consumed, but what is it exactly that he wants? By the end of the play it is clear that knowledge, voluptuousness, and power are each mere approximations of the goal for which he sells his soul and body; what that goal is remains maddeningly unclear. "Mine owne fantasie / . . . will receiue no obiect," (136–37), he tells Valdes and Cornelius, in a phrase that could stand as the play's epigraph. At first Barabas seems a simpler case: he wants wealth, though there is an unsettling equivocation between the desire for wealth as power and security and desire for wealth as an aesthetic, even metaphysical gratification. But the rest of the play does not bear out this desire as the center of Barabas's being; he seeks rather, at any cost, to revenge himself on the Christians. Or so we think until he plots to destroy the Turks and restore the Christians to power. Well then, he wants always to serve his own self-interest: *Ego mihimet sum semper proximus* (I. 228). But where exactly is the self whose interests he serves? Even the Latin tag betrays an ominous self-distance: "I am always my own neighbor," or even, "I am always *next* to myself." Edward II is no clearer. He loves Gaveston, but why? "Because he loues me more than all the world" (372). The desire returns from its object, out there in the world, to the self, a self that is nonetheless exceedingly unstable. When Gaveston is killed, Edward has within seconds adopted someone else: the will exists, but the object of the will is little more than an illusion. Even Tamburlaine, with his firm declaration of a goal, becomes ever more equivocal. "The sweet fruition of an earthly crowne" turns out not to be what it first appears—the acquisition of kingship—for Tamburlaine continues his restless pursuit long after this acquisition. His goal then is power, which is graphically depicted as the ability to transform virgins with blubbered cheeks into slaughtered carcasses. But when Tamburlaine views the corpses he has made and defines this object for himself, it immediately becomes something else, a mirror reflecting yet another goal:

> Al sights of power to grace my victory:
> And such are obiects fit for *Tamburlaine*,
> Where in as in a mirrour may be seene,
> His honor, that consists in sheading blood.

(1 Tam. 5.2.2256–59)[30]

It is Tamburlaine, in his celebrated speech "What is beauty saith my sufferings then?" (1 Tam. 5.2.1941 ff.), who gives the whole problem of reaching a desired end its clearest formal expression in Marlowe: beauty, like all the goals pursued by the playwright's heroes, always hovers just beyond the reach of human thought and expression. The problem of elusiveness is one of the major preoccupations of Renaissance thinkers from the most moderate to the most radical, from the judicious Hooker to the splendidly injudicious Bruno.[31] Marlowe is deeply influenced by this contemporary thought, but he subtly shifts the emphasis from the infinity that draws men beyond what they possess to the problem of the human will, the difficulty men experience in truly wanting anything. Kenneth Burke remarks that for Saint Augustine the essence of evil is that anything should be "sought for itself, whereas things should be sought only in terms of the search for God."[32] Marlowe's heroes seem at first to embrace such evil: they freely proclaim their immense hunger for something that takes on the status of a personal absolute, and they relentlessly pursue this absolute.

The more threatening an obstacle in their path, the more determined they are to obliterate or overreach it: I long for, I burn, I
will. But, as we have seen, we are never fully convinced by these
noisy demonstrations of single-minded appetite. It is as if Marlowe's heroes wanted to be wholly perverse, in Augustine's
sense, but were incapable of such perversity, as if they could
not finally desire anything for itself. For Hooker and Bruno
alike, this inability arises from the existence of transcendent
goals—it is a proof of the existence of God; for Marlowe, it
springs from the tragic fact that all objects of desire are fictions,
theatrical illusions shaped by the characters. And those characters are themselves fictions, fashioned in reiterated acts of
self-naming. The problem is already understood in its full
complexity by Montaigne, but, as Auerbach observes, "his
irony, his dislike of big words, his calm way of being profoundly at ease with himself, prevent him from pushing on
beyond the limits of the problematic and into the realm of the
tragic."[33] Marlowe, whose life suggests the very opposite of that
"peculiar equilibrium" that distinguishes Montaigne, rushes to
embrace the tragic with a strange eagerness.

Man can only exist in the world by fashioning for himself a
name and an object, but these, as Marlowe and Montaigne
understood, are both fictions. No particular name or object can
entirely satisfy one's inner energy demanding to be expressed or
fill so completely the potential of one's consciousness that all
longings are quelled, all intimations of unreality silenced.
Throughout the sixteenth century, Protestant and Catholic
polemicists demonstrated brilliantly how each other's religion—
the very anchor of reality for millions of souls—was a cunning
theatrical illusion, a demonic fantasy, a piece of poetry.[34] Each
conducted this unmasking, of course, in the name of the *real*
religious truth, but the collective effect upon a skeptical intellect
like Marlowe's seems to have been devastating. And it was not
only the religious "deconstruction" of reality to which the

playwright was responding. On the distant shores of Africa and America and at home, in their "rediscovered" classical texts, Renaissance Europeans were daily confronting evidence that their accustomed reality was only one solution, among many others, of perennial human problems. Though they often tried to destroy the alien cultures they encountered, they could not destroy the testimony of their own consciousness. "The wonder is not that things are," writes Valéry, "but that they are *what* they are and not something else."[35] Each of Marlowe's plays constitutes reality in a manner radically different from the plays that preceded it, just as his work as a whole marks a startling departure from the drama of his time. Each of his heroes makes a different leap from inchoate appetite to the all-consuming project: what is necessary in one play is accidental or absent in the next. Only the leap itself is always necessary, at once necessary and absurd, for it is the embracing of a fiction rendered desirable by the intoxication of language.

Marlowe's heroes *must* live their lives as projects, but they do so in the midst of intimations that the projects are illusions. Their strength is not sapped by these intimations: they do not withdraw into stoical resignation or contemplative solitude, nor do they endure for the sake of isolated moments of grace in which they are in touch with a wholeness otherwise absent in their lives. Rather, they derive a tragic courage from the absurdity of their enterprise, a murderous, self-destructive, supremely eloquent courage.

In his turbulent life and, more importantly, in his writing, Marlowe is deeply implicated in his heroes, though he is far more intelligent and self-aware than any of them. Cutting himself off from the comforting doctrine of repetition, he writes plays that spurn and subvert his culture's metaphysical and ethical certainties. We who have lived after Nietzsche and Flaubert may find it difficult to grasp how strong, how courageous Marlowe must have been: to write as if the admonitory purpose

of literature were a lie, to invent fictions only to create and not
to serve God or the state, to fashion lines that echo in the void,
that echo more powerfully because there is nothing but a void.
Hence Marlowe's implication in the lives of his protagonists and
hence, too, his transcendence of this implication in the creation
of enduring works of art. For the one true goal of all these
heroes is to be characters in Marlowe's plays; it is only for this,
ultimately, that they manifest both their magnificent energy
and their haunting sense of unsatisfied longing. And they alone
survive a life that was violent, sordid, and short.

NOTES

1. "The voyage set out by the right honourable the Earle of Cumberland,
in the yere 1586 . . . Written by M. John Sarracoll marchant in the same
voyage," in Richard Hakluyt, ed., *The Principal Navigations, Voyages,
Traffiques & Discoveries of the English Nation* (Glasgow: James MacLehose
& Sons, 1904), 11:206-7.

2. At the opening of *Tamburlaine,* there is a wry reminder of how exotic
Europe would appear to a Persian: *"Europe, wher the Sun dares scarce
appeare, / For freezing meteors and coniealed colde"* (*1 Tam.* 1.1.18-19).
Quotations of Marlowe's plays, with the exception of *Doctor Faustus,* are
from *The Works of Christopher Marlowe,* ed. C. F. Tucker Brooke (Oxford:
The Clarendon Press, 1910). Quotations of *Doctor Faustus* are from the A
text of W. W. Greg's *Marlowe's "Doctor Faustus" 1604-1616: Parallel
Texts* (Oxford: The Clarendon Press, 1950). My own reading of the play
supports recent arguments for the superiority of the A text; see Fredson
Bowers, "Marlowe's *Doctor Faustus:* The 1602 Additions," *Studies in
Bibliography* 26 (1973): 1-18, and Constance Brown Kuriyama, "Dr. Greg
and *Doctor Faustus:* The Supposed Originality of the 1616 Text," *English
Literary Renaissance* 5 (1975): 171-97.

3. See Ernst Cassirer, *The Individual and the Cosmos in Renaissance
Philosophy*, trans. Mario Domandi (New York: Barnes & Noble, 1963),
esp. ch. 1, "Nicholas Cusanus." In *Doctor Faustus*, Marlowe plays upon
the residual religious symbolism of the Elizabethan stage (though this is
more true of the B text than of the A text), but he does so only to subvert
it, locating hell psychologically rather than spatially.

4. Here, as elsewhere in my discussion of *Doctor Faustus*, I am indebted to conversations with my colleague Edward Snow and to his essay, "Marlowe's *Doctor Faustus* and the Ends of Desire."

5. "Experience" may also have the sense of "experiment," as if Faustus's whole future were a test of the proposition that hell is a fable.

6. The futility of naming cities after oneself was a commonplace in the period; see, for example, Ralegh's *History of the World* (1614): V,v,2, p. 646: "This was that *Seleucia*, whereto *Antigonus the great* who founded it, gave the name of *Antigonia:* but *Seleucus* getting it shortly after, called it *Seleucia;* and *Ptolemie Evergetes* having lately won it, might, if it had so pleased him, have changed the name into *Ptolemais*. Such is the vanitie of men, that hope to purchase an endless memoriall unto their names, by workes proceeding rather from their greatnesse, than from their vertue; which therefore no longer are their owne, than the same greatnesse hath continuance."

7. The cutting edge of this career was the conquest of the New World where fertile lands, rich mines, and whole peoples were consumed in a few generations. It is estimated that the Indian population of New Spain (Mexico) fell from approximately 11 million in 1519 to approximately 1.5 million in 1650, and there are similarly horrifying figures for Brazil. In 1583, a Jesuit, José de Anchieta, observed of the latter that "the number of people used up in this place from twenty years ago until now seems a thing not to be believed" (Immanuel Wallerstein, *The Modern World-System* [New York: Academic Press, 1974], p. 80, n. 75); appropriately, it is on this great enterprise (among others) that the dying Tamburlaine, with infinite pathos, reflects.

8. E. E. Evans-Pritchard, *The Nuer* (Oxford: The Clarendon Press, 1940), p. 103; quoted in E. P. Thompson, "Time, Work-Discipline, and Industrial Capitalism," *Past and Present* 38 (1967): 96.

9. See Keith Thomas, *Religion and the Decline of Magic* (London: Weidenfeld and Nicolson, 1971), p. 621; likewise, Christopher Hill, *Society and Puritanism in Pre-Revolutionary England*, 2nd ed. (New York: Schocken Books, 1967), ch. 5.

10. See Natalie Zemon Davis, "Some Tasks and Themes in the Study of Popular Religion," in *The Pursuit of Holiness in Late Medieval and Renaissance Religion*, ed. Charles Trinkhaus and Heiko A. Oberman (Leiden: E. J. Brill, 1974), 307–36. I am also indebted to Professor Davis's essay, "Ghosts, Kin and Progeny: Some Features of Family Life in Early Modern France," forthcoming in *Daedalus*.

11. C. L. Barber, " 'The form of Faustus' fortunes good or bad'," *Tulane Drama Review* 8 (1964): 99.

12. For a typical expression of this view, see Ralegh's *History:* II, xix, 3, pp. 508–09: "The same just God who liveth and governeth all thinges for ever, doeth in these our times give victorie, courage, and discourage, raise, and throw downe Kinges, Estates, Cities, and Nations, for the same offences which were committed of old, and are committed in the present: for which reason in these and other the afflictions of *Israel*, alwaies the causes are set downe, that they might bee as precedents to succeeding ages."

13. See, for example, the Edwardian proclamations: #287 (393–403), #313 (432–33), in *Tudor Royal Proclamations*, ed. Paul L. Hughes and James F. Larkin, vol. 1 (New Haven: Yale University Press, 1964).

14. This characterization of the period's legal procedure is Christopher Hill's: "The Many-Headed Monster in Late Tudor and Early Stuart Political Thinking," in *From the Renaissance to the Counter-Reformation: Essays in Honor of Garrett Mattingly*, ed. Charles H. Carter (New York: Random House, 1965), p.303. Hill's view is close to Thomas More's in *Utopia:* Thieves "were everywhere executed, . . . as many as twenty at a time being hanged on one gallows" (*Utopia*, ed. Edward Surtz [New Haven, Yale University Press, 1964], p. 20). Statistics are inexact and inconsistent, but, for example, seventy-four persons were sentenced to death in Devon in 1598, and the average number of executions per year in London and Middlesex in the years 1607–1616 was 140 (Douglas Hay, "Property, Authority and the Criminal Law," in Hay et al., *Albion's Fatal Tree* [New York: Random House, 1975], p.22n.).

15. *The Mirror for Magistrates* is typical for its tireless repetition of the same paradigm of retributive justice, while both tragedy and comedy are quite characteristically concieved by Sidney, in the *Apology for Poetry*, as warnings and lessons. This conception continues to dominate sociological theories of literature; see, for example, Elizabeth Burns, *Theatricality* (New York: Harper & Row, 1973), p. 35.

16. There is a preliminary but perceptive exploration of this aspect of Marlowe's work by J. R. Mulryne and Stephen Fender, "Marlowe and the 'Comic Distance'," in *Christopher Marlowe: Mermaid Critical Commentaries*, ed. Brian Morris (London: Ernest Benn, 1968), pp. 49–64.

17. Max Bluestone, "*Libido Speculandi:* Doctrine and Dramaturgy in Contemporary Interpretations of Marlowe's *Doctor Faustus*," in *Reinterpretations of Elizabethan Drama*, ed. Norman Rabkin (New York: Columbia University Press, 1969), p. 82.

18. Edward Said, *Beginnings* (New York: Basic Books, 1975), p. 58. As *The Prince, The Courtier, The Governor*, and *The Schoolmaster* bear witness, these intermediate beings fascinated the Renaissance. See Stephen J. Greenblatt, *Sir Walter Ralegh: The Renaissance Man and His Roles* (New Haven: Yale University Press, 1973), ch. 2.

19. See Georg Lukács, *History and Class Consciousness*, trans. Rodney Livingstone (Cambridge, Mass.: M.I.T. Press, 1971), p. 15. The fountain-head of all modern speculation along these lines is Vico's *New Science*.

20. In *The Marx-Engels Reader*, ed. Robert C. Tucker (New York: W. W. Norton, 1972), p. 437.

21. See C. L. Barber, " 'The Form of Faustus' fortunes good or bad'," esp. p. 107. This does not, however, establish Holy Communion as the healthy, proper end that Faustus should be pursuing; on the contrary, Marlowe may have regarded Holy Communion as itself perverse. There are, in *Doctor Faustus* and throughout Marlowe's works, the elements of a radical critique of Christianity, a critique similar to that made with suicidal daring in 1584 by Giordano Bruno's *Expulsion of the Triumphant Beast* (*Lo spaccio de la bestia trionfante*). Here, in a scarcely veiled satirical allegory of the life of Christ, the Greek gods, sensing a waning of their reputation on earth, decide to send Orion to restore their credit among men. This Orion "knows how to perform miracles, and . . . can walk over the waves of the sea without sinking, without wetting his feet, and with this, consequently, will be able to perform many other fine acts of kindness. Let us find him among men, and let us see to it that he give them to understand all that I want and like them to understand: that white is black, that the human intellect, through which they seem to see best, is blindness, and that that which according to reason seems excellent, good, and very good, is vile, criminal, and extremely bad. I want them to understand that Nature is a whorish prostitute, that natural law is ribaldry, that Nature and Divinity cannot concur in one and the same good end, and that the justice of the one is not subordinate to the justice of the other, but that they are contraries, as are shadows and light . . . With this he [Orion] will persuade them that philosophy, all contemplation, and all magic that could make them similar to us, are nothing but follies, that every heroic act is only cowardice, and that ignorance is the best science in the world because it is acquired without labor and does not cause the mind to be affected by melancholy" (*Expulsion*, trans and ed. by Arthur D. Imerti [New Brunswick: Rutgers University Press, 1964], pp. 255–56).

22. See C. L. Barber, "The Family in Shakespeare's Development: The Tragedy of the Sacred," a paper delivered at the English Institute, September, 1976; also Peter Laslett, *The World We Have Lost* (New York: Charles Scribner's Sons, 1965).

23. *The City of God*, trans. Henry Bettenson (London: Penguin Books, 1972), II, xii, 26, p. 506. See Georges Poulet, *Studies in Human Time*, trans. Elliott Coleman (Baltimore: The Johns Hopkins University Press, 1956), p. 19.

24. "The victor in any competition for honour finds his reputation

enhanced by the humiliation of the vanquished. . . . It was believed at
one time in Italy by the common people that one who gave an insult thereby took to himself the reputation of which he deprived the other. The
Church of England hymn puts the point succinctly: 'Conquering Kings
their titles take / From the foes they captive make.' " Cf. Julian Pitt-Rivers,
"Honour and Social Status," in *Honour and Shame*, ed. J. G. Peristiany
(London: Weidenfeld and Nicolson, 1965), p. 24.

25. The Vulgate is worth quoting for its subtle play on *consummo*:
"Postea sciens Iesus quia omnia consummata sunt, ut consummaretur
Scriptura, dixit: Sitio. Vas ergo erat positum aceto plenum; illi autem
spongiam plenam aceto hyssopo circumponentes obtulerunt ori eius. Cum
ergo accepisset Iesus acetum, dixit, Consummatum est. Et inclinato capite,
tradidit spiritum."

26. See Mario Untersteiner, *The Sophists*, trans. Kathleen Freeman (Oxford: Blackwell's, 1954), p. 106. Untersteiner's account of the place of
tragedy in Gorgias has considerable resonance for a student of Marlowe.

27. Kathleen Freeman, *Ancilla to the Pre-Socratic Philosophers* (Cambridge, Mass.: Harvard University Press, 1948), p. 129.

28. "With complete assurance and certainty, tragedy solves the most difficult problem of Platonism: that of discovering whether individual things
have their own Idea and their own Essence. And the reply which it gives
reverses the order in which the question is put, since it shows that it is
only when what is individual—that is to say, a particular living individual—is
carried to its final limits and possibilities that it conforms to the Idea and
begins to really exist" (Lucien Goldmann, *The Hidden God*, trans. Philip
Thody [London: Routledge & Kegan Paul, 1964], p. 59). Marlowe's
heroes are extremists of the kind called for by this conception of tragedy,
but Marlowe treats their extremism with considerable irony.

29. Gilles Deleuze, *Différence et Répétition* (Paris: Presses Universitaires
de France, 1968), p. 96. The idea originates with Hume.

30. In the very moment of Tamburlaine's triumph, a gap is opened between the self and its object, indeed, a gap *within* both self and object.
Similarly, when one of his admirers says that Tamburlaine is "In euery
part proportioned like the man, / Should make the world subdued to *Tamburlaine*" (*1 Tam*. 2.1. 483–84), his words inadvertently touch off a verti-
ginous series of repetitions and differences.

31. "For man doth not seem to rest satisfied, either with fruition of that
wherewith his life is preserved, or with performance of such actions as ad-
vance him most deservedly in estimation; but doth further covet, yea often-
times manifestly pursue with great sedulity and earnestness, that which
cannot stand him in any stead for vital use; that which exceedeth the reach

of sense; yea somewhat above the capacity of reason, somewhat divine and heavenly, which with hidden exultation it rather surmiseth than conceiveth; somewhat it seeketh, and what that is directly it knoweth not, yet very intentive desire thereof doth so incite it, that all other known delights and pleasures are laid aside, they give place to the search of this but only suspected desire. . . . For although the beauties, riches, honours, sciences, virtues, and perfections of all men living, were in the present possession of one; yet somewhat beyond and above all this there would still be sought and earnestly thirsted for" (Richard Hooker, *Of the Laws of Ecclesiastical Polity* [London, Everyman's Library, 1954] : I, I, xi, 4, pp. 257-58). "Whatever species is represented to the intellect and comprehended by the will, the intellect concludes there is another species above it, a greater and still greater one, and consequently it is always impelled toward new motion and abstraction in a certain fashion. For it ever realizes that everything it possesses is a limited thing which for that reason cannot be sufficient in itself, good in itself, or beautiful in itself, because the limited thing is not the universe and is not the absolute entity, but is contracted to this nature, this species or this form represented to the intellect and presented to the soul. As a result, from that beautiful which is comprehended, and therefore limited, and consequently beautiful by participation, the intellect progresses toward that which is truly beautiful without limit or circumscription whatsoever." (Giordano Bruno, *The Heroic Frenzies*, trans. Paul E. Memmo, Jr., *University of North Carolina Studies in Romance Languages and Literatures*, No. 50 (1964), pp. 128-29). There are strikingly similar passages in Cusa and Ficino.

32. Kenneth Burke, *The Rhetoric of Religion* (Berkeley: University of California Press, 1961), p. 69.

33. Erich Auerbach, *Mimesis*, trans. Willard R. Trask (Princeton: Princeton University Press, 1968 edition), p. 311. The relevance of this passage to the present context was suggested to me by my colleague, Paul Alpers.

34. The essential positions are already laid out in England as early as the More-Tyndale controversy; see Thomas More, *A dyaloge of syr T. More* (London: W. Rastell, 1529), William Tyndale, *An answere vnto Sir Thomas Mores dialoge* (Antwerp: S. Cock, 1531), Thomas More, *The confutacyon of Tyndales answere* (London: W. Rastell, 1532; part two, 1533). A splendid new edition of the latter has recently appeared in three parts as volume 8 of the Yale edition of *The Complete Works of St. Thomas More*.

35. Paul Valéry, *Leonardo Poe Mallarmé*, trans. Malcolm Cowley and James R. Lawler, Volume 8 of *The Collected Works of Paul Valéry*, ed. Jackson Mathews, Bollingen Series XLV (Princeton: Princeton Univ. Press, 1972), p. 93.

Edward A. Snow

Marlowe's *Doctor Faustus* and the Ends of Desire

Perhaps the most difficult thing about writing on Marlowe is finding some way of formulating and discussing his themes that will not betray the radically questioning nature of his work. For instance, if we were forced to venture a statement about the central topic of *Doctor Faustus*, it would probably not be untrue to suggest that the play, like all of Marlowe's work, is about the fulfillment of will.[1] Yet this would scarcely suggest the extent to which the play puzzles about what the will is, and what fulfillment consists of, and how words like "will," "want," and "have" can victimize the speaker who tries to make them serve his purposes. Every time the drama raises the issue of what Faustus wants, it does so in a way that subtly deflects attention away from the ostensible objects of his desire toward the onto-logical ambiguities at its origin. All of his specific desires, the more randomly and recklessly they accumulate, and the more compulsively he *speaks* of them, begin to seem mere epiphe-nomena, attempts to rationalize an alien, anxiously prior inward restlessness by creating around it the appearance of a self that wills it and has it as "its" desire. (The problem about the sub-ject of this sentence is the problem at the heart of the play it-self.) Willing itself eventually begins to seem less a natural habitus than, as Faustus himself at one point unwittingly calls it, a "desperate enterprise." The Faustian project, we might say, becomes a matter of stabilizing the "I" by converting "wanting" in the sense of "lacking" into "wanting" in the sense of "desir-ing": the formula by which he characteristically aspires is not even "I will" or "I want" but "I'll have . . . I'll have . . . I'll have," so anxious is he to feel himself a containing self rather than merely the voice of a nameless emptiness or an impersonal rush to the void. It is not so much that there are things that he wants as it is that he needs to ensure himself that there will always be some object out there, marking extension in space and time, toward which he will be able to project "his" desire, in terms of which he can experience himself as an interior distance alive in the present and stretching continuous and intact into the future. All his negotiations with Mephastophilis leave the question of wishes to be granted pointedly unspecified and open-ended:[2]

> I charge thee wait upon me whilst I live,
> To do whatever *Faustus* shall commaund, . . .
>
> (281–82)

> To give me whatsoever I shal aske,
> To tel me whatsoever I demaund . . .
>
> (339–40)

> *Thirdly, that Mephastophilis shall do for him,*
> *and bring him whatsoever.*
>
> (544–45)

And Mephastophilis is in turn reassuring Faustus at the level of his deepest anxieties when he promises that "I wil be thy slave, and waite on thee, / And give thee more than thou hast wit to aske" (486–87). Mephastophilis (besides insinuating that Faustus will get more than he bargained for) is not so much promising him "the unimaginable" as telling him not to worry about not really knowing what he wants, nor about running out of things to ask for, coming to the *end* of desire. Ultimate fulfillment or satiety can be the most fearful prospect of all for a self that suspects it has created itself out of nothing (in order to protect itself from nothingness), and can thus only sustain itself in the "conceited" space between desire and possession:

> *Cornelius:* The spirits tell me they can drie the sea,
>   And fetch the treasure of all forraine wrackes,
>   I, all the wealth that our forefathers hid
>   Within the massie entrailes of the earth.
>   Then tell me *Faustus*, what shal we three want?
> *Faustus:* Nothing *Cornelius*, O this cheares my soule,
>   Come shew me some demonstrations magicall . . .
>
> (177–83)

It is only with difficulty that an actor's voice, in attempting to
express Faustus's enthusiasm, can overcome the resistance of
the laconic, inward-turning, brooding tendencies of "Nothing,
Cornelius," and block out the ominous effect of the pause that
follows it. The prospect of wanting (lacking) nothing evokes
just for a moment the subliminal dread of wanting (desiring)
nothing, and perhaps lacking it—as if by a demon in language
itself, *that* were what were on the other side (and at the heart)
of all imagined desires. Longing and dread are an extremely
unstable antithesis in this play. Like the Good and Evil Angels,
they are always co-present, inseparable poles of a single impulse
(and at times it seems that this impulse as a whole is what is
called "the will"). It is hoped that this essay will, among other
things, provide a validating frame for Empson's perception of
the way in which the difficulty of giving rhetorical emphasis to
the negatives in Faustus's penultimate "Ugly hell gape not,
come not *Lucifer*" (1507) tends to make the voice that speaks
it impatiently, even desperately invoke that which it is attempting to keep at arm's length.[3] Whatever it is that strains against
those negatives is also what resists the earlier, impatient *invocations* that the line so pointedly recalls: "come Mephastophilus, /
And bring glad tidings from great *Lucifer:* / Ist not midnight? /
Come *Mephastophilus*, / *Veni veni Mephastophile*" (466–69).
The same erotic energy charges both utterances, and the later
one is the genuine consummation of the earlier one as well as
its ironical inversion.

★

The focus of the play, then, is not so much on a theme as on
the field of "terministic" ambiguities in which all its central
issues are mutually implicated.[4] An approach needs to be found
that can indicate how it is that the play, being about desire, is
also, necessarily, about damnation, guilt, self-transcendence,
and fear of death; about the body, about self-reference, about

cause, motion, place, and duration; about, ultimately, "the whole philosophical mythology concealed in language."[5] Even more than themes and images, we need to look at the *terms* by which the play is organized—and in the process shift the focus of our attention from character-analysis and its attendant ethical judgments to the phenomenological contours of the world of the play and their relationship to those of the consciousness at the center of it. Following the language of inside-outside, or here-there, or now-then, or fast-slow, or motion-rest, through the complications of the text would, I think, put us in closer touch with the intentionality of the play than do the restrictive, morally-biased generalizations to which an approach such as "the theme of damnation" seems inevitably to condemn us.

I propose to start with the term "end" and its cognates, and follow it, especially through its interweavings with terms for body, will, and time, into whatever corners of the text it happens to lead. Of all the words in the play, it is probably the one that opens most directly upon central complexities. The language of achieving ends, making an end, coming to an end, etc., is a continual refrain of the opening soliloquy, and it recurs throughout the course of the play ("Now will I make an ende immediately" [513], "*Consummatum est*, this Bill is ended" [515], "Thy fatall time doth drawe to finall ende" [1170]), climaxing in the vacillations of the last soliloquy ("'Twill all be past anone" [1482], "O no end is limited to damned soules" [1488]), and not culminating until the final "authorial" inscription: "*Terminat hora diem, Terminat Author opus.*" And in virtually every instance there is a tension between the speaker's attempt to say one thing, and mean it, and the tendency of the words themselves to generate ambiguity, irony, and paradox. Consider, for instance, "O no end is limited to damned soules." It is possible to take "limited" as an adjective qualifying "end," rather than as an active verb, in which case the focus of the sentence shifts from the doctrinal to the psychological, and we

find ourselves on the verge of a purely phenomenological definition of the state of damnation. Even when we do hear "limited
to" as a verb, there is a certain resistance to understanding it as
"granted" or "allotted" (we normally think of "to limit" as the
opposite of "to bestow"); and in the time it takes us to adjust
to this meaning, we may hear the grammatically easier and
utterly subversive "no particular end is peculiar to damned souls
(all men suffer the same fate)." Finally, the awkward, apparently
tautological predication of "end" by "limited" can suggest two
phenomenologically opposed senses of an ending struggling
within Faustus's confrontation with finality—end as extension
or as circumference, as an abyss or as the boundary that keeps
one from falling into it. In "Now will I make an ende immediately," to take another example, there is a rich paradox potentially involved in the notion of *making* an *end;* a possible
equivocation between the volitional and temporal senses of
"will"; and a transition from one experience of the time of the
present to its opposite effected by the extension of "now" into
the five anxious syllables of "immediately" (not unlike the transition from "dying" to dying an "everlasting death"). Or, as a
last example, consider " 'Twill all be past anone." The phenomenological ambiguities of "past" tend to focus the line on the
imaginative process by which the mind experiences time and
death, and on the various ways in which it unconsciously pre-
serves, gives substance to what no longer exists: "It will all have
finished passing by" (on the model of "til I am past this faire
and pleasant greene, / ile walke on foote"), or "It will all be the
past, or in the past" (with Homer, Alexander, the Trojan War,
the old philosophers, and Faustus's student days in Wittenberg).
And there is an irony about transposing into the context of
death itself the rather common (but still curious) act of imagining a future in which the present will be past; we are encouraged
to contemplate the difficulty the mind has in including itself in
the "all" or the "it," and the process by which it contrives to

survive its death in the very act of projecting into it. In every instance, the more we attend to implicit ambiguities, the more we find a sceptical, nonjudgmental exploration of human consciousness tending to take the place of either an heroic, dramatistic identification with Faustus or a theological, homilectic disapproval of him.

It is in the opening soliloquy, with its careful delineation of not so much the characteristics as the *symptoms* of a Faustian personality, that the play on "end" and its cognates is most elaborately developed; it seems as a consequence the natural place for this analysis to begin. But before encountering specific instances of the term, something needs to be said about certain peculiarities of the overall texture of the soliloquy. It is virtually a patchwork of different languages: Greek, Latin, bastardized, proverbial Italian, and the "Lines, circles, sceanes, letters, and characters" of magic; or, on another axis, the specialized idioms of metaphysics, logic, ethics, medicine, law, and Christian theology. Every one of these languages implies, to a certain degree, its own world and world view: the word "end" will have slightly different connotations depending upon whether you are a Platonist or an Aristotelian, a pagan or a Christian, a Catholic or a Protestant, a metaphysician or a moralist, or a physician or a theologian. But this "Faustian" discourse, which seems capable of translating and absorbing all other languages into itself, seems correlatively to have no point of view of its own, no commitment to any particular world view or governing set of values. And it seems likewise incapable of recognizing difference or distance, or of understanding any other discourse on its own terms. The act of translation (and, less obviously, the resistances of a text) is itself a central motif of the soliloquy, and it is invariably attended by ironies of misattribution or reductive misreading.[6] "*On cai me on*" (A's "*Oncaymaeon*") is, according to one editor, not from Aristotle, but from Gorgias, as cited by

Sextus Empiricus;[7] and if it seems implausible that Marlowe's intentions should extend to such minutiae (however appropriate it would be to the ironical tenor of the whole to discover the subversive presence of Sextus's radical scepticism lurking within Faustus's absolutist, transcendental presumptions), it surely is an aspect of the ironical design of the speech that "being and not being" connotes for Faustus not the metaphysical and onto-logical issues that were the heart of ancient Greek philosophy, but merely the formal, scholastic paradigms by which logical disputation is taught and mastered. *Bene disserere est finis logices* is not even from the *Analytics* to which Faustus has re-duced Aristotle's works, but from the *Animadversiones Aristo-telicae* of Pietrus Ramus, who "reformed" Aristotle by breaking down the division between logic and rhetoric and devising other shortcuts for mastering him—in both respects symptomatic of the character to whom this soliloquy introduces us. (In *The Massacre at Paris*, Ramus is denounced as a "flat dichotamest," and accused, in words that *Doctor Faustus* pointedly recalls, of "having a smack in all, / Yet didst never [*sic*] sound anything to the depth." If Faustus would seem to be antithetical in his resolve to "sound the deapth" of all that he professes [32], the condemnation of Ramus nevertheless describes perfectly the shallowness he betrays in the process.)[8] His inability to attend to the full contexts of the Biblical passages has become a critical commonplace; it may also be of ironical significance that he quotes (with slight mistakes) from *Jerome's* Bible, thus empha-sizing that it is already a translation with which he is involved (and scarcely the translation one would expect a precocious stu-dent at Wittenberg to be reading, given Marlowe's anachronisti-cally contemporary dramatization of Faustus), intrigued even here by the presumptuousness of human authorship (underscored by the rhythmic stress on "*Jeromes*"), and haunted as well by its derivative, interpolated nature.

It is interesting to compare, as a means of grasping at least one aspect of Marlowe's elusive critical perspective, the way in which this opening soliloquy reduces every "foreign" language that enters it with the manner in which "*O lente lente curite noctis equi*" (1459) intrudes into the final soliloquy. Here, too, technically, is misquotation: the original is "lente currite, noctis equi." Here too, if you wish, is a flagrant violation of the original context: what in Ovid is a wish to extend a night of erotic pleasure serves for Faustus as an expression of apocalyptic dread. Once again a pagan (or epicurean) sensibility is distorted when it is appropriated by a Christian (or Faustian) one. Yet the difference in effect is complete. The line from Ovid wells up spontaneously from the depths of Faustus's being: it *originates* in him (no time or need for translation here!). Burning his books will not get it out of his system. Beneath its apparent inappropriateness, it is profoundly expressive of the obscure erotic energy involved in his religious passion. And against the feeling that Ovid's guilt-free, flesh-and-blood eroticism is betrayed in this Faustian setting, there is an equal sense that the setting deepens the Ovidian sense by creating a cosmic and spiritual background against which the erotic embrace it celebrates can take on its full, intrinsic value. (Jump comments that the transposition "adds immeasurably to [the words'] power and poignancy.")[9] Faustus's misquotation here seems literally an improvement of the original, in its own language—as if he were further inside the poetry, feeling it more deeply, than Ovid himself. And the haunting, paradoxical inwardness of the line can become even more complex if it happens to remind us that Marlowe himself began his literary career and first achieved notoriety with a translation of the *Elegies*. The contrast between the line's perfunctory Englishing there—"Stay night, and run not thus"—and its spontaneous, originative upwelling (and remembering) at the end of *Faustus* then takes its place as a facet of a complex meditation by Marlowe, implicit throughout the play, on authorship and its consequences—specifically, on his relationship to his protagonist, and on the distance that bringing him into being places between him and his more superficial, complacent Ovidian origins. Certainly no less crucial to the final, lingering effect of the play than Faustus's own passionate breakdown is the accompanying collapse of the authorial perspective, from the ironical, mocking detachment established by the opening soliloquy into the experience of immediacy and emotional identification that the closing soliloquy thrusts upon us. Whatever the actual chronology of Marlowe's plays, no work of art—not even *The Tempest*—communicates more powerfully the *sense* of a "last work" than does *Doctor Faustus*.

When we turn specifically to the motif of "end" and "ending" in the opening soliloquy, what seems crucial about the method of reiteration is a discrepancy between the pointed awareness in the text of the different words that can be translated as "end"— and the correspondingly different senses of "end-ness" that language can suggest—and the speaker's incapacity to respond to the concept in any other than an eschatological, self-alienating sense of "end-point" or "termination." For instance: "disputing well" (already a symptomatically Faustian translation of the potentially less disputatious *bene disserere*) is the "end" (*finis*) of logic in the sense of final cause, abiding concern, reason for being: one is always in the midst of logic, once one *has* achieved its end. Yet Faustus seems instinctively to assume that having "attained" this end means that he has arrived at the end of it, used it up, finished with it—and that as a result there is nothing to do but move on to something new. It is much the same with *ibi desinit philosophus, ibi incipit medicus*. This is what amounts to an ethical statement about the limits of the *field* of philosophy, a reminder that the health of the body and the knowledge of its functions and its orders lie outside the scope of philosophy, yet that philosophical wisdom should involve a respect for the body and the knowledge by which physical well-being is maintained. (And in the context of Marlowe's own "post-Christian" vision, the aphorism acquires a gnomic significance beyond anything Aristotle would have intended: that to go all the way in the realm of philosophy is to arrive at the all-important starting-point of the body, to discover it as the unanalyzable phenomenon toward which every thread of philosophical speculation, no matter what its ostensible subject, ultimately leads us. As if *only* a philosopher could know the true significance of medicine.) But Faustus seems to take it to mean simply that when you are finished with philosophy, then it is time to take up medicine.[10] His experience as a physician has no bearing on his experience as a philosopher, nor vice versa. One art follows directly upon another, each beginning precisely where the last left off, each neatly condensed, predigested, and encapsulated within the covers of its own book.[11]

If Faustus were more at home within the metaphor of "sounding the depths," then the "end" of an art might be a moment of creative fulfillment, an opening upon immanent horizons. But "levelling at the end," which seems so much more obviously expressive of the acquisitive impatience and narrow, projective vision that characterize him throughout the soliloquy, condemns him to traverse only surfaces, and to arrive only at terminations. It seems paradoxically the very nature of his will to go forward, his eyes aiming at a goal posited beyond him, that fates him to find himself always back where he started, empty-handed. As the soliloquy unfolds, the impression of an heroic capacity to originate and conclude ("Settle thy studies *Faustus*, and beginne") gradually yields to that of a more passive, compulsive insertion into the ambiguities of "having commencde." The spectacle of a virtuostic progress through the human sciences is displaced by a growing awareness of static self-imprisonment; the gestures of an insatiable thirst for the profound gradually betray the existence of a grasp that turns everything it touches into "external trash."

Against the emphasis in the first soliloquy on the order of books—on compartmentalization and inventory, on hierarchical ordering, on the programatic acquisition of knowledge—and against the goal-oriented obsession with horizon and transcendence that it reinforces, the shape and texture of the play itself poses an altogether more complicated picture of the structures within which a human life unfolds:

> As are the elements, such are the spheares,
> Mutually folded in each others orbe,
> And *Faustus* all jointly move upon one axletree,
> Whose terminine is tearmd the worlds wide pole . . .

(667–70)

On the one hand, of course, this is simply Mephastophilis' devilishly laconic recapitulation of the Ptolemaic commonplace: against Faustus's desire for privileged awareness, he reasserts the truth of what has always been and what every schoolboy already knows; against Faustus's submerged longing for a pluralistic universe ("Tel me, are there many heavens above the Moone?" [664]), he insists upon the closed world of classical and medieval order. But the words themselves, excerpted from their immediate context, are descriptive less of a classical world picture than of a field of Pyrrhonist or Montaignian "experience" (or of what a modern sensibility might term a "problematic"): the various spheres of what we experience as the world are not discrete and hierarchically ordered but "mutually folded in each others orbe"; the same is true even of the elements themselves. The very notion of distinct, separable professions, or of explanatory and evaluative sets of finite, static irreducibles (whether it be the four elements, the seven deadly sins, the faculties of psychology, or the entities with which the language of religion populates and fragments the inner life) is an arbitrary imposition upon an "ever moving" field of circulation where everything is made up of and interanimated by everything else. All revolves upon a single axis, while the concept of end-point and polarity (Good and Evil Angels as well as East and West, North and South) is just a "terministic" reduction of what is really spherical extent. Although any attempt to prove that the play endorses, as well as evokes, this vision of things would ultimately become problematical,[12] one can feel a cherished atmosphere of human kindness and well-being, a sense of grace itself, suddenly descend over the play when Faustus describes to the Duke and his pregnant Duchess a circular movement within which the mind's and language's divisive oppositions and linear sequences are imperturbably accepted and contained:

> *Duke:* Beleeve me master Doctor, this makes me wonder above the rest, that being in the dead time of winter, and in the month of January, how you shuld come by these grapes.
>
> *Faustus:* If it like your grace, the yeere is divided into twoo circles over the whole worlde, that when it is heere winter with us, in the contrary circle it is summer with them, as in *India, Saba*, and farther countries in the East, and by means of a swift spirit that I have, I had them brought hither, as ye see, how do you like them Madame, be they good?
>
> *Dutchess:* Beleeve me Maister doctor, they be the best grapes that ere I tasted in my life before.
>
> *Faustus:* I am glad they content you so Madam.

(1245–57)

If one looks at the form of Faustus's fortunes rather than at the frames in terms of which he consciously experiences himself, one can also discover a "whole worlde" in which all disciplines, all approaches to knowledge, are simultaneously implicated in one another, lead to one another not sequentially but dialectically. The Biblical texts at which Faustus balks confront him with what would seem strictly a matter of divinity; yet it is with an ethical sensibility (however impure) that he instinctively responds to it, while both ethical and theological crisis unfold within the framework of an exercise in elementary syllogistic reasoning.[13] The language of magic, which seems so opaque and autonomous in the opening soliloquy, borrows heavily from the language of Christianity, and its invocations turn out to be efficacious (or so at least the devil claims) only because of the negative significance that theology attributes to them. Blasphemy, too, turns out not to be self-consummating, but must be accomplished through a legal contract. The congealing of blood is a resistance to pacts with the supernatural that can be understood either medically or theologically, as a confirmation of either Augustinian or Epicurean wisdom—ultimately at stake are two antithetical visions of the nature of Faustus's damnation. When Lucifer responds to Faustus's desperate cry for salvation with "Christ cannot save thy soule, for he is just" (714), part of our difficulty in coming to terms with the reply has to do with the convergence of theological, ethical, and contractual perplexities on the single word "just."

Nothing that Faustus dismisses in the opening soliloquy really goes away; whatever he banishes returns as a theme woven into the very fabric of the play. The result is a curious disjunction between the gestures that he makes and the fortunes that befall him, between what he undertakes at the level of consious, rhetorical selfhood and what he undergoes at the level of flesh and blood, "textual" experience. He is strangely out of place in this play that seems at first glance but the logical extension of his personality: if he is the prototype of the "forward wit" condemned by the final chorus, he seems conceived and framed by the "patient judgment" to whom the opening chorus appeals. In the moments when the issue of what is happening to him most concerns Faustus himself, there is always an exasperating feeling of the inability of the mind to make contact with the sphere where its life is taking place, in spite of what would seem the stable locus of the body. This obscure sensation crystallizes in moments such as Faustus's attempt, as he watches his blood congeal, to interpret what it means, and only succeeding when he can manage to *read* it as a text; it is present most obscurely but intensely throughout the final soliloquy.

This disjunction between the organization of Faustus's mind and the shape and rhythm of the experience to which the play submits him (along with the growing conviction that, *contra*

Mephastophilis, no amount of the latter will ever "change" the former) is what is at the bottom of the feeling that he is fated, in spite of all his compulsive gestures of bidding farewell and making final ends immediately, to experience it all over and over again ad infinitum—beyond even the twenty-four years of the contract, into the fatal round of the play itself. As the play takes its course, one can sense evolving, through the dialectic between Faustus's forward progress and the depths of the work that Marlowe is shaping around it, a meditation on what is really involved in "settling" and taking stock of a life, and on what is really required in order to "get over and done with, conclude, come to a form, achieve resolution in the self and of the self's works."[14] Against all of Faustus's conclusions and resolutions, Marlowe allows himself only that final, laconic "*Terminat hora diem, Terminat Author opus*"—an ending that, in spite of all *its* ambiguities, rings true with the force of an epitaph.[15]

★

Especially symptomatic of Faustus's habits of mind in the opening soliloquy is translating "*summum bonum*" as "end," and then bidding the discipline farewell because he has already "attained" that end. The character that emerges here is radically alienated from the very notion of a *summum bonum*. (Faustus is so temporally, eschatologically determined that the language of final ends will come instinctively to mind only in the context of death and whatever lies on the other side of it: "Thy fatall time doth draw to finall ende" [1170].) His undertakings accumulate in the absence of any sense of a highest good—there seems no ultimate rationale for doing or not doing anything (hence the presence of something ominously nihilistic always lurking just at the edges of his aspirations *and* his despair—boredom is to the world of Marlowe what dread is to that of Kierkegaard). Nor can one really imagine Faustus, in spite of his desire to "have" his joys "in full possession" (185), inhabiting any achievement, living and dying *in* any work. He seems able to imagine assimilation, incorporation, and containment only as violent, destructive acts: he characteristically "consumes" his objects, while his passions and enthusiasms correspondingly "ravish" him. Desire and despair generate with equal frequency images of assault upon the body and the boundaries of the self.

Where these prereflective aspects of Faustus's character are concerned, the unstressed, apparently insignificant habits of his language can be especially revealing. When he rejects one of his studies, for instance, as fit only for those who "aim" at nothing but "externall trash" (65), we need not, like him, merely take for granted the pejorative connotations borne by the word "external." The insistence in the language of the play as a whole on a complex, often paradoxical interplay between the inside and the outside worlds (as in Mephastophilis' "for where we are is hell, / And where hell is, there must we ever be" [568–69]), and on the manner in which that interplay is experienced by—or *as* —the subject, should alert us to the ethical and ontological issues that are at stake in Faustus's instinctively negative relationship to the word.[16] The Faustus of the opening soliloquy is initially fascinated by things "external" to him: he values an object to the extent that it does exist out there, as a resistance to be desired, pursued, and taken in. It is only after his objectives have yielded to him, and he has digested them, that he discovers them to be "externall trash." And Marlowe dramatizes the process in a way that suggests that the problem is less with the objectives themselves than with the subjective mechanisms through which Faustus incorporates them. (Part of the "magic" of magic no doubt has to do with its capacity to remain a wholly alien language even in his mastery of it, thus retaining the sense of potency that seems lost to whatever he succeeds in converting into his own substance.) It is as if his inner being were like that of the body politic in *Coriolanus:* all digestive system, without any interior space where the knowledge or experience that enters him could remain in some sense alive and intact. Only by being so incorporated could what is outside the self be experienced as meaningful and sustaining; and—such is the radical dialectic of the play—as long as "external" remains synonymous with "superficial" and instinctively qualifies "trash," then the "internal" will be characterized not by profundity so much as by sterility and emptiness. One of Faustus's rare moments of grace occurs when an uncharacteristic and unpredictable perception of the world in all its mere externality, as apparently no more than a passing diversion, temporarily frees him from his anxiousness to "make haste" to Wittenberg and the end that awaits him there: "Nay, til I am past this faire and pleasant greene, ile walke on foote" (1142). Here a simple, unwilled pleasure in the natural world as something imperturbably out there, wholly manifest and at rest, indifferent to desire and despair alike, becomes the correlative of a leisurely, fertile space within the self where all is well. For once, instead of "aiming at" or "longing to view," Faustus just happens to see. For just a moment the inner life is open upon external circumstance, upon what is given it in the unimaginable present. Vision here seems to originate in the external world, and pass into the subject, instead of remaining the destination at the end of the gaze. And what is seen survives and thrives upon the seeing of it—Faustus intuitively understands that this fair and pleasant green will still be here, just as fair and pleasant, once he is "past" it. The conviction of reality is perhaps stronger here than anywhere else in the play: for just this moment Faustus is allowed to experience not the desire but the *capacity* for experience.[17]

But when Faustus is most "Faustian," he suffers the ironic non-fulfillment of one whose "dominion . . . stretcheth as farre as doth the minde of man" (90–91). Fixed, in spite of all his movement through space and time, at the center of a scene that never really changes, where nothing every really happens, where his only fellow creatures are the projections of his own inner demons and Mephastophilis, his *"fratris imagine"* (278), he can take sight of the external only through megalomanic or hallucinatory fantasy, and arrive at it only as something that is "gone," "past," or yet to come.

It would be possible to adopt an Augustinian point of view from which to understand this profane, cursed mode of hunger that compels Faustus, and speak of the experience of "sacramental intake" from which he is cut off. But the problem is that Christianity, as it manifests itself in this play, both exacerbates and in turn lives off the self-perpetuating, destructively projective mechanisms of desire in which his "Faustian" appetite originates. The Faustus who begins his incantations with "Now that the gloomy shadow of the earth, / Longing to view *Orions* drisling looke, / Leapes from th' antartike world unto the skie, / And dimmes the welkin with her pitchy breath" (244–47), is essentially the *same* Faustus who cries out from the heart of his Christian despair, "O Ile leape up to my God: who pulles me downe? / See see where Christs blood streames in the firmament" (1462–63). Grace for Faustus would be not a drop of this hallucinatory blood but a cure from the mode of utterance that generates his vision of it. It is in fact only Faustus's rare moments of fully *secular* experience (e.g., the episode with the pregnant Duchess and the dish of ripe grapes) that have a sacramental *feeling* about them. This is the paradox at the heart of the play's vision, and the one upon which the orthodox and the "diabolonian" reading of the play alike founder.

Thus when Faustus ridicules with Mephastophilis "a troupe of bald-pate Friers, / Whose *summum bonum* is in belly-cheare" (870–71), he is both more like them than he knows and less like them than he has wit to ask. For Marlowe's subject is itself a certain Faustian appetite, an insatiability that is finally less a sign of inner capacity than emptiness, a metaphysical lack where one would hope to find a set of abiding, natural appetites. The clown would sell his soul for a well-roasted shoulder of mutton (but not for a raw one), and the pregnant Duchess, longing like Faustus for that which is not, asks in the dead of winter for a dish of ripe grapes. But Faustus, unlike the Duchess, is "swolne with a *selfe* conceit," and wishes to glut the longing of his *heart's* desire; and just what this heart is, or longs for, Faustus himself seems to have not the slightest inkling. Certainly neither the origin of its longings, nor the conditions for their fulfillment, turn out to be as straightforward as those of the belly or the womb—even though the violent onomatopoeia of its language insists upon a relationship to primal, erotically charged experiences of the body's feeling:

Till swolne with cunning of a selfe conceit,

. . .

And glutted more with learnings golden gifts,
He surffets on cursed Negromancy . . .

(21, 25–26)

How am I glutted with conceit of this?

(110)

One thing, good servant, let me crave of thee
To glut the longing of my hearts desire . . .

(1348–49)

Her lips suckes forth my soule, see where it flies:

(1360)

The "gluttony" expressed in such passages seems too ontologically puzzling to be come to terms with moralistically.[18] It seems too violently oral to qualify as the expression of a bodily need. The desire voiced here sounds like a disincarnate presence inside a body, sensing that for its fulfillment (or extinction) it requires the incorporation of something into the body, or some sort of reincorporation by it. The ambivalent feelings involved are expressed most elaborately in the desperation of the final soliloquy. There a desire to withdraw into a body is confused with a desire to escape out of a body; a desire to return to the womb with a desire to be born from it; a desire to escape death with a desire for self-extinction. Dismemberment is both feared and longed for, as are devouring and suffocation:

> Mountaines and hilles, come come, and fall on me,
> And hide me from the heavy wrath of God.
> No no, then wil I headlong runne into the earth:
> Earth gape, O no, it will not harbour me:
> You starres that raignd at my nativitie,
> Whose influence hath alotted death and hel,
> Now draw up Faustus like a foggy mist,
> Into the intrailes of yon labring cloude,
> That when you vomite foorth into the ayre,
> My limbes may issue from your smoaky mouthes,
> So that my soule may but ascend to heaven:

(1470–80)

Every imagined refuge winds up being experienced in oral terms, and thus ultimately reinforces the negative feelings about the isolation, destructiveness, and imminent dissolution of the self that Faustus is trying to resolve or escape from by conjuring it up. The earth into which he will run "headlong" (the reverse-birth fantasy seems very conscious on Marlowe's part) immediately becomes a gaping mouth, and once a mouth it will not "harbour" him: the very image of what terrifies him, he experiences it as both rejecting (it refuses him entrance) and threatening (instead of protectively containing him and concealing him from the wrath of the father, it wishes to swallow him whole, consume him). He asks to be drawn up into a "labring" cloud, in order to be harbored and to be given birth to as well. But within that cloud are "intrailes": gestation is confused with digestion, the pregnant womb with an over-glutted, sickened stomach. The moment of birth is thus interpreted as a cathartic vomiting, a violently reflexive image of self-disgust and its aggression upon the body that contains and somehow engenders it. Birth itself is experienced in imagery of rejection and disintegration.

The first fantasies that enter Faustus's imagination as he anticipates his magic powers express this "oral-narcissistic dilemma"[19] at the heart of his longings: a plundering of the maternal, enveloping realm ("Ile have them . . . Ransacke the Ocean for orient pearle" [114-15]) is juxtaposed to a defensive walling-in against external threat ("Ile have them wall all *Germany* with brasse, / And make swift *Rhine* circle faire *Wertenberge*" [120-21]). And his apostrophe to Helen develops in accordance with the same underlying compulsions. What begins as a simple gesture of courtesy and friendship ("Gentlemen, for that I know your friendship is unfained, / and Faustus custome is not to denie / the just requests of those that wish him well, / you shall behold that pearlesse dame of *Greece*" [1284-87]), attended by the partly sceptical, partly cautious, partly respectful distance that a creator might be expected to take toward the works of his inspiration ("Be silent then, for danger is in words" [1290]), returns, under the pressure of guilt and fear, as a desperate fantasy of ecstatic sexual union—envisioned, again, in oral terms ("Her lips suckes forth my soule" [1360]). This incestuously erotic embrace is then transformed, as if by the force of an internal momentum, into a relationship with a benign maternal presence where he will "dwell," and to whom he will return at the end of each day's hazards for comfort, reward, and renewal. Finally, at the climax of the fantasy, Faustus-Helen undergoes a metamorphosis into Semele-Jupiter, with Faustus himself identifying with *both* Jupiter and Semele. His vision thus culminates on the apparently inevitable note of conflict, invasion, wounding, violation, consumption of the other, an aggressive tearing-open of the womb, and on the correspondingly passive longing for ravishment and self-extinction.

Even when Faustus desires most enthusiastically, we can usually hear a note of desperation in his language. A phrase like "glut the longing," for all its voraciousness, conveys a sense of suffocation and choking: it sticks in the throat, makes swallowing and breathing difficult. Such desires are being experienced as impediments, or as threats. One feels that when Faustus "craves" of Mephastophilis to "glut the longing of my hearts desire," he is not asking to be given something out of the fullness of his being, but wishing, more literally, that the desire itself, which is alien to him, living off him, might be extinguished, quenched. This negative orality might be contrasted to Cleopatra's "I have / Immortal longings in me," where the sounds of swallowing open up an interior fullness, and establish effortless yet powerful rhythms of breathing. Cleopatra's longings, even though they are more than her and take her out of and beyond herself, are still *hers*, and they are *in* her, and their unquenchableness is for her an authentic self-affirmation. She generates her desires. Even when she is breathless, she breathes forth power. But Faustus, when he sees hell "gaping" for him, cries out "Adders, and Serpents, let me breathe a while" (1506), imploring those inner, alien monsters that give the self no peace, whose insatiable oral demands consume everything that might nourish or sustain it, even for "a while."

In this context, *summum bonum medicinae sanitas* begins to acquire gnomic resonance. Within the pre-Christian, pre-dualistic ontology that informs Aristotle's ethical vision, *sanitas* can be understood not merely as physical health but, more comprehensively, as regularity, soundness of being, discretion, good sense, etc.—as if (to translate the vision back into the terms of post-Christian experience) what we term psychic or spiritual "sanity" *were* in the final analysis a matter of "our bodies health" (and madness the fear of or for it, or disgust with it, or a fever in it), the state of being grounded and stabilized in the continuity of physical existence. The values implied would seem to be in equal opposition to both Christian and Faustian man—who, from this point of view, seem but two manifestations of a single phenomenon.

C. L. Barber, in a beautiful perception of the way in which the play characteristically works, has noted the counterpoint between Faustus's fearful response to his devils' threats of dismemberment and the clown's contrastingly "sane" reaction to

Wagner's threats to "turne al the lice about thee into familiars, and they shall teare thee in peeces":

> Doe you heare sir? you may save that labour, they are too familiar with me already, swowns they are as bolde with my flesh, as if they had payd for my meate and drinke.
>
> (388-91)

Barber stresses the *felt* value of "the clown's independence, and the *detente* of his common man's wit which brings things down to the physical."[20] Yet he seems to back away from the logical implications of his insight when he goes on to suggest that the ultimate effect of the contrast is to "set off the folly of Faustus' elation in the bargain," and to underscore the serious consequences of that bargain: "Mephastophilis, Faustus' familiar, will pay for him meat and drink, and ultimately 'make bold with his flesh'."[21] In this interpretation, the common man's sanity of the clown is, by a dramatic irony, made to reinforce the intimidating power of the latent psychotic fears to which it seems so affirmatively immune. But surely what it most strikingly sets off is not the folly of Faustus's elation in his bargain but his terror-stricken response to the threats with which both Christian doctrine and its devils intimidate him once he has entered into it. The clown seems more a benign dialectical alternative than merely an ironical foil. (He plays Barnardine to Faustus's Claudio, or Calyphas to Faustus's Tamburlaine.) Here is someone who has lived so long with his personal demons, and become so intimately—so woefully and lice-bittenly—acquainted with them, that he is immune to attempts to threaten him with them as if they were external, alien, persecutory forces—the strategy, it should be noted, of the Christian God as well as of the devil who is his servant *malgré lui*. (Wagner's intimidation of this clown is, in fact, a more accurate analogue of one of Christianity's methods of conversion than it is of diabolic temptation—"wel, wilt thou serve me, and Ile make thee go like

Qui mihi discipulus?" [374–75].) The clown's life of poverty
makes the presence of his body, with its needs, demands, and
vulnerabilities, the central, inescapable reality of his experience,
and thus paradoxically grants him an easy, intimate relationship
with the physical that Faustus lacks. Yet the judgment at Faustus's expense, it needs to be emphasized, remains problematical:
Marlowe's focus is here as elsewhere less on willfully chosen,
self-created personalities than on given, instinctual natures.

Thus when the opening chorus describes Faustus as "swolne
with cunning of a selfe conceit," there is beneath the melo-
dramatic surface a morally and ontologically complex situation.
"Conceit" can mean either "vanity," or "fancy," "idea," etc.
(with only potential, and at any rate less simplistically pejorative connotations of "unreal" or "illusory"), or "engendering,"
"conception," evoking the image of a physical pregnancy.
"Cunning" can mean "craft" or "guile," but it can also be
understood in a less negative sense as a sort of ontological po-
tentiality, a knowing that, though neither quite being nor doing,
is also a "canning," a "being-able-to." "Swolne" reinforces the
metaphor of pregnancy, but (in pointed contrast to the great-
bellied Duchess) associates it with a pathological condition—the
swollenness of enflamed or diseased parts of the body. "Selfe
conceit" can correspondingly be taken as either "vain pride,"
or as "self-engendered," or, somewhere in between, as "an idea
or imagination or illusion of [a] self"; and, within this third
possibility, the idea of self could be a "conceit" either because
it is a false or vain one, or, more problematically, because the
"selfe" is *essentially* a conceit, and perhaps a necessary one. If
this conceit is the sickness that inflames and alienates Faustus,
it also seems to be the only thing that offers him the possibility
of peace and rest, the only refuge to which he can entrust himself in self-relinquishment: "Tush, Christ did call the thiefe
upon the Crosse, / Then rest thee Faustus quiet in conceit.
(*Sleepe in his chaire*)" (1173–74). Even if the moment of grace

Faustus experiences here is begot of nothing but vain fantasy and grounded in sophistry and evasion, the positive feelings that accompany it are only enhanced by comparison with the theologically-approved version that he is urged to seek, with its enjoinder to "Breake heart, drop bloud, and mingle it with teares" (1306). Beyond the superficial moral disapproval of the phrase there arises the potential of a more tragic, poignant Faustus, burdened with his conceit of self as the Duchess with her child (the last soliloquy his final labor), attempting to be born, to give birth to himself, to a self where he can be, and be at rest: having (for whatever reasons) to engender upon himself, through consciousness, what the Robins and Wagners and Emperors and Horsecoursers of the world are prereflectively rooted in: and thus fated (or chosen) to confront the ontological void in which ordinary experience is so imperturbably suspended.

Again, it is Shakespeare who offers us a sympathetic rather than a reductively judgmental contrast. Faustus's closest Shakespearean relative is Falstaff ("O Hal, I prithee give me leave to breathe a while"). The latter, derived more intimately (but no less subversively) from the Gluttony of the morality tradition, embodies the needs, the anxieties, and perhaps ultimately the tragedy of the human self, the embodied self. (Mistress Quickly knows that Falstaff is *dead* when she lays her hand over the parts of the continuous, whole object that his body is, and feels that "all [is] as cold as any stone"; the scholars know that Faustus is burning in hell—or "gone," as the final chorus more evasively puts it—when they find his limbs scattered over the floor of his study.) When Falstaff speaks of his body, it is always with a wry acceptance of it as the locus of his being; and the result is always to consolidate his connections with a world in whose otherness he is so elaborately implicated. ("Oversolitariness" is Faustus's sickness; "company" is Falstaff's ruin, as he himself remarks.) But Faustus's hunger is radically alienated from the wisdom (and the tragic knowledge) of the body. So projective both in space and time, it seems really a hunger *for* a self, for some interior, habitable space where the outside world as well might appear intact and actual—where real desires might originate and real responses to them might be received. When Faustus speaks of (or to) his body—or his soul, or his heart, or "Faustus"—a sense of inner isolation, dislocation, and abstraction results. His wording of the contract with Lucifer (it is Faustus who authors it) provides a telling instance of how unreal and abstractive, yet compulsive, the act of self-reference is for him:

> *I John Faustus of Wertenberge, Doctor*, by these presents, do give *both body and soule* to Lucifer prince of the East, and his minister Mephastophilis, and furthermore graunt unto them, that 24. yeares being expired, the articles above written inviolate, full power to fetch or carry *the said John Faustus body and soule, flesh, blood, or goods*, into their habitation wheresoever.
> By *me John Faustus.*
>
> (550–57; italics mine)

All this in spite of the fact that Mephastophilis never asks for anything except Faustus's *soul*. The threat of dismemberment is already latent in such language. It is as if Faustus, unsure of where to locate himself amidst the constellation of words that he possesses with which to refer to himself, always elsewhere than where he points, unconsciously wishes to insure that there is no loophole in the contract that would allow the devil to claim something that is his yet leave "Faustus himself" behind. (Yet again, to what does the grammatical subject of my own sentence so complacently refer?) In the final soliloquy, as Faustus attempts to confront (and evade) what is going to "become" of him when the clock strikes twelve, his terms of self-reference begin to whirl desperately about the blind spot at their center. The stars are asked to draw up "Faustus" like a foggy mist, but this image of the dissolution of the whole (composite?) self, named from the outside, is promptly cancelled when it is extended to involve clouds subsequently belching forth "my

limbes" so that "my soule" may ascend to heaven (1474–80).
The body survives its gentle dissolution, only to be torn violently apart; the "I" continues to speak and to name its posses-
sions, only to be left behind, abandoned to the void that remains
when "its" body and "its" soul have gone their separate ways.
If it is "my soule" that will be in hell forever (1483), it is "my
incessant paine" that God is asked to end (1485), and this in
turn will involve letting "Faustus" live "a thousand yeeres, a
hundred thousand"—before "at last" being saved (1486–87).
When the possibility of the transmigration of souls is envisioned,
the "I" identifies not with the soul that flies to a new embodiment and identity, but with what remains behind when it is
gone: "Ah *Pythagoras metemsucossis* were that true, / This soule
should flie from me, and I be changde / Unto some brutish beast
(1491–93). But the beast into which this "I" would be changed
is in the process imbued with its own mode of eschatological
consciousness: "al beasts are happy," it now turns out, not because they are "wanting soule" (1489), but because "when they
die, / Their soules are soone dissolvd in elements" (1493–94).
The lines that deny a Pythagorean transmigration of souls thus
enact the curse of an inverted, Faustian metempsychosis. It is
appropriate that Faustus should reject this doctrine by returning
to a "mine" that "must live still to be plagde in hel" (1495).

What is it that so doggedly persists in this soliloquy, that resists
or actively refuses every image of transmigration, metamorphosis,
or dissolution of identity that is seized upon? Amidst all this
naming and owning, can one discover a central core of being that
Faustus *is?* Where and what is the voice that speaks these lines,
that says "Faustus," and what becomes of *it* when the clock
strikes twelve? Can the straightforwardness of the final stage
direction, "exeunt with *him*" (italics mine), fail to be contami-
nated by these referential ambiguities and the metaphysical perplexities they generate? Can all our nagging questions about the
whereness of Faustus ("—How now sirra, wheres thy maister?—

God in heaven knows" [206-7]), and all our related difficulties with that phrase "body and soul" ("for is not he *corpus naturale*, and is not that *mobile*" [221-22]), really be put to rest by the spectacle of several stage-hand devils carrying an expired body off Marlowe's stage? In *The Will to Power*, Nietzsche compares our belief in the subject to the error we commit when we say "the lightning flashes," thereby adding to the event (the flash) a transcendent entity (the lightning) that causes or performs the event. If we could imagine this "lightning which flashes" given a language with which to speak of itself (or better yet, imagine the flash of light itself as that language), and then attempting during its span to think in that language about "what will become of me when my flash expires," we might be very close to understanding what it is that Marlowe is attempting to dramatize in this final soliloquy.

Yet certain qualifications become necessary here. For what we have left altogether unaccounted for are the unexpected nuances of Marlowe's own attitude toward this Faustian egotism and the nothingness at the heart of it. The play is always analytical, often ruthlessly ironical, yet Marlowe's distance from his protagonist is never without a strangely benign sense of humor, a bemusement that ranges from exasperation to wry affection. The very aspects of Faustus's personality that should make us remorselessly critical of him so often wind up disarming us instead, perhaps even endearing him to us. When he responds, for instance, to Lucifer's and Belsabub's entrance by prematurely crying out, "O Faustus, they are come to fetch away thy soule" (719), we could describe him as a cowering wretch, and take righteous, moralistic pleasure in this collapse of his facile, stoic-promethean bravura, but in so doing we would miss entirely the gentle laughter that colors his dramatization here. Marlowe's regard for him seems not so far at times from that with which he contemplates the folly of his creatures (and the creatures of his folly) in *Hero and Leander*. There is about Faustus, even at his worst, a certain innocence, a certain childlike guilelessness. Burning with desire to be initiated into the forbidden arts, his instinct is to enhance his plunge into evil by postponing it until after a hearty dinner shared with Valdes and Cornelius: "Then come and dyne with me, and after meate / Weele canvas every quidditie thereof" (196–97). Just after having signed away his soul, and delighted with his newly purchased wantonness and lasciviousness, the best he can do is ask Mephastophilis, to the latter's dismay, for a *wife*. Informed by Mephastophilis that they are going to stay in the Pope's privy chamber while they are in Rome, Faustus replies, again to the exasperation of his companion, "I hope his holinesse will bid us welcome" (847). He responds to the silliness of the pageant of the Seven Deadly Sins with the naive, egocentric delight of a child watching a Punch-and-Judy show. And when he soliloquizes, he seems to be doing the same thing that children do when they talk to themselves, and for essentially the same reasons. Where a less radical humanism would insist upon a central self or a stable core of being, and a more romantic, self-mystified nihilism upon a heart of darkness or a "dumbfoundering abyss,"[22] Marlowe's vision perceives, quizzically, a conversational circuit ("Settle thy studies *Faustus*, and beginne . . .")—which, for all the effects it creates of an inner life that is imaginary, ungrounded, discontinuous, and tenuously verbal, still achieves at its happiest an ingratiating mode of self-intimacy ("Now *Faustus*, thou art Conjurer laureate" [276]), and expresses at its most disturbed nothing more damnable than the terror of a child's fear of being left alone in the dark and the despair of a parent's attempt to comfort it ("Then feare not *Faustus*, but be resolute" [257]), "Then rest thee Faustus quiet in conceit" [1174], "Ah Faustus, / Now thou hast but one bare hower to live" [1450–51]).[23] Thus the final soliloquy, a nightmare of self-fragmenting solipsism, a final yielding of the mind to its own hypothetical terrors, yet unexpectedly culminates on a note of pure tenderness,

as fear for self turns so far inward that what comes out has the
sound of a deep, urgent altruism:

> O it strikes, it strikes, now body turne to ayre,
> Or *Lucifer* wil beare thee quicke to hel:
>> *Thunder and lightning.*
> Oh soule, be changde to little water drops,
> And fal into the *Ocean*, nere be found:

(1500–1504)

One can hear in these lines both the child's fear and the parent's
protective affection for it. The word "little" carries with it the
same feelings that so often rush in through it to flood the Shakespearean void, as in Lear's "Stay a little," Cleopatra's "yet come
a little" and "the little O, the earth," Prospero's "our little life
is rounded with a sleep," and, perhaps closest of all to the present context, Hal's "could not all this flesh / Keep in a little life?"

★

It might help to clarify Marlowe's perspective if we were to
think of Faustus as the dialectical, ironical counterpart of Tamburlaine (rather than as a developmental, autobiographical
recantation of him), and the two of them together as comple-
mentary considerations of a single human problematic. (Their
respective deaths might be seen, for instance, as two morally
neutral, dialectically opposed, phenomenologically considered
ways of responding to the same existentially definitive, yet in-
trinsically meaningless human event.) The latter asserts that
"Wil and Shall best fitteth *Tamburlaine*," and his tour de force
consists of making good on those terms strictly in the declarative mood. To will for him *is* to do—even if the single-mindedness
of such a commitment ultimately generates around him the
same ontological void that Faustus is always trying to keep at
arm's length. The only rationale even for saying "I will" or "I
shall" is to ensure that events will be recognized as deeds, extensions of the will, rather than will a response to circumstance or

perhaps only a retrospective fiction. He posits his object, then he "cuts a passage" straight through to it. The time is always *now*—yet this presentness is merely the attribute of a vectorial will, not a mode of spontaneous or contingent duration independent of the subject.

"Will" and "shall" are also the words that best fit Faustus ("What doctrine call you this, *Che sera, sera*, / What wil be, shall be?" [77-78]), but they ensnare him in the field of human ambiguities to which Tamburlaine remains—perhaps ironically, absurdly—immune. Throughout the play, they shuffle back and forth between their temporal, declarative, interrogative, imperative, fatalistic, and conditional moods, creating for the subject a subjunctive limbo between past and future, volition and contingency, reality and imagination, necessity and (im)possibility:

> *Good Angel:* Faustus, repent yet, God wil pitty thee.
> *Evill Angel:* Thou art a spirite, God cannot pitty thee.
> *Faustus:* Who buzzeth in mine eares I am a spirite?
>   Be I a divel, yet God may pitty me,
>   I God wil pitty me, if I repent.
> *Evill Angel:* I but Faustus never shal repent.
> *Faustus:* My hearts so hardned I cannot repent . . .

$$(641-47)^{24}$$

The words that for Tamburlaine are the cornerstones of the will to power and sovereignty betray, when Faustus utters them, the deeply conditional nature of the self and its compromises with circumstance, situation, other wills, and its own inner tensions. Instead of emphasizing the speaker's capacity to found and enact his own reality, they suggest a sense in which everything that happens to him remains merely possible, imminent, infinitely postponed. Employed by the subject to pronounce its power over time, they reveal that subject instead to *be* an unstable complex of dread, anticipation, reluctance, waiting, remembering, and delay. Even Faustus's most emphatically declarative uses of "will" and "shall" seem fated to arrive in the future conditional. The very existence of a will to something in this play, the very need to say the word "will," implies both a resistance and a reluctance as well as a desire and an intent. Time and again, Faustus will begin a speech on the heroic, self-assured note of "now," attempting to posit (or conjure) the present through force of will; but inevitably its momentum will extend and return upon itself until the moment has been hollowed out into a space of purely virtual, speculative anticipation, whether inhabited in a spirit of longing or dread:

> Now that I have obtaind what I desire,
> Ile live in speculation of this Art,
> Til *Mephastophilis* returne againe.

(357-59)

> Now Faustus must thou needs be damnd,
> And canst thou not be saved?

(438-39)[25]

The "now" in which Faustus discovers himself is thus just as radically circumscribed by eschatological imaginings as the present that Tamburlaine asserts by force of will. What makes it so much more complex and openly problematical is the internal resistance of what has the appearance of a conservative, self-preservative impulse, a preoccupation with containing, dwelling, "living in"—in his study, in Aristotle's works, in all voluptuousness, in speculation, in conceit, in Helen's arms, in hell forever. As fundamentally constituted by teleological, apocalyptic drives as Faustus seems to be, his instinct is nevertheless not so much to fulfill them as to create out of them a habitable, sustaining space for himself and his will—his resolution is to *make* an end immediately. (The ontological status of this "impulse" or "instinct" is crucial for the play's vision of human nature and value: does it have to do merely with a dread constituted wholly within and in terms of the apocalyptic energies of Faustus's desire, or is it the manifestation of "life instincts" that have a positive, autonomous existence of their own, and thus resist

from without his "Faustian" tendencies? How are we to interpret the congealing of his blood?) For Tamburlaine, projects
exist straightforwardly to be realized, as perpetual demonstrations of the self; for Faustus, they are "self conceits" that can,
at least *until* they come to fruition, be imaginatively inhabited.
Where the one thrusts forward, his sword erect, the other reaches
out to draw a magic circle round himself.

Nothing, in this respect, could be more characteristic of Faustus and the temporal ambiguities that make him up than to
specify of his own accord a twenty-four year limit to his contract with the devil. To have Mephastophilis wait on him for "as
long as he lives" (as Faustus first demands and Mephastophilis
himself later proposes), besides leaving a loophole open for the
devil, would be to reinforce the sense of life as an open, aimless
extension into indefiniteness that he is haunted by in the first
place. The feeling of time's contingency, and of the self's accidental, precarious dispersal into it would be intensified—the
paradigmatic moment of death would occur when the clock
struck not twelve but "one." (It is such a sense of things at
which Hamlet seems eventually to arrive: "If it be now, 'tis not
to come; if it be not to come, it will be now; if it be not now,
yet it will come.") The twenty-four years, on the other hand,
become "his" (as, conversely, "the interim" becomes Hamlet's),
and at the same time they contain him, concentrate him, *dramatize* him—it is of the essence that they amount to *less* than a
normal life span. Contingency and flux are transformed into "thy
fatall time," death from one moment among many into "thine
houre," the "finall ende" toward which *all* points and rushes.

"Endlessness" is thus a matter of crucial ambivalence for
Faustus: if it is the goal that he pursues, it often seems in turn
precisely what he is fleeing from. "O no end is limited to damned
soules" can be taken as a phenomenological definition of
damnation for Faustian consciousness, and not just as an article
of faith concerning the nature of existence in hell. The form of
the expression makes ends and limitedness feel like things that

are bestowed upon you, like grace. ("The *reward* of sinne is
death: thats hard.") Without the sense that life ends (terminates)
there could be no sense that life has an end (direction, purpose,
goal), even if all invented ends then become means for annulling
or evading the end upon which they are predicated. Without the
imposition of limits, real or imaginary, there could be no striving, straining, aspiring, transgressing, or overreaching—and this
would surely be hell for the Faustian sensibility. And, from the
opposite direction of whatever it is in Faustus that resists him,
only an end given to him as a limit could save him from his own
overreaching nature, which, left to itself, would *be* his damnation: "The damned souls *are* those who are deprived the sense
of death as a limit, a termination"; or (taking "limited" as an
adjective), "The damned souls are those who are unable to respond to any end as limited, terminal, bounding; for whom
every goal becomes a means of reaching for infinity or transcending the self; for whom the necessity of dying becomes an
issue of living or dying an 'everlasting' death." [26] Again, in hidden tension with the apparently inclusive choice between eternal
damnation or salvation is what may be an even more fundamental alternative between mortality and immortality per se (for
after all, no end is limited to the souls that are in heaven, either)
—as if the Christian soul and the Faustian soul at its most outcast
were phenomenologically identical, and both were denied the
grace of all that is embodied in a dish of ripe grapes.

The specification of exactly twenty-four years further reinforces this interplay between Faustus's "Faustian" instincts and
that in him which holds out for the sanity of a "natural" life.
By subliminally drawing upon the paradigm of twenty-four
hours, the span reinforces the sense of a human life as something
short and urgent, cut off from the larger, enduring rhythms of
nature, moving ever further from home and origins, haunted by
the linear "passing" of a purely subjective, instrumental time
that is yet suffered as something external and daemonically

alien to the self ("O, it strikes, it strikes"). Yet one can also feel
in Faustus's insistence upon twenty-four years a desire to experience himself installed within the natural order of things
(compare his initial eagerness to conjure "in some lustie grove"
[184]), his life taking its course as if it were a "naturall day"
[1457], with time revolving in an endless round about the self
at the center of it, containing it, replenishing it, and ultimately
returning it to its beginnings (as if minutes, hours, days, weeks,
months, years, lives, and the ever-moving spheres of heaven
were concentric circles).[27]

It is interesting in this regard that when Faustus's internal
time sense unaccountably registers that the end of his twenty-
four years is approaching, his instinct is to "make haste to
Wertenberge" (1138–39), back to the *place* where it all began.
It is as if his life were literally coming full circle, and the study
in Wittenberg were where his death were going to happen, and
he had to hurry in order not to arrive there too late for it. (Again,
beneath the fear of death, a fear of being abandoned, left behind.) And while we could take this as symptomatic of Faustus's
inability to internalize fully his own death, to take it upon
himself as something that happens in him, within the limits of
his self—yet there is something very positive about the instinc-
tive conviction it implies that, in spite of Mephastophilis' lessons,
life does take place in the external world, and that places do
exist apart from and independent of the self that occupies them.
(Something similarly affirmative is implicit in Faustus's explanation to the Duke and Duchess that our time encompasses places
where we are not, and where things are different, yet where life
goes on, as if it were merely a continuation of our own. Time
here is not what erodes but what unifies and encompasses, what
is held in common [". . . that when it is heere winter with us,
in the contrary circle it is summer with them . . ."], assuring
us that the green world is even in the dead of winter present and
magically at hand.) The mood of the play becomes for a moment

extraordinarily benign. Death is associated with returning home (and fear of death with exile), with a finite life coming full circle. The temporal anxieties out of which life is made do not disappear, but for a moment they are resolved: time still "runne[s]" a "restlesse course," but it runs it with "calme and silent foote"; Faustus still feels the urge to "make haste," but in that very moment he looks out and sees a "faire and pleasant greene," and decides to "walke on foote" till he is "past" it (1134–42). The world remains at a distance (though for a change, so near at hand!), and the human relationship to it remains one of passing, and passing by; yet for once this relationship seems the source of a deep contentment: the world abides, and Faustus's movement past it is the measure of his freedom within it.[28] Faustus's leisurely walk interacts most beautifully with his apprehension of the calm and silent foot of time. We realize how complex the relationship between subjective and objective experience is: the language suggests a sense in which Faustus is time, and time Faustus. At least the time in which Faustus is caught up and the time that takes place inside of him seem for a moment to share a common rhythm, and through that sharing both gain composure, both are released from Faustian energies that drive them.

Such experiences of grace never amount to anything more than brief, elusive interludes in the play; they remain wholly invisible to Faustus's conscious grasp of himself and his fate, and have no influence at all on the larger, compelling form of his fortunes—one can in fact observe their potential affirmations being systematically converted into terror and despair in the final soliloquy. Marlowe is too self-critically implicated in his protagonist, too intent on pursuing ambiguities and contradictions to their radical conclusions, too insistent on both the fatality and the inexplicable contingency of a human nature, to bestow upon his character a creaturely grace predicated upon an authorial transcendence. Yet these interludes—the fellowship of the Scholars, the walk past the fair and pleasant green, the pregnant Duchess and her dish of ripe grapes, even, in a strange way, the practical jokes at the expense of the Knight and the Horsecourser—are, nevertheless, privileged moments in the deepest sense: they contain the experience that is not only held up for critical reflection and questioned from within but also deeply *valued* for its own sake by the play. It is they, in all their apparent inconsequentiality, that adumbrate the presence of a single, resolved point of view brooding imperturbably, even benignly, over all the play's internal ambiguities and fluctuations. When the Emperor of Germany, given the opportunity to fulfill his heart's desire, cautiously approaches a vision of Alexander's paramour to inspect the mole (or wart) that was rumored to have grown on her neck, and expresses his wonder and naive, self-satisfied delight in actually finding it there, surely we are being invited to cherish—more than through all of Faustus's transcendental projects combined—the sweetness of a human life, precisely *for* its limitedness, for the littleness of its absurd, gently laughable epiphanies. It is, in fact, the background of Faustus's own restless striving, and the religious unhappiness it attracts to itself, that bestow upon what might normally pass as "the trivial" such a deep sense of value. (What pastoral strategy could do for the green world what Faustus's casual, momentary appreciation of it accomplishes?) Conversely, it is the play's drive toward an *acknowledgment* of the Faustian predicament that gives its critical distance and its insistence upon other values the quality of *radical* gestures. And if in the end the play nevertheless remains the "tragicall History" of Doctor Faustus, it is by reference to the touchstone of human happiness and sanity embodied in these moments, and not to one of either heroic overreaching or Christian self-abnegation (the one merely the inverted image of the other), that his tragedy is contemplated and his losses ultimately measured:

> As for the most central of our senses, our inner sense of the interval between desire and possession, which is no other than the sense of duration, that feeling of time which was formerly satisfied by the speed of horses, now finds that the fastest trains are too slow, and we fret

with impatience between telegrams. We crave events themselves like food that can never be highly seasoned enough. If every morning there is no great disaster in the world we feel a certain emptiness: "There is nothing in the papers today," we say. We are caught red-handed. We are all poisoned. So I have grounds for saying that there is such a thing as our being intoxicated by energy, just as we are intoxicated by haste, or by size. . . . We are losing that essential peace in the depths of our being, that priceless absence in which the most delicate elements of life are refreshed and comforted, while the inner creature is in some way cleansed of past and future, of present awareness, of obligations pending and expectations lying in wait.[29]

NOTES

1. "Fulfillment of will" has been called the "central topic" of *Tamburlaine* by J. R. Mulryne and Stephen Fender in their richly suggestive account of Marlowe's calculated, dialectical employment of ambivalence: see "Marlowe and the 'Comic Distance'," in *Christopher Marlowe: Mermaid Critical Commentaries*, ed. Brian Morris (London, 1968), p. 53.

2. All quotations from *Doctor Faustus* are from the A text of W. W. Greg's *Marlowe's "Doctor Faustus": Parallel Texts* (Oxford, 1950). Opting for the A text involves, needless to say, basic interpretative decisions in itself. In spite of the arguments by Kirschbaum and Greg in favor of the B text, I find myself in agreement with C. L. Barber (in "'The form of Faustus' fortunes good or bad'," *TDR* 8 [1964]: 92n.) about the overall superiority of the readings in the A text, and about its basic formal and theatrical integrity as well. For a persuasive, closely argued challenge to Greg's preference for the B text, see Constance Brown Kuriyama, "Dr. Greg and *Doctor Faustus:* The Supposed Originality of the 1616 Text," *ELR* 5 (1975): 171-97. I plan to present my own case for the A text in a separate article, but for now I must simply assert that the present essay is about the A text, and that my ground for concentrating on it rather than the B text is that it is both more Marlovian in feel and measurably the greater work of art.

3. *Seven Types of Ambiguity* (Edinburgh, 1939), p. 206. Representative of the level at which Empson's reading is usually dismissed are J. B. Steane, *Marlowe: A Critical Study* (London, 1964), pp. 368-69, and Robert H. West, "The Impatient Magic of Dr. Faustus," *ELR* 4 (1974): 222n.

4. The word "terministic" is borrowed from Kenneth Burke, *The Rhetoric*

of Religion: Studies in Logology (Berkeley, 1961), passim; see esp. p. 14 for an interesting distinction between a "mythological" concern with imagery and a "logological" or "terministic" concern with words. This book casts a fascinating, often revelatory light on the text of *Doctor Faustus*—primarily, it seems to me, because Burke's demystificatory attitudes toward Christianity and its rhetoric so closely approximate those of the play itself.

5. The phrase is Nietzsche's: see *The Philosopher and His Shadow*, Part 2.

6. Only the language of magic remains immune to translation and rhetorical embodiment in this soliloquy; instead of voicing it, Faustus encounters it as a purely visual phenomenon: "Lines, circles, sceanes, letters and characters: / I, these are those that *Faustus* most desires" (81–82). His description, in fact, sounds like a response to the textuality of language per se by someone who was wholly a speaker. (Greg's emendation of A's "sceanes" to "signs" seems in this light especially persuasive.)

7. *Doctor Faustus*, ed. John D. Jump (London, 1962), p. 7n.

8. For a more extended discussion of the misattributions, misquotations, and misunderstandings embedded in the soliloquy, see Gerald Morgan, "Harlequin Faustus: Marlowe's Comedy of Hell," *HAB* 18 (1967): 29–31.

9. Ibid., p. 100n.

10. The pattern of quotation established in the soliloquy leads us to expect that *ubi desinit philosophus, ibi incipit medicus* and *Summum bonum medicinae sanitas* are from Galen, the author that Faustus has just taken up; yet both are in fact from Aristotle. It could be argued that Marlowe means to dramatize here not a naive protagonist but a superficially ironical one, who willingly distorts Aristotle's meaning and uses it against him: "Seeing that Aristotle himself says that medicine picks up where philosophy leaves off, then so much for Aristotle and his philosophy: where's my Galen?" But it seems to me that the Faustus of this soliloquy is conceived less as the author than as the comic and tragic victim of its ironies. The blind spots he locates are of a radical, constitutional nature. Note how silent and inaccessible the realm of the physical remains: of all the authors who appear in this scene, Galen is the only one from whom nothing ultimately is quoted.

11. It is to the very degree that Faustus in all this merely characterizes the orthodox Renaissance itself, with its fascination with the mystique of books and its oft-elaborated schema for systematically acquiring the encyclopaedic knowledge contained within them, that he *is* the object of Marlowe's critique. I think in fact that we may be *intended* to hear the echoes in this opening speech of the moment in Lyly's *Euphues* when its hero

finally sees the light: "Philosophie, Phisicke, Divinitie, shal be my studie. O ye hidden secrets of Nature, the expresse image of morall vertues, the equall ballaunce of Justice, the medicines to heale all diseases, how they begin to delyght me. The *Axiomaes* of *Aristotle*, the *Maxims* of *Justinian*, the *Aphorismes* of *Galen*, have sodaynelye made such a breache into my minde that I seeme onely to desire them which did only earst detest them" (quoted by Jump, p. 6n.). Marlowe situates us not with a spectacle of forbidden practices (as the prologue might lead us to expect) but with just such a note of typical Renaissance enthusiasm; then, as the soliloquy unfolds, we are made to feel its superficiality, and sense the desperateness beneath it, and experience the inevitability with which it collapses time and again into disillusionment before finally arriving, with a sense of utter continuity, at a fear of everlasting death and an embrace of obscurantist magic. I mean to suggest throughout this essay that *Doctor Faustus* involves a critique of the Renaissance itself, an attempt to understand its driving energies and get at the rationale of its internal contradictions by a playwright who could obviously suffer their embodiment.

12. Martin Versfeld, for instance, can take these same lines as evidence of Mephastophilis' alienation from the true metaphysical ground of things: "He is entirely at home in a world of process, but he cannot tolerate a universe which is an analogical procession": see "Some Remarks on Marlowe's Faustus," *ESA*, 1 (1958): 134–43.

13. Max Bluestone explores the implications of the confusion among Faustus's critics over whether to condemn him for being illogical or for bringing logic to bear on a matter of theological faith in "Libido Speculandi: Doctrine and Dramaturgy in Contemporary Interpretations of Marlowe's *Doctor Faustus*," in *Reinterpretations of Elizabethan Drama: Selected Papers from the English Institute*, ed. Norman Rabkin (New York, 1969), pp. 60–65.

14. The phrases in quotation marks are assembled from Stanley Cavell, *The World Viewed* (New York, 1971), p. 112.

15. The only critic who attempts to discuss at any length the relationship between Marlowe and his character as an aspect of the play's intrinsic design is C. L. Barber; what he ultimately decides to stress is Marlowe's authorial survival and transcendence of his work: "At the end of the text of *Doctor Faustus*, Marlowe wrote 'Terminat hora diem, Terminat Author opus.' . . . The final hour ends Faustus' day; but Marlowe is still alive. As the author, he has been in control: *he* has terminated the work and its hero. . . . Marlowe has earned an identity apart from his hero's—he is the author. He has done so by at once conceiving and subduing the protagonist" (" 'The form of Faustus' fortunes'," p. 118). Yet if such a note of triumph is at all to be

heard in this epigraph, it is mitigated by an even more forceful sense of fatalism and submissive anonymity. The analogy stresses the impersonal manner in which a work takes its course and comes to a conclusion, overtaking and absorbing its author and his will—"As the hour [and not "as the Creator"] ends the day, so ends the author his work [or vice versa]." As Barber suggests, it is as though Marlowe finishes the play at the stroke of midnight; yet what that suggests more than anything else is that there is a *similarity* between the "ending" of the author and the "ending" of his protagonist, not simply that one perishes while the other survives at his expense.

16. For an interesting, if philosophically and phenomenologically naive discussion of this theme, see Witold Ostrowski, "The Interplay of the Subjective and the Objective in Marlowe's *Dr. Faustus*," in *Studies in Language in Honour of Margaret Schlauch*, ed. Mieczyslaw Brahmer, Stanislaw Helsztynski, and Julian Krzyzanowski (Warsaw, 1966), pp. 293–305.

17. The affirmations implicit in this moment of perception become even more resonant if it is compared with Faustus's earlier, more characteristic expression of interest in the world of nature: "Nay let me have one booke more, wherein I might see al plants, hearbes and trees that grow upon the earth" (622–24).

18. The contrast with the figure of Gluttony, who actually appears in the pageant of the Seven Deadly Sins, could, in fact, scarcely be more extreme. This vice seems remarkable (unlike the more "Faustian" vices of Covetousness, Wrath, and Envy) primarily for his ontological security; Marlowe goes out of his way to present him as an infinitely likeable paragon of human well-being: "O I come of a royall parentage, my grandfather was a gammon of bacon, my grandmother a hogs head of Claret-wine: My godfathers were these, Peter Pickleherring, and Martin Martlemas-biefe, O but my godmother she was a jolly gentlewoman, and welbeloved in every good towne and Citie, her name was mistresse Margery March-beere: now *Faustus*, thou hast heard all my Progeny, wilt thou bid me to supper?" (773–81). Such an acknowledgment and celebration of parentage is especially remarkable in the context of Marlowe's work; it certainly seems meant to contrast favorably with Faustus's miserable "Curst be the parents that ingendred me" (1496).

19. The term is borrowed from Philip Slater, *The Glory of Hera: Greek Mythology and the Greek Family* (New York, 1969). My understanding of the dilemmas being expressed in the passages under discussion has been greatly influenced by Slater's analysis of similar patterns in Greek myth and tragedy. C. L. Barber also discusses, from a rather different point of

view, the oral character of Faustus's desire: see " 'The form of Faustus' fortunes'," pp. 95–115.

20. Barber, p. 112.

21. Ibid., p. 112.

22. Wallace Stevens, "Saint John and the Back-ache."

23. Marlowe seems in this play to have a conscious insight into the existence of internalized parental figures and voices within the self.

24. See also ll. 111–14, 485–86, 799–803, and the whole of the final soliloquy.

25. See also ll. 244–49, 470, 513, 862–67, 1134–39, 1433–34, and 1450–54.

26. Note, in the admonition with which the Old Man recalls Faustus to Christian self-awareness, the suggestion (reminiscent of the ironies of Blake's "Ah! Sunflower") of perpetual deferral, of the tendency of goals to become redundant means to further goals: "Ah Doctor Faustus, that I might prevaile, / To guide thy steps unto the way of life, / By which sweete path thou maist attaine the gole / That shall conduct thee to celestial rest" (1301–5).

27. *"Terminat hora diem, Terminat Author opus"* subjects the play itself to these same ambiguities.

28. The relevant contrast is the final soliloquy, where Faustus, fixed and suspended at the center of a subjective void, experiences time and "all" passing him by.

29. Paul Valéry, "Le Bilan de l'Intelligence," trans. Denise Folliot and Jackson Mathews, in *History and Politics*, vol. 10 of *The Collected Works of Paul Valéry*, ed. Jackson Mathews, Bollingen Series XLV (New York, 1962), pp. 141–42.

BEN JONSON

Gabriele Bernhard Jackson

Structural Interplay in Ben Jonson's Drama

I should like to begin by suiting my paper's structure to Ben Jonson's drama: placing before my main demonstration a prologue or induction—general, explanatory, with allusions to other playwrights, and of a certain magnitude, to provide the context for what is to follow. In brief, my preplay argument is that what is to be shown here about Jonsonian comedy holds true in many ways for English Renaissance drama in general, and perhaps indeed for comedy and tragedy at large, though I confine them at present because "we would make known, / No country's mirth is better than our own" (*Alch*. Prol., 5-6). My only apology to the audience is that Jonson's mirth will not really be treated as mirthful; yet I hope to balance this heaviness of subject with some levity of style.

Less cryptically, my induction to Jonson's comedy moves away from the notion that comedy and tragedy are different kinds of action, or even different ways of developing an action, to the view that they are opposed *perspectives* on an action. Taking a dramatic action to be a series of movements, by one or more characters, towards a goal or set of goals, we might say that in the tragic perspective, movements towards a goal that threatens established reality are seen as basically serious, as potentially successful, and as crucial to the value system of the real world. In the comic perspective, on the other hand, such goal-oriented actions are seen as amusing because they cannot succeed in the real world nor, if they did, would they be of value to it. The goals and actions themselves may not be very different in tragedy and comedy; the difference lies in the view shared by dramatist and audience.

Perhaps the readiest example for these assertions comes from Shakespeare, so often seen as Jonson's polar opposite that I should like for once to bring them together. The goals and actions of *Othello* and *Much Ado About Nothing* are nearly the same right through the rejection of bride by deceived bride-groom, and even beyond.[1] But though the bride in *Much Ado* does fall senseless, she is secretly revived and rewedded, dis-guised as her (invented) purer cousin: that is, disguised as she really always was. Desdemona, of course, must really die of Othello's misapprehension before he can believe in the truth of her guise.[2] The comic or tragic perspective on these phenomena is selected by the dramatist (assuming he can control his choice) and communicated by certain signals to the audience.

Of these signals, the most definitive is naturally the play's ending; but the opening is also of great importance in notifying the audience whether a tragic or a comic perspective is more likely to be appropriate. The comic contract between play-wright and audience depends heavily on a conviction, established early, of where basic or stable reality lies. With a conviction of stable reality, conflicting or threatening goals can be seen as comic: as *fantasies* doomed to explosion by reality or, at least, to a radical alteration that will allow them to fit in with what social possibility really is. The threatening characters can be seen as impotent or laughable or both, because they are blind and deaf to the authoritative reality understood between audi-ence and playwright. So, to return to our examples, at the beginning of *Much Ado*, we learn that the most potent figure of social reality, the Prince, is in favor of the marriage of Claudio and Hero—he furthers it actively himself; and that the arbiter of Hero's particular social reality, her father, also favors the mar-riage. At the beginning of *Othello*, on the contrary, we learn that Desdemona's father has had to be deceived and escaped from, while the Duke of Venice, though not prepared to hinder the match, cannot provide the buttress of social reality because Othello and his bride are going to Cyprus: the island—not incidentally—sacred to the goddess of love. Here Othello himself will be supreme commander, even creator, of social reality. The status of Iago's threatening fantasies, then, will depend upon the degree of accord possible between Othello's Cyprian and Cypriot rules. Confronted with this unprecedented sociological experiment, the audience has no clear predictive signal as to whether the bond between Othello and Desdemona can hold up. It will be tried on ground as remote from established social support as their union is already remote—in its very nature—from accepted social conjunctions.[3]

In tragedy, then, the audience is soon signaled either that there is no authoritative social reality that guarantees the failure of threatening fantasy goals; or—more ominous yet—that the threatening fantasy goal is actually suited to the prevailing social reality: as in *Hamlet*, where the vision of a ghost demanding revenge fits in all too well with the Queen's hasty, semi-incestuous marriage and with the King's circumvention of political process.

To refer to comedy and tragedy as containing fantasies is convenient for two reasons: it suggests that there is an idea in the mind of a central character that he is attempting to act out; and it reminds us that the dramatist is acting out for the audience an idea from his own mind—an idea that, in the manner of its acting, includes the perspective of the dramatist. The terms "reality" and "realization," therefore, are double. Ultimately, the "reality" presented by a tragedy or comedy rests upon its author's tragic or comic view of his own idea. Its "realization" is its achievement of convincing form. The play's givens, however, become a reality in themselves if we suspend (as we usually do) our awareness of the author.

For the purpose of returning to comedy, and particularly Jonsonian comedy, I would like to have the best of both words. Jonson's extended prologues and inductions make it exceptionally difficult for us to rule the author out; he often goes so far as to announce overt directives or compacts for accord between playwright and audience. His work provides a useful, because explicit, paradigm in which an announced perspective governs the audience's perception of reality, while at the same time an announced fantasy is acted out within the play. In the following discussion, I shall take the central action of each Jonsonian comedy as an initial fantasy in the mind of one or more characters, whose goal is to act out that fantasy completely in the "real" world. As the "realization" of the fantasy comes nearer and nearer, the audience receives more and more signals that reversal impends. Finally, the attempt to achieve the goal, to impose the fantasy fully upon the real world, results in the collapse or drastic alteration of the fantasy, and reality prevails.

In tragedy, on the other hand, an initial fantasy is acted out or realized with greater and greater success, until it is fully imposed on the real world and causes the collapse of what had previously been reality, as well as the destruction of the fantasizer.[4] Without prejudice as to the comparative value, much less beauty, of social reality and fantasy in any given play, tragedy can be tentatively designated the drama of the unliveable, while comedy is the drama of liveability. Liveability means accommodation, and there can be little doubt that in the great Jonsonian comedies, at any rate, this societal self-preservation is seen as a primary value.

The structural interplay to which my title refers, then, will be treated here as the typical interplay between a Jonsonian drama's central fantasy and some of the many methods by which the dramatist presents its comic development. I shall leave aside tone, characterization, and a multitude of other contributing techniques, in order to concentrate on the movement towards attempted realization, which is, simultaneously, a movement towards reversal. A play's individual manner of getting from its beginning to its end is what I mean by its structure: some elements of this structure are the selection of characters (one might call this a part of the premises), the logic of movement from scene to scene, the signals provided that an action is fantasy out of accord with a stable reality, the indications that a reversal of action is in the offing, and, of course, the final accommodation or conclusion. By the central action of a Jonsonian drama I mean essentially its main plot line and what that plot line signifies to my critical eye when looked at symbolically. Therefore my choice of "central action" in each case must be to some extent arbitrary; but I believe that whatever appropriate reformulation might be chosen by another critic, the same typically Jonsonian constructions of symmetry between action and structure would hold good. To minimize the potential distractions of central critical disagreement, I have chosen to work with two plays on which there is much critical accord about plot and significance: *Volpone* and *The Alchemist*. In order to add a more difficult and complicated test case, I shall deal also with *Bartholomew Fair*, though in less detail.

It will be seen that the subject of this paper falls into two parts. One is identification of the fantasies that determine each play's central action. The second is identification of ways in which each central action is related to the particular comic construction of its play.

I

It has often been suggested that a major Renaissance dramatic motif is "the real energy and appetite for transcendence that animated the Renaissance."[5] In particular, this overreaching has been explored in the tragedies of Marlowe and the comedies of Jonson, especially *The Alchemist*. I should like now to reformulate and limit this notion of transcendence, or overreaching, to the fantasy of *self-sufficiency*, and to suggest that it is indeed a basic—perhaps *the* basic—Renaissance fantasy, holding sway in the real world over the minds of absolute monarchs, of lone explorers, of merchants seeking patents for monopolies—as well as, in the fictional dramatic world, dominating the imaginations of dozens of comic and tragic characters from Dr. Faustus to

Vittoria Corombona asserting, when sentenced to a house of correction for whores: "It shall not be a house of convertites; / My mind shall make it honester to me / Than the Pope's palace" (*The White Devil* 3.2.285–87). The mind is its own place. Given space enough and time, we could find examples from nearly every Renaissance dramatist claiming that self-sufficiency is an attempt at spiritual heroism.[6]

Of special interest are two dramatic boasts that may conveniently (though not precisely) demarcate the period when this notion was dominant. The first is Tamburlaine's (1587–88): "I hold the Fates bound fast in iron chains, / And with my hands turn Fortune's wheel about" (1.2.173–74). The last is Giovanni's very similar utterance in *'Tis Pity She's a Whore* (1632), when "in human scorn of men" he declares: "in my fists I bear the twists of life" (5.3.70–72). Indeed, these claims *are* alike in deriving from a sexual definition of self-sufficiency: the dream of self-completion through union with a counterpart. Tamburlaine's triumphant tone is part of his dream come true in "Divine Zenocrate," "The only paragon of Tamburlaine" (3.3.119). Giovanni's defiant despair is a shard of the same dream shattered by *his* "only paragon," his sister and faithless lover, whose heartstrings in his murderous hands represent the bonds that were his "twists of life."[7]

It is while the cycle is running from the optimism of Tamburlaine's era to the despair of Giovanni's that fantasies of sexual self-sufficiency rule in the real as well as the fictional realm, from the adroitly preserved virginity of Elizabeth through the homosexuality of James I to the continued royal patronage of Charles I for Buckingham—now his licentious alter ego. In this sexual form, the completeness of the self is displayed in its self-surrender to some surrogate, either an extension or a mirror image (or both). In such a sexual relationship, that basic drive that most undeniably and urgently threatens the notion of self as self-contained is directed into the service of self-preservation.

The union of self with other becomes a unity of self with self, and the world as other is both excluded and dominated by that all-powerful doubling intensification. Politically, the semi-mythical status of the omnipotent ruler is asserted and reinforced. More and more clearly, however, both the period's history and its drama seem to set forth the incommensurability of reality with this fantasy's imaginative pull—not only towards personal power, but towards intimations of harmony in an inviolate inner world, and correspondent resonances of ultimate unity. The social realm parallels the drama in extruding the fantasy as imposed by its contemporary political incarnation, electing the tragic denouement that destroys what has hitherto been reality:

> That thence the *Royal Actor* born
> The *Tragick Scaffold* might adorn:
>   While round the armed Bands
>   Did clap their bloody hands.
> *He* nothing common did or mean
> Upon that memorable Scene:
>   But with his keener Eye
>   The Axes edge did try . . .
>   (Andrew Marvell, "An Horatian Ode . . ." 53 ff.)[8]

The tragic hero, seen gathering into himself the salient functions of executioner and instrument of execution—testing and exhibiting deadly keenness—remains an embodiment of self-sufficiency in the very manner of his death. Certainly the prayer, copied out of the *Arcadia*, that Charles put into the hands of an attendant clergyman suggests that he, like his audience, saw death as an affirmation of self against other: "Let calamity be the exercise, but not the overthrow, of my virtue. . . . let never their wickedness have such a hand, but that I may carry a pure mind in a pure body" (3.5). For this tragic actor as for contemporaneous fictional ones, death becomes the final assertion of self-sufficiency when reality refuses to countenance it. A glimpse of comic perspective tempts me to agree with Milton

that there may have been, in the choice of this particular
"virtuous" prayer, a flash of sardonic defiance—a dying sparkle
of the age, allied in spirit to Giovanni's "scorn of men," to the
tortured Princess Calantha's "smile in death" (Ford's *Broken
Heart*, 5.3.98), or, better, to Cleopatra's notion of her suicide
as a royal joke:

> Who would have imagined . . . so little . . . sense of his afflictions or
> of that sad hour which was upon him as immediately before his death
> to pop into the hand of that grave bishop who attended him, for a
> special relic of his saintly exercises, a prayer stolen word for word
> from . . . no serious book, but the vain amatorious poem of Sir Philip
> Sidney's *Arcadia;* . . . full of worth and wit, but among religious
> thoughts and duties not worthy to be named . . .
>
> (Milton, Iconoclastes, Ch. I)

Self-aware or not, the doomed absolute monarch holding in
his hand a prayer from a vain amatorious book may stand as
one emblem of his times. Whether tragically or comically
illuminated, the search for independence of all social require-
ments is powerfully expressed by the metaphor of a vain
amatorious commitment. In the drama of the period, this may
range from the deliberate choice of a counterpart to some
half-recognized partnership with a subordinate version of the
self, a version banned from reality by "common" circumstance.
Consider the isolated Viola, developing in her independence an
alter ego as male wooer of Olivia—a woman whose name comes
close to identifying her anagrammatically with Viola herself.[9]
Alternatively, a sexual partner who acts as an extension of self
can be a projection, like Helen of Troy, out of one's own
mental powers, or be created, like DeFlores in *The Changeling*,
out of an actual servant. It may be true to say that in the earlier
part of the period this fantasy more clearly appears as some
sort of mental construct, while by the time of *The Changeling*
(1624) it has become an attempt at a real self-enriching fusion.[10]
Insofar as it posits a self-reinforcing sexual merger, the central

fantasy of self-sufficiency is connected with the metaphorical figure of the androgyne so important to Renaissance philosophy and iconography. This sexual formulation of the Renaissance ideal is of special interest for Jonsonian comedy, since I would like to argue that *Volpone, The Alchemist*, and *Bartholomew Fair* present differing individual versions of the androgynous fantasy, and that these successive versions form a progression toward transcendence or abandonment of the idea in two ways: in a recognition, however qualified, of a sexual tie between independent entities; and in the substitution of an ideal of social union among miscellaneous equals. Before that freedom is attained, however, the androgynous fantasy presents itself in many versions: one is simple narcissism ("androgynous" only in that lover and beloved are indivisible); another, a hermaphroditic view of the self; others, homosexuality, heterosexual eroticism, and even marriage. I have deliberately arranged these options in order of further and further removal from self-absorption, both to prepare for the ensuing discussion and to suggest that, as these versions dramatically present ever more recognition of other-ness, they more nearly approach, metaphorically, acceptance of life in a society. Thus they make progressively more possible for the dramatic characters an accommodation to social givens—and so facilitate for the dramatist a truly agreeable transformation of fantasy into reality, or comic ending.

Volpone is well known to offer no such comfortable conclusion. Compact artifact that it is, it combines instead convenient and unmistakable examples of alienated narcissism, hermaphroditism, and homosexuality. The general narcissism of both Volpone and Mosca is of course self-evident, but it is interesting that Mosca's self-admiration in particular is sexually focused:

> I fear I shall begin to grow in love
> With my dear self and my most prosp'rous parts,

> They do so spring and burgeon; I can feel
> A whimsy i' my blood. I know not how,
> Success hath made me wanton.   (3.1.1ff)

Mosca's figurative self-projection is echoed by the true hermaphrodite figure who acts the main role in Mosca's introductory
playlet; this hermaphrodite, appropriately, also belongs to
Volpone: he is a member of the household menagerie and pos-
sibly Volpone's offspring. In this figure, the audience of Mosca's
playlet is told, the once philosophical soul of Pythagoras has
presently come to rest. Subhuman self-sufficiency defines
Mosca's notion of the soul's condition—and, the soul's set
speech declares, "even here would I tarry" (1.2.63).

Volpone, however, would like to go further. As the mutual
action of the Volpone/Mosca unit springs and burgeons, success
makes Volpone wanton: his reactions change from "Loving
Mosca!" (at the end of Act 1, scene 2) to "Mosca! / Come
hither, let me kiss thee" (at the end of Act 1, scene 3), rising at
the end of scene 4 to "I cannot hold; good rascal, let me kiss
thee" (137). Thus long Mosca ignores and evades Volpone's
actions, busying himself with his own part. But after the next
gulling, when Volpone rather alarmingly announces that "The
Turk is not more sensual in his pleasures / Than will Volpone"
(1.5.88–89), Mosca exits—returning to divert his patron with
an account of Celia's beauty. So the spirit informing the
Volpone/Mosca unit remains, as Mosca's playlet has predicted,
merely hermaphroditic, until the unit divides and narcissism
prevails. Even before the split into narcissism, Volpone's last
word of admiration for their mutual masterwork is only a
lecherously wistful accolade: "Let me embrace thee. O that I
could now / Transform thee to a Venus" (5.3.103–04).

In this consciously unworkable suggestion, as in Volpone's
more serious delusion that private theatricals may indeed
metamorphose Celia into his mistress, and again in the real
miseries of Celia's real marriage, we see that all forms of

heterosexual desire in *Volpone* are presented as mistakes. The play's central fantasy is identified by the working out of its narcissistically imposed limitation. The fantasy, in cheaters as in cheated, is that self-sufficiency will be achieved through refusal of lasting relationship: the refusal, or rather incapacity, of most animals—and particularly those named as the characters of this play.

In *The Alchemist*, on the other hand, the dependence of self-sufficiency on relationship is explicit from the first scene, in which Dol Common vigorously reminds her quarreling colleagues that disunity will leave them all "a prey unto the *marshall*" and their "sober, scirvy, precise neighbors" (1.1.120, 164). The trio of characters who want simultaneously to secede from and control this social world must adhere to their "indenture tripartite" (5.4.131), one condition of which is a heterosexual bond between Dol Common and both her male associates. Homosexual fantasy is minimal, though Sir Epicure does offer to bite Face's ear at a particularly gratifying moment (2.3.326) and contemplates having him gelded (2.2.35); Face's narcissism seems to find no firmer sexual expression than a harmless preference for his own anatomy over what he describes as Subtle's "no-buttocks" (1.1.37). On the contrary, much manipulative success is projected in terms of heterosexual unions and marriages, one of which actually comes off.

Alchemy, on which it is reckoned that more than 113 books appeared between 1595 and 1615,[11] was in fact the science of the creation of bonds: of indissoluble bonds between metals. When from the original "base earth," as the foundation matter of the experiment was called, had been extracted the basic substances sulphur and mercury, these were refined from their ordinary physical state into alchemically workable sulphur and mercury, of which sulphur was regarded as male and mercury as female. The ultimate object was to *marry* these metals. To that end, they were purged of all impurities by repeated distillation in a closed vessel, which raised their state until, heated and reheated, they fused and became gold. In the highly influential version of this process described by Paracelsus, a third basic material was added: salt, which was necessary to fix the color of the ultimate fusion. In this version, all three originally disparate materials had to unite more and more completely in order to produce the union of male and female metal, called in alchemical terminology "the hermaphrodite." This union was followed by a state of temporary inactivity, known as a concealed "death," after which the male and female substances revived and entered the condition entitled "the mystic marriage," productive of the elixir or philosopher's stone, a higher form of gold than physical gold. This, fixed by the stabilizing salt, could turn all baser metals to physical gold.

That the trio in Lovewit's closed-up vessel of a house join together in more and more complicated fusions, to derive gold from whatever material happens along, could hardly have escaped critical notice, and there have been some attempts to identify the three cheaters with specific metals and to deduce interpretations from such correspondences.[12] I myself identify Dol—obviously—with mercury, because she is female and is described within the play as performing her appropriate type of distillation: "She'll mount you up, like quicksilver / Over the helm, and circulate" (2.3.254–55). Sulphur I take to be Subtle, not only because of the similarity in sound but also because he has, like that element, "Combustibility" (see, e.g., Act 1.1) and "the right *color* for making gold" (Kernan, Appendix I, p. 230; italics mine). Besides, he is the male counterpart of Dol and escapes with her at the end, fused though not married. Face is salt, not only because of his inexhaustible wit in the experiments, but also because (being in charge of the house during his master's absence) he is the element necessary to fix the golden nature of the outcome, to provide all this airy vaporization with a local habitation and a name.[13] In *The Alchemist*, then, the central fantasy of self-sufficiency is again sexually expressed as hermaphroditic fusion, but it abandons narcissism and looks forward to some version of marriage, a lasting bond between separates.[14]

The next step in the movement away from the goal of isolation to the goal of social interaction is the journey to *Bartholomew Fair*, in which the original fantasy requires the success of a number of marriages: that already existing between the Littlewits, that contracted by Cokes and Mistress Grace, and that hoped for by the Widow Purecraft and her rival suitors. Yet even this heterosexual marital fantasy, close as it may seem to the most conventional of authoritative realities in or out of drama, is in truth still another version of the dream of self-sufficiency.

That fact becomes very clear in the opening scene between the Littlewits. Doting John has prevailed upon his wife to enact his wishes by wearing a velvet hat and "fine high shoes," items of clothing unsuited to her social rank. Despite her reluctance, he requires her—most lovingly, of course—to perform for him: "I would fain see thee pace" (18ff). Having admired her beauty, he rewards her, and gratifies himself, with a kiss. This is still a self-extending hermaphroditic fusion, though under the warrant of legal marriage. The scene introduces a central fantasy, borne out by the comments of other marital aspirants: that the happiness of marital matches is measured by the self-extension of the husband—unless he is a madman, the kind of husband sought, in fact (in fulfillment of a prophecy), by the experienced widow Dame Purecraft. If the man is *not* mad, mutual satisfaction will best result—according to the play's opening premise—from a situation in which the wife is young, handsome, compliant to her spouse, and in some admirable way a pretender to a status above his—that is, she should be someone fit to be put on a pedestal, be it only because of her fine high shoes.[15] In other words, the initial romantic fantasy of

Bartholomew Fair is the commonest romantic fantasy of our own time.

Not only in Jonson, not only in the Renaissance, and not only in fiction, then, is a basic fantasy of self-sufficiency often dramatized by the insistent acting out of an erotic fantasy. Yet in order to recapture Jonson in his immediate context, recalling also its dark side, we might remind ourselves of Edward II's tragic insistence on equating the integrity of his absolute kingship with freedom to choose homosexual eroticism—or remember the Duchess of Malfi's similar equation between loyalty to her forbidden marriage and her stable identity as "Duchess of Malfi still" (4.2.167).

The fantasy of total integrity or self-sufficiency, however, as one might expect, is various in form and not always sex-linked. Certainly the sexual aspect of the Jonsonian versions I have been describing is one very useful reflector of similarities and differences among them. I should like now to broaden my focus to include other angles of vision on the central actions of these same plays, in order to demonstrate some ways in which Jonsonian comedy structures itself in symmetry with its subject matter. This shaping process, in accordance with the covenant between dramatist and audience, should progressively clarify— or, rather, construct—a shared perspective in which the action can be identified as an artifice originating in a deluded mind, working itself out simultaneously towards realization and reversal.

II

Typically, Jonson allows us just a glimpse of some authoritative reality very early in the play. A glimpse suffices for the purpose; it appears as something explicitly excluded by the characters in their initial actions, like the glimpse of the rising sun from which Volpone turns. This absolute outside norm need not, however, define the nature of "reality" as the play's ending will present it. What a working reality will turn out to be is gradually revealed to the audience through the introduction of a counterfantasy; fantasy and counterfantasy delimit the space within which reality exists. The development of the counterfantasy is the second term of the author's dialectic; the comic resolution is a socialized version of the original fantasy, tempered by recognition of the claims made by an absolutely opposing psychological position. The conclusion is thus established by a combination of social and emotional imperatives.

Simultaneously, Jonson charts the progress and breakdown of the initial fantasy by converting some of its component notions into rules for dramatic action, and advancing the play through mutations of these. Striking here are the hierarchies of characters he constructs, hierarchies that accord with the play's central fantasy and govern the order in which characters are introduced and reappear—for the deployment of these hierarchies is one signal as to the status of the central action. Against this mobility we can place the fixed points of orientation at which a concept originally part of the fantasy action is repeated in a different key, so to speak, on its way to reality. The most economical example is probably "explosion" in *The Alchemist*, verbally enacted by the cheaters as the play opens, realistically counterfeited by them for Mammon as crisis impends, and actually forced upon them at the end.

Since *Volpone* is the simplest of the plays under discussion, it will be useful to take it as paradigm case for examination of some of the above devices. In its central action, the fantasy of self-sufficiency appears as movement towards the goal of acting more and more like animals: that is, as we have already seen, of denying all lasting emotional ties. In order to include Volpone's three household grotesques and the peripheral Lady Would-Be, we might redefine this goal as acting more and more subhuman, for the securing of that invulnerability of self that Volpone sees as "far transcending / All style of joy in children,

parents, friends, / Or any other waking dream on earth"
(1.1.16ff).

Total counterfantasy is introduced into the play by Celia and
Bonario, prompted by their names to act not subhuman but
superhuman. Resisting Volpone's attempted seduction, Celia
invokes the abstractions "honor," "virtue," and many another
waking dream on earth, including the protection of "heaven"
(3.7.38, 259, 243). But the main defense of her limited imagination, too, centers on self-sufficiency: she is glad not to
possess "a mind affected / With . . . delights" and claims that
perfect innocence leaves her invulnerable: "but I . . . / . . . /
Cannot be taken with these sensual baits" (3.7.205ff). Bonario,
less hyperbolic, is equally reliant on self-sufficiency. Asked at
the first trial to produce witnesses of his and Celia's innocence,
he replies, "Our consciences"; while Celia adds: "And heaven,
that never fails the innocent." But the official response of the
real authorities is unsympathetic: "These are no testimonies"
(4.6.14ff). To fallible judges of real relationship, who must
work on the basis of real observation, such fantasies of super-
human integrity are as irrelevant as are, in the end, fantasies
of subhuman unaccountability. The normative courtroom is
the site of the play's first collision between both these fantasies
and reality (if we bow to simplicity and agree to discount
metafantasy, that is, Volpone pretending to be a pretender
when he impersonates Scoto in the mountebank scene). What
signals have by then passed from dramatist to audience to
indicate the probable outcome, or even the approach of such a
dangerous intersection?

Because we have had some brief indication of a simple outside reality at the very beginning of Act I, in the rising of the sun
already mentioned and the allusion by Volpone to the normal
custom of saying matins, the action in Volpone's chamber
opens immediately as internal fantasy. As further emphasis,
the curtains of Volpone's shrine are opened to show what is

inside; on this cue, Volpone, in his morning service to his gold, begins the enactment—though as yet only verbal—of his fantasy of self-sufficiency, expounding it as simultaneously financial, intellectual, emotional, hedonistic, reliant on subhuman "sport" soon to be presented by his grotesques, and *in potentia* narcissistically sexual: "What should I do / But cocker up my genius and live free / To all delights . . . ?" (1.1.70ff).

This opening of the curtain signals, and not only in Jonson's dramas, the beginning of a fantasy action as well as the exposure of a material reality. The gold is revealed simultaneously in its fantasy value and as an integral object with its own implications, perceived by the audience though not the fantasizer. The play's conclusion will force the fantasizer to take into account the mute pressure of this independent existence, which shapes events the obsessive eye cannot foresee.[16]

The next move in the attempted realization of Volpone's fantasy is the playful acting out of his ideal by his deformed jesters, in particular the grotesque hermaphrodite; and this play becomes itself the prologue to Volpone's own. In Act 1, scene 2, he dons his furry costume, another obvious signal of fantasy action, lies down behind the open curtains of his bedstead, and becomes the werefox, to whom the fowls that are his proper prey appear in their proper order. For they *have* a proper order, a formal hierarchy symmetrical with the central action, and the preservation or violation of that order is a signal that the central fantasy is working out or is in a state of disarray.

Of Volpone's birds, the vulture, first to appear in the person of Voltore, was distinguished in bestiary description for its predatorily oriented eyesight, its ability to "notice cadavers even when they are beyond the seas" and to "perceive from a height, while flying, many things which are hidden from us by the mountains in between."[17] The lawyer Voltore is first not only through predatory expertise but also by spiritual proximity, for vultures were believed to isolate themselves from their own kind and to be sexually self-sufficient: they eschewed copulation, and were thought "not to mingle in a conjugal manner. . . . The females conceive without any assistance from the males and generate without conjunction" (White, 109).

The second arrival, Corbaccio the raven, is less far-ranging and not gifted with the oversight of the vulture, according to bestiary lore. Nevertheless an effective predator, the raven destroys sight in its victim, beginning its meal with the eyes and proceeding to attack the brain (White, 141–42). (It is to Corbaccio on his first visit that Mosca says of Volpone: "His speech is broken, and his eyes are set," 1.4.38; "his eyelids hang" 42; "and from his brain . . . / Flows a cold sweat" 47–48. Throughout this scene Volpone does not speak.) Though not an avoider of its kind, the raven was said to refuse to feed its young unless its offspring exactly resembled it. (Cf. 3.9.2 ff: "*Mosca.* Your son, I know not by what accident, / Acquainted with your purpose to my patron / . . . / Sought for you, called you wretch, unnatural, / . . . / *Corb.* This act shall disinherit him indeed.") Further, it was symbolically related to solitude, probably because of its biblical (as Jonsonian) habit of feeding hermits (White, 141–42).

Corvino the crow, who arrives last, is not properly a predator at all, though of course notorious for greed of the harvest. The crow is a dutiful family bird and, easily tamed by man, can even learn to pronounce some human words (White, 142). (Cf. Corvino's original reaction to Volpone's condition: "'Las, good gentleman. / How pitiful the sight is!" 1.5.20–21, as well as the ensuing dialogue in which Mosca "teaches" Corvino how to describe Volpone: ibid., 59–66.)

It would be impossible to expound all the correspondences between these birds and the social as well as psychological characteristics of the men in *Volpone* who take their roles. What is clear is that they appear, given the fantasy goal, in a descending hierarchy: moving away from the characteristics of

Volpone himself, they diminish in power, size, and self-sufficiency while they more and more nearly approach the level of social man.

When the visitors next appear in Volpone's house, in Act 3, scene 7, they arrive in reverse order, a development unforeseen by Mosca in his role as Volpone's *arbiter fantasiae*. This reversal, like the arrival of Volpone's reverse fantasist Celia at the very start of this second round of visits, signals the approach of a general reversal for Volpone's fantasy. The upset duly takes place by the end of Act 3 in the private unmasking of Volpone by Bonario. But by Act 4, Mosca has marshalled his three birds in the courtroom in such a way that they will speak in their proper original order. Voltore first exhibits his powers as lying lawyer, then Corbaccio disowns his son, and finally Corvino deposes that his wife is a whore. In this sequence, the central action is back in working order and the central fantasy of having no ties and no social obligations moves forward further into reality—out of the private house and into the state. The goal of subhumanity, too, is closer to attainment. Voltore is now acting out what was earlier merely a fantasy-description of Mosca's: "Hood an ass with reverend purple / So you can hide his two ambitious ears, / And he shall pass for a cathedral doctor" (1.2.111ff); Corvino points to his forehead to show "here / . . . the horn" of the cuckold (4.5.124–25). One of the judges is "turned a stone" (4.5.154), while Volpone, as Kernan has pointed out, represents himself as "simply an object to be carried about."[18] Celia and Bonario are described as the dregs of animal society: Bonario is a swine, goat, wolf, viper (4.5.111–12); Celia, a partridge, chameleon, and hyena, who "neighs like a jennet" in her sexual cavorting (4.5.118, 4.6.2–3, 4.5.119). With such total and unresisted enthusiasm is the surrealistic illusion projected that, unexpectedly, it balances the retreat of reality by becoming laughable. Yet the laughter remains undeniably uncomfortable; in the central action's first test against

reality it has advanced in its own due order, an outcome potentially tragic.

Integrated into this forward march of fantasy are the actions of
the semianimal subgroup centered around Sir Politic Would-Be.
Since Sir Pol and his baiter Peregrine are only half bird (their
names, obviously, have human meanings first), they are properly
produced after the fully fledged (in Act 2, between the first
two sets of visitations to Volpone's house). The Lady Would-Be
is last and least, making the pivotal visit that both ends the
profitable first series and begins the inverted second. Her animal
aspirations barely qualify her for entrance; she merely chatters
so excessively as to make Volpone cry out, "Ay me, I have ta'en
a grasshopper by the wing!" (3.4.54–55), and contributes
animal misidentifications of Celia. Her more engagé husband,
Sir Pol the parrot, is appropriately an imitator, who takes his
values from the behavior of animals without actually playing
the game. His assessment of public actions is entirely based on
the behavior of animals, such as "a raven, that should build / In
a ship royal of the King's," the whelping of a lion in the Tower,
the appearance of three porpoises above London Bridge, and the
report of "a whale discovered in the river, / . . . that had waited
there, / Few know how many months, for the subversion / Of
the Stode fleet" (2.1.22f,34–35,40,46ff). Sir Pol, encouraged in
his deductions by Peregrine, comes to a natural end when he
attempts the subhuman game itself. Disguising himself as a tortoise to escape Peregrine's staged onslaught by the police, he
has, suitably for a tortoise, just got in Act 5 to the stage of
donning his costume. Poor Pol as tortoise, his political notes destroyed, is also acting out unknowingly the favorite Renaissance
emblem of the tortoise carried high into the air—usually by an
eagle (here, a Peregrine falcon)—only to be dropped to earth
with a smashed case.

Act 5 smashes and reverses all fantasy, but the action pro-
ceeds by easy stages. It copies Act I in the opening dialogue

between Mosca and Volpone on their previous success and future plans; but now Volpone, pushing his obsession to its logical extreme, will act out the ultimate fantasy of subhuman self-sufficiency: death. The characters enter in their original order, and Mosca, himself demolishing the previous action, expels them in reverse order, though he realizes that this may be the endgame. It plays out too well the fantasy of lack of bonds and lack of obligation, dissolving the bonds and obligations among the players themselves. Volpone's irreducible self-sufficiency throws each gull into enforced parallel isolation. "I doubt it will lose them" (5.3.108), Mosca warns. With himself and Volpone as the only remaining players, Mosca makes the final move by dissolving the last bond. Winner of the game, he is revealed as the lowest animal of all, a parasitic fruit fly that devours its host. Fantasy action has reached the verge of complete success, and must go a second time to a real court for judgment.

Here Voltore's attempt to reverse his earlier testimony (schematically reinforced by his appearing last) proves as unconvincing to the judges as Volpone's attempt to reinstate it (and the original gulling hierarchy). The only possibilities remaining are total acceptance of the fantasy, or recognition and repudiation of the entire game as game. The outcome rests on the choice of Volpone himself, initiator of the fantasy, who alone has the power to bring it to an end by choosing reality. As he throws off his disguise, his decisive motivation is social: Mosca must not be allowed to marry into a respectable family. Better, for Volpone, to live with any heavy punishment than with the fully worked out implications of his dream—the anarchic double threat of Mosca's advancement and his own degradation by whipping. Celia's counterfantasy of superhuman mercy is rejected by the judges, and the accommodation to reality is grimly enforced as the conspirators and gulls, sentenced in their proper order, receive punishments that are versions of the animal game in removing the actors from all human bonds to various versions of isolation and self-contemplation. Indeed, real authority comes so close to sanctioning the central fantasy, though of course in a negative form, that the audience could be pardoned for getting its comic and tragic signals crossed if it were not explicitly requested to "fare jovially, and clap your hands."

A typical Jonsonian comic ending, though untypically harsh, this judgment substitutes suitable real terms for the fantasy concepts of the deluded characters—a corrective emendation. So here the "mortifying of a fox" (5.12.125) with cramping irons provides an appropriate final point of orientation about a fantasy in which gradual dying has appeared first as a pleasure and then as a public necessity (in the first courtroom scene). The unifying modulation of this notion corresponds to the development of "explosion" already noted in *The Alchemist*.

A detailed further comparison of structural progression in *The Alchemist* and *Bartholomew Fair* would be unending. Let me, then, rather indicate which of the structural features we have seen in *Volpone*, differentiating fantasy from reality and pointing to the victory of the latter, are most clearly common to the three plays.

An opening indication, characteristically glancing, of an out-side norm appears in the identification of the abnormal circum-stances in *The Alchemist* that render Lovewit's house both available and temporarily sealed up; in *Bartholomew Fair*, such an indication is given by the fact that John has insisted on his wife's violating, however playfully, the prescriptions of their social status. Although neither of these later plays has a curtain-drawing scene, both begin almost immediately with an analo-gous action, in which one set of characters is clearly putting on a show for another, who act as believing audience. In *The Al-chemist*, this is the first gulling scene, in which Subtle and Face communicate in double entendres impenetrable to Dapper; in *Bartholomew Fair*, it is the opening scene in which Win unwillingly performs for her uncomprehending husband. Donning of costume is also an early and obvious evidence of attempt to act out fantasy; in *The Alchemist*, Subtle changes into his doctor's robes before the first gull appears, while in *Bartholomew Fair*, Win has already had to change costume before the play begins.

Each play contains a challenge to its initial action by one or more counterfantasists. In *The Alchemist*, the counterbeliever is Surly, who rejects all notion of the possibility of transmutation as completely as the alchemical trio accepts the idea that *anything* can be transformed. Surly disqualifies his position when he counters the alchemical costume act (which he hopes to expose) by means of a costume act of his own, unintentionally demonstrating that even the most unpromising material *can* be transmuted upward (he is disguised as a nobleman). In *Bartholomew Fair*, the counterfantasy becomes a second major action: going to the Fair, which develops in turn its own counterfantasists, Overdo and Busy. How these fantasy actions interconnect can best be seen in their effect on the destruction of hierarchies, a major Jonsonian (as well as Shakespearian and Marlovian) signal of the impending failure of a central action.

Both the cheaters and the gulls in *The Alchemist* go through a hierarchical heightening process symmetrical with the hierarchy of alchemical experiment. Though the correspondences are often tangled, the heightening of the cheaters parallels the increasing complication of the "experiments" as well as the increasing value of the major materials, or gulls. These appear initially in an ascending order based on social status, closeness to alchemical ideals, and productivity in yield of gold.[19] Dapper, the lawyer's clerk, hopes to become a minor cheat with the aid of absurd ritual conjuring; guildsman Drugger wishes to guarantee business success through white, or natural, magic; Sir Epicure, to create unlimited wealth and a new golden age by alchemy itself. Each aspirant, gradually refined above his original sense of self, produces increasingly valuable matter as he approaches the grand goal—the mystic marriage. To Dapper, this means merely an unspecified alliance with the invisible divine Queen (an alchemical term for mercury sublimed); Drugger is taught to attempt a rich young widow; and Sir Epicure is provided with a lady of his own social elevation, with whom he yearns to unite when they have reached what he calls "a free state" (4.1.156).[20]

As the base matter becomes more elevated, so do the alchemical practitioners. At the start, Subtle is for Dapper simply "the cunning man," "a doctor" as opposed to a clerk (1.2.8,9), who speaks ordinary if dignified English; to Drugger, "Master Doctor" (1.3.20) is specifically necromantic (and perhaps connected with physic), referring easily by name to planets, religious spirits, and occult arts; to Mammon, he is not only "a rare physician, . . . an excellent Paracelsian," who "deals all / With spirits, he" (2.3.229ff), but in his alchemical learning a holy man, properly addressed as "father" (2.3.1). Similarly, Face advances first to "Captain" and then to alchemical initiate; while Dol becomes "a lord's sister" and finally the Faery Queen, in which sublimity she is joined by Subtle as a Priest of Faery.[21]

Within this overall heightening process, as within the overall lowering process of *Volpone*, the hierarchy of the gulls becomes reversed and disorganized in signal of the central action's progressive disarray. Nothing could reduce the inspired chaos of *The Alchemist* to the relatively schematic organization of *Volpone*, but a similar line of development remains visible. The order in which the major gulls enter is reversed by the long pivotal scene in which Mammon, last to arrive, becomes first to see his mystic mate. This is also the scene in which the intransigent counterfantasist Surly appears and forms his plan. Thereafter, Drugger returns before Dapper, signalling a movement of the experiment back towards base earth—perhaps confirmed by the surfacing of a new gull, Kastril, later called by Subtle (in a pun differently intended) "terrae filius" (4.2.13). Although the

ensuing double scene with Dapper allows the cheaters to re-
fashion the original hierarchy by their inexhaustible delaying
tactics, those delays force on them an alchemical inversion:
golden Mammon precedes leaden Dapper ("You may wear your
leaden heart still"—3.5.49) in Dol's company, and ultimately
the gulls have to be disposed of in reverse order. The whole
derangement can be traced to Surly's influence, for the false
Spanish count displaces Mammon at the top of the hierarchy—
enforcing its status as part of a delusive fantasy—and thereby
both throws off the experiment's timing and redirects it towards
a patently nonexistent goal.

As in *Volpone*, however, the central action's first and private
reversal is overcome; the contest between total transmutation
and rocklike resistance remains in suspense until the unexpected
appearance of an outside norm—here in the shape of Lovewit.
As the gulls return in disillusionment and reverse order, the
fantasy action is accommodated to reality by the compromise
that *some* sorts of real transmutation are possible: some gulls
are capable of an increase in understanding, and some ingenious
gentleman may really end up magically enriched—if not by a
mystic union, at least by a surprise marriage. The glorious
object of the magus, to discover "the harmony of the spheres
and the order of the cosmos, which would put into his hands
the power of God Himself" (Kernan, *Alch.*, 12), is reduced to
Lovewit's comprehension of mysterious goings-on in the neigh-
borhood, restoration of household order, and power over those
forces of nature and fortune located in his house: Dame Pliant
in the bedroom and the metal goods in the basement.

Let us deal now as succinctly as possible with the diffuseness
of *Bartholomew Fair*'s pursuit of hierarchical reversals. As
Waith has pointed out, the Fair booths have a hierarchy of
their own, from Joan Trash's stall to Leatherhead's booth to
Ursula's double structure.[22] I would suggest that this order
reflects the ability of the booths to cater to the Fair-going

fantasy: gratification of natural desire. This fantasy goal lies opposite that of the initial marriage fantasy, which promises gratification through imposed artifice. The potential happy spouses appear in Act 1 hierarchically—in order of progressive disinclination: Littlewit uxorious, with a reticent wife; Winwife a suitor, but only to the widow's money; Quarlous not interested in marriage at all; and Cokes actually reluctant to marry Grace, who would like to be rid of him. In every case, the projected match is unequal, with the wife superior to the husband in some way that benefits him only.

One might expect the hierarchy of the Fair booths, then, to threaten that of the marital aspirants. Sure enough, the characters conceive their desires to go to the Fair, and proceed in that direction, in an order just opposite to that in which they originally appeared to further their various courtships. Once at the Fair, each reverses the marital goal itself: Cokes loses Grace in the crowd; Quarlous, uninterested in the widow, is first to become interested in Grace; while Winwife, first with the widow, becomes Grace's second suitor. The Littlewits initially achieve their marital liberty from outside restraint, shaking off Purecraft and Busy so that, as John puts it, "Now we may go play" (3.6.107); but having reached Ursula's booth, they separate, and Ursula's cohorts quite naturally begin to break down the very concept of marriage by persuading Win that she should become a whore: "Never know ty husband from another man" (4.5.50–51).

The gratification fantasy, Fair as it is, leads towards social disruption and not Jonsonian reality. Breaking the marriage bond is reluctantly played at by Win in the beginning as part of the marriage fantasy itself (her husband insists that both young gallants kiss and fondle her); it is repeated at a midpoint of corrective deception (in Grace's escape), and finally in its full meaning, as is Jonson's wont. But even more finally, in an almost precisely inverted hierarchical order, the Fair's reversals

are reversed into appropriate matches. Winwife becomes first
with Grace; Quarlous settles for the widow and she for him
instead of a genuine madman (he gains money, she a more
interesting kind of life—unillusioned but comparable improvements). The Littlewits are reunited with a truer comprehension
of the strength, or weakness, of their doting marriage bond. So
the Fair's tendency toward a predatory state of nature is countered, like the original state of artifice, by accommodation of
both fantasies to a social contract—a contract seen at last as
transcending sexual self-sufficiency, in Adam Overdo's miscellaneous banquet for married and unmarried, honest and
dishonest alike.

It is in *Bartholomew Fair*, too, that the contract between
dramatist and audience becomes explicit. The Induction, which
develops it, is an argument: the stagekeeper rejects the action
to be presented, as a mistaken fantasy about a given reality;
the prompter who supersedes him offers the play as a special
version of reality itself. On behalf of the dramatist, he presents
to the audience a covenant for acceptance before the play can
begin, an agreement that the author's perception of reality be
understood as a fantasy accommodated "to delight all" who can
"think well of themselves" (74–75)—an insistent reminder that
comedy is a deliberate construct, demanding audience collabo-
ration. I think I am fair, then, in adding from among our
collection another Jonsonian prologue, which defines the goal
of this Jonsonian covenant:

> All gall and copperas from his ink he draineth,
> Only a little salt remaineth,
> Wherewith he'll rub your cheeks, till red with laughter
> They shall look fresh a week after.

Although this is the prologue to *Volpone*, it uses what should
now be readily recognizable terms of alchemical transformation.
All corrosives having been refined away, Jonson leaves the

audience with pure salt or wit, the indispensable transmuting material. With this he creates the redness that, in alchemical literature, signifies the height of the alchemical fusion, bringing about no mystical transmutation but a realistic version of the goals of eternal health and youth—red cheeks.

In this sense, the dramatist's comedy and the audience's appreciation fuse into the true elixir, sanitive laughter. Finally, the fact that the effect is not really eternal, but only realistically temporary—say a week, while memory of the play lasts—suggests what even a great comic poet may realize: that comic insight, though pleasurable and healthful, is itself only a *perspective* on reality. The laughable fantasy could be, if one's angle of vision shifted or even wavered, the fatal fantasy, and the poet who can write both comedy and tragedy respects the strength of the delusions he can mock.

NOTES

1. Both stories could without distortion be told in much the same way. A successful soldier, highly regarded by his supreme commander, is about to be joined in marriage with an innocent young girl. After an initial unsuccessful attempt by a malcontent villain to disrupt the match, the bridegroom is successfully deceived into thinking his beloved untrue, because he is brought to witness a scene in which the behavior of a young woman of loose morals is misinterpreted for him by the villain. The bridegroom takes fatal revenge on his bride and is emotionally overcome by his own action; the villain, apprehended, confesses; the bridegroom is horrified by his own injustice and makes what restitution he can, rejoining his bride in the only way he sees possible.

2. Compare his opposed apprehensions of her almost identical appearance (and its cosmic backdrop) before and after the murder: "Let me not name it to you, you chaste stars! / It is the cause. Yet I'll not shed her blood, / Nor scar that whiter skin of hers than snow, / And smooth as monumental alablaster" (5.2.2-5). "Now, how dost thou look now? O ill-starr'd wench! / Pale as thy smock! . . . / . . . / . . . Cold, cold, my girl, / Even like thy chastity" (5.2.272-76).

3. The opposition at the end of Act 1 can be seen as a struggle over the realistic power of this bond. Desdemona's plea to go with Othello to Cyprus rests on her need (issuing even in "downright violence and storm of fortunes") to realize in the outside world—"I did love the Moor to live with him"—the tenuous inner bond they have constituted: "I saw Othello's visage in his mind" (1.3.249,248,252). Othello supports her request by appeal to the same value: "to be free and bounteous to her mind," but goes further (or not as far) in asserting the compatibility of this inwardness with social function and control: "And heaven defend your good souls that you think / I will your serious and great business scant / For she is with me" (1.3.265-68). Iago, on the other side, well comprehends that his attack on the effective power of their bond is possible because such inward union deviates from all established social usage; it is vulnerable as a notion that has not found its context: "If sanctimony and a frail vow betwixt an erring barbarian and a supersubtle Venetian be not too hard for my wits . . ." (1.3.356-58). The tragic outcome he engineers breaks through the possibilities of the existing social structure: "this would not be believ'd in Venice, / Though I should swear I saw't" asserts the Venetian ambassador (4.1.240-41) even before the murder; afterwards, of course, Othello is entirely stripped of social context: "Your power and your command is taken off, / And Cassio rules in Cyprus" (5.2.331-32). Cassio's Cyprian behavior, a lukewarm liaison with a courtesan, falls well within the social norm—though this is not the overt reason for his promotion.

4. To work out this sketch more fully and match it to various tragedies and comedies (not to mention mixed modes), even within the Renaissance period, would require a determined delicacy in respecting differences and adjusting values. Let me suggest only two major considerations: (1) The precipitating fantasy of a tragedy may be (and in Jacobean drama, often is) more valuable than the social givens it disrupts. (2) The author may entertain comic and tragic views of his idea simultaneously and to the very end; within our period, consider the unrepentant, unabated enactment of a minority tragic view by Shylock, Malvolio, Sir Giles Overreach—or the magnificent comic view shared by Cleopatra and the asp.

5. Alvin Kernan provides this concise formulation of the well accepted idea in the Introduction to his edition of Jonson's *The Alchemist* (New Haven and London: Yale University Press, 1974), p. 8.

6. From Shakespeare, we might select Prospero on his desert island; from Jonson, Adam Overdo, sole understander and judge of Bartholomew Fair: "defy all the world, Adam Overdo, for a disguise, and all story; for thou

hast fitted thyself, I swear" (2.1.2ff). To Marlowe, Shakespeare, Jonson, Webster can be added Chapman with Bussy D'Ambois's epigrammatic claim: "Who to himself is law, no law doth need, / Offends no law, and is a king indeed" (2.1.203–04); and Massinger with Sir Giles's mad self-assertion: "Why, is not the whole world / Included in myself? To what use then / Are friends and servants?" (*A New Way to Pay Old Debts*, 5.1.355ff).

7. His earlier furious accusation against the cause of his fall from self-sufficiency is even closer to Marlovian ideology: "why, I hold fate / Clasped in my fist, and could command the course / Of time's eternal motion, hadst thou been / One thought more steady than an ebbing sea" (5.5.11ff).

8. For the explicit appeal to tragedy, H. M. Margoliouth cites in addition the contemporary account, *Tragicum Theatrum Actorum & Casuum Tragicorum Londini* (Amsterdam, 1649), in his edition of *The Poems and Letters of Andrew Marvell*, I, 2nd ed. (Oxford: The Clarendon Press, 1963), p. 239.

9. Indeed, Viola slips into Olivia's place in the Duke's affections with a smoothness and speed not impossibly facilitated by the conceptual lubrication of the spelling. We should also compare Viola's devotion to her role (in which she wears clothing just like her "dead" brother's) with Olivia's devotion to the memory of *her* dead brother. Both self-sufficient attachments must be broken down before the women can form socially viable emotional ties.

10. I should like at least to try to say this. In order to deal with Marlowe, I should emphasize Tamburlaine's long imaginative speech about Zenocrate (1.2.87ff), conceived not in terms of interaction or personality, but of a static, pictorial conceptualization of her value and symbolic attributes; and Edward II's obsessive attachment to the *notion* of a male counterpart, superseding his specific attachment to Gaveston—for the instantaneous substitution of young Spencer seems independent of that gentleman's personal attractions, if any. *The Changeling* itself is a special case, since Beatrice does not expect her self-aggrandizing union with DeFlores to be sexual. She relocates her sense of self-sufficiency in a love bond with him, however, once she experiences the value of his sexually motivated service (5.1). This change resembles the progression I have outlined, here contained within one play.

Certainly a hypothetical development from mental construct to real attempt would suit Jonson's major comedies as I treat them below, leaving an appropriate gap for *Epicoene* and his/her marriage/non-marriage.

11. S. Musgrove, ed., *The Alchemist* (Berkeley: University of California Press, 1968), Introduction, p. 4, n. 10.

12. See, e.g., Herford and Simpson's notes to the play; Musgrove's introduction, p. 5, for suggestive though not very specific parallels, and his notes for locally illuminating identifications, though these are not systematized. For a longer analysis, see C. G. Thayer, *Ben Jonson, Studies in the Plays* (Oklahoma: University of Oklahoma Press, 1963).

13. I would argue that these are the primary identifications, though—as in the alchemical texts themselves—there is justification for seeing interchanges of properties among the trio. Musgrove points out (in his note to 2.5.31) that mercury, in alchemical literature, is sometimes called *servus fugitivus* (runaway slave or servant); hence he identifies mercury with Face. But it would be just as plausible (or more so) to make an identification with Subtle, who actually concocts a plan to run away (with Dol and the profits) from the meeting agreed to by the trio in their escape plan (5.4.74ff). Face is no doubt more mercurial than Subtle in his changes of personality, his comings and goings, and his roles as messenger and intermediary. Dol, though, is ahead of Face in linguistic volatility; she even reports in 1.4.5 having impersonated a spirit, and thus has four distinct personalities to Face's three. Besides, she is a pickpocket, appropriate representative of the god of thieves. Interestingly, mercury is referred to in 2.5.31ff with the masculine pronoun, though there is no doubt that in all alchemical treatises it plays the female role; but cf. Subtle's throwaway comment in his explanation to Surly (2.3.164–65): "Some doe beleeve *hermaphrodeitie*, / That both doe act, and suffer." (He refers to sulphur and mercury here, not to the grand alchemical hermaphrodite.) This, of course, turns out true of both Subtle and Dol. There is even a *sub rosa* suggestion that Dol Common, who is expected to produce gold when touched to Dapper, Mammon, and the supposed Spanish count, could be thought of as the very stone itself: "*Mammon.* Sisiphus was damn'd / To roule the ceaslesse stone, onely, because / He would have made ours common. (DOL *is seene*.)" (2.3.208ff). Jonson was probably having more fun than we can ever trace.

14. But "marriage" in this sense, like true alchemy, remains quite out of the question in *The Alchemist*. Crucial to my argument and to the failure of the cozeners' triunity is the conviction of each cheater that the others are subordinate—though necessary and even admirable—agents of his or her fulfillment. In the opening scene, all three argue for superiority

(though Dol uses hers to restore the needful opportunistic balance). There-after, the precarious triple compound keeps separating into equally unstable doubles: Face and Dol unite against Subtle (1.1.149), Face and Subtle against Dol (in their decision to pursue the Widow Pliant, 2.6.85–92), and finally Subtle and Dol against Face (in their plan to make off with the booty, 5.4.72–91).

15. Appropriately, Quarlous suggests that Grace's match with Cokes might even be legally considered a "disparagement" or unequal marriage (3.5.255).

16. A benevolent example of the same device is Olivia's removal of her mourning veil when she falls in love with the disguised Viola: "we will draw the curtain and show you the picture" (1.5.220). "The picture," as Viola immediately grasps, is a design of nature that mandates reproduction, not fantasies of unrequitable passion. A less pleasant Shakespearean instance of determining revelation is the discovery of dead Polonius behind the arras—an object who figures in Hamlet's first lunge toward revenge only as "the guts," a corpse who is not the king. This inert body in its independent meaning activates the catastrophes of Ophelia, Laertes, and Hamlet himself. There are many variations of such a scene; in reverse it may terminate a fantasy when all is understood, as for instance the unbearable gap created between obsession and reality by Iago, the results of which cannot be contemplated by balanced minds: "Look on the tragic loading of this bed. / . . . The object poisons sight; / Let it be hid" (5.2.364–66). (We might think also, though outside our period, of Hedda Gabler's suicide behind the curtains, which are opened to evoke Judge Brack's incredulous response: "People don't do such things.")

17. T. H. White, *The Book of Beasts: A Translation from a Latin Bestiary of the Twelfth Century* (London: Jonathan Cape, 1956), p. 109. Further references to this book will be given in the text.

18. Alvin Kernan, ed., *Volpone* (New Haven: Yale University Press, 1968), p. 24.

19. After the first round of visits the account stands: Dapper, five angels (ca. fifty shillings); Drugger, a portague (eighty or more shillings); Mammon, ten pounds (plus two unspecified tips to Face).

20. Each promised union is preceded by a suitable version of the culminating vapor bath. (See 2.3.101–03: "*Mammon:* When do you make projection? *Subtle:* Son, be not hasty; I exalt our med'cine, / By hanging him in *balneo vaporoso*.") Dapper sits it out in the privy ("Only the fumigation's somewhat strong"—3.5.81); Drugger gets a lick and a promise (he

is sent "back again, to wash his face"—5.4.95); Sir Epicure invents his own: "My mists / I'll have of perfume, vapored 'bout the room, / To loose our selves in; and my baths like pits" (2.2.48-50). Even Dol's suitor the supposed Spanish count has his prepared: "in your *bathada*, / You shall be soaked, and stroked, and tubbed, and rubbed, / and scrubbed, and fubbed, dear Don, before you go" (4.4.96-98).

21. The frequent changes of costume by both cheaters and cheated are signs of the experiments' progress and regress, clothing images being a standard vocabulary for the crucial alchemical transformations, which also fluctuated precariously. So Dapper is instructed to begin his venture for fortune by putting on a clean shirt, which would bring him to the "embrion" condition of the putative glass H mentioned in 2.3: "H has his white shirt on" (83). Later, in preparation for his meeting with the Queen of Faery, he is made to put on a robe (3.5.7)—compare Subtle's "The work is done: bright Sol is in his robe" (2.3.29). In fact, all the projected "marriages" demand an elevating change of clothing; even Drugger's widow is first identified as "a *bona roba*" (2.6.30). Jonson does not work out such shifts systematically nor for every character, but at the play's center the three cozeners are noticeably elevated and lowered by their clothing, references to which are obtrusively insistent. Face's sartorial collapse towards the end is very evident as he declines in rapid sequence (4.5, 4.6, 4.7) from alchemical getup to Captain's suit to butler's clothing —the last demanding a quick shave.

22. E. M. Waith, ed., "The Yale Ben Jonson," *Bartholomew Fair* (New Haven: Yale University Press, 1963), Appendix II, 208-11.

Ian Donaldson

Jonson and the Moralists

The first serious critic of Ben Jonson's work is Ben Jonson himself. Serious in all senses of the term: rigorous, high-minded, touchy, firm to associate inferiority in art with delinquency in morals: "*I cannot but be serious in a cause of this nature*," he writes, while lamenting the current state of the English theater, in the epistle dedicatory to his greatest comedy.[1] His critical language has a solemnity and elevation that at times may sound almost Arnoldian. "Purity," "truth," "doctrine," "nobility," "innocence," "goodness," "profit," "liberality," "understanding," "sweetness," "light" are words that come naturally to Jonson when he speaks about his art. Jonson is not a critic whom we can easily avoid; his voice is constantly to be heard, in prologues, inductions, dedications, choruses, epilogues, apologetical dialogues. His poems, as we read them, comment gravely upon themselves. This somber critical presence is at once powerful and disconcerting. There often seems to be a curious disjunction between commentary and work, a sense that Jonson's critical genius and Jonson's creative genius are at a loss to know what they should do with each other. Jonson the critic, surveying Jonson the poet, seems oddly tight-lipped, unable either to perceive the rich and various energies of his own work, or alternatively to concede that he does perceive them. Jonson's prime, and at times sole, concern seems to be to assure us that his work is morally impeccable. Take the case of the *Epigrams* for example, that very heterogeneous collection of poems of praise and insult; poems that are by turns haughty, humorous, affectionate, contemptuous, tender, complimentary, skittish, and scatalogical. The longest and last of the group, "The Famous Voyage," was too much even for Swinburne: "all English readers, I trust," he wrote, "will agree with me that coprology should be left to Frenchmen."[2] No hint of these exceedingly diverse qualities is conveyed in Jonson's characteristically demure

146

and single-minded description of the collection as "my chast booke."[3] A description of this sort may, of course, be partly protective, an indication of the poet's awareness of the presence of other elements in his work that might attract quite another kind of description. (It may be relevant to recall that certain words were omitted from poems in Jonson's posthumous 1640 folio, evidently because they were thought to be obscene or blasphemous or both.[4]) Yet the official view of Jonson's work, the view that he himself propounded, seems from an early stage to have won general acceptance among his admirers. The official view dominates the volume of commemorative poems that appeared after Jonson's death in 1637. "Nothing but what *Lucretia* might rehearse," murmurs one of Jonson's mourners, respectfully surveying his works. And another tells

> How no spectator his chaste stage could call
> The cause of any crime of his, but all
> With thoughts and wils purg'd and amended rise,
> From th' *Ethicke Lectures* of his *Comedies* . . .[5]

Jonson has had a powerful influence on the criticism of his own work not merely in his time but also in ours. Jonson's work still seems to be thought of at times as a series of ethic lectures, upon which it is the critic's task to deliver further lectures of like tone. The verses just quoted are indeed cited admiringly in one recent book on Jonson's comedy, by way of testimony that the writer's approach to the plays is in accord with that of Jonson's contemporaries.[6] What I have called the "official" view of Jonson is also to be found in recent criticism of his poetry, with which I shall be principally concerned in this paper. Jonson's work offers peculiar temptations in this respect. When Byron writes to John Murray, "In my mind, the highest of all poetry is ethical poetry, as the highest of all objects must be moral truth,"[7] we are likely to recognize that such a statement, noble as it is, is applicable to Byron's own poetry—and to that of Pope, which he is here concerned with defending—only in a highly complex and perhaps paradoxical way. What delights us in the poetry of Byron, of Pope, and (I suggest) of Jonson himself is not primarily the ethical truths, abstractly considered, that their poetry might be thought to convey. It is, rather, the poets' deftness of wit, their warmth, their tolerance, their exasperation, their alertness to human absurdity, that, in diverse and even at times contradictory ways, assure us of their fundamental humanity, good humor, and good sense. Where such qualities are absent, the poetry, ethically irreproachable though it may be, may appear merely petulant, strident, or overpitched.

Unlike a poet such as Byron, who often speaks in genial amazement of his own inconsistencies and fluctuations of mood and opinion, Jonson seldom admits officially to being anything other than constant in outlook. It has consequently become something of a commonplace in recent years to assert that Jonson's work is, in moral terms, all of a piece. "In a long and productive career," writes George Parfitt in an article entitled "Ethical Thought and Ben Jonson's Poetry," "Jonson's views changed remarkably little, and except for his views on woman, they all contribute to a coherent whole." "Throughout a long career," writes Alan Dessen in his book *Jonson's Moral Comedy*, "Jonson's goals are markedly consistent." And Gabriele Jackson begins her book on Ben Jonson's drama with a similar statement that his moral ideals are expressed throughout the various plays in a "basic structure" that remains "absolutely consistent, irrespective of individual plot."[8] This coherence and consistency is normally adduced as evidence of Jonson's moral integrity and stability. These are virtues that deserve respect. Yet at times we may wonder: for it is also possible that a writer who shows no capacity for changing his mind, no ebb and flow of mood or of moral opinion, no disposition to regard human behavior in various lights, may have limitations not merely of an emotional and imaginative kind, but—consequently, and for these purposes most importantly—of a moral kind as well. We may also perhaps remember that Jonson's satiric contempt in his plays, his poems, and his masques is often directed toward those who are shown to be incapable of change—"Go, you are, / And wilbe stil your selfe, a *Mere-foole*" (*The Fortunate Isles*, 432-33)—or whose capacity for change is merely superficial, such as Inigo Jones: "your Trappings will not change you. Change yor mynd" (*Ungathered Verse*, XXXIV.25).

Such praise of Jonson in terms of his moral consistency may sometimes seem, then, gently to subtract even while it strives to add: as when Parfitt speaks cautiously of "that limited created world which is Jonson's achievement as a poet," and declares that "Jonson's achievement depends upon the restrictions of his world view."[9] Jonson's created world seems to me larger, more various, more imaginatively and morally capacious than such a statement allows. Nor am I convinced that Jonson's poetry, still less his work as a whole, shows such moral coherence and consistency as is sometimes suggested. Parfitt instances as evidence of such consistency the persistent way in which Jonson returns to the notions of the Golden Age and of human degeneracy. And yet if we look at Jonson's work as a whole, it may well be the variousness rather than the consistency of Jonson's treatment of such notions that strikes us most forcibly. Jonson's views of the relative intractability or perfectability of his society are quite differently expressed, for example, in his plays written for the public stage and in his court masques. To turn from the endings of, say, *Volpone* or *The Alchemist* to those of, say, *The Golden Age Restored* or *Mercury Vindicated From the Alchemists at Court* is to turn from a morally untransmutable world to a world that is seen as capable of moral transmutation; from a world in which folly and knavery seem ubiquitous and perpetual, to one from which they may indeed be expelled:

> For spight is spent: the iron age is fled,
> And, with her power on earth, her name is dead.
>
> (*The Golden Age Restored*, 82-83)

Such sharply contrasting outlooks are not to be accounted for simply in biographical or historical terms, for they may often be found in works written in much the same period of Jonson's life; it is not just a matter of his lapsing from optimism into gloom, or vice versa. The two kinds of vision represent two quite contrary rhetorical cases, as do Pope's *Messiah:*

> See Heav'n its sparkling Portals wide display,
> And break upon thee in a Flood of Day!

(97–98)

and Pope's *Dunciad:*

> Thy hand, great Anarch! lets the curtain fall;
> And Universal Darkness buries All.

(B, IV.655–56)

A common tendency in Jonson criticism—noticeable, for example, in L. C. Knight's important and pioneering study, *Drama and Society in the Age of Jonson* (1937)—is to present Jonson as a consistently somber and pessimistic critic of his age, and to ignore or minimize the very different evidence concerning Jonson's social outlook that is to be found in his masques.[10] It is over half a century since T. S. Eliot laconically remarked that what was needed in order to understand Ben Jonson was "intelligent saturation in his work as a whole."[11] And the more one regards Jonson's work as a whole, the more various, I suggest, it appears, not only in its technical and emotional range, but in its moral outlook as well.

Within the nondramatic poetry alone, one finds a perplexing variety of moral attitudes. Take this passage from "An Epistle to a Friend, to Persuade Him to the Wars":

> . . . what we call
> Friendship is now mask'd Hatred! Justice fled,
> And shamefastnesse together! All lawes dead,
> That kept man living! Pleasures only sought!

(*The Underwood*, XV. 38–41)

Astraea, goddess of justice, fled to heaven at the end of the Golden Age, and (Jonson suggests) it is now only in heaven—if indeed there—that she is to be found: "Justice fled, / . . . All lawes dead." It is tempting to argue, as one recent critic has done, that this poem represents Jonson's real and deeply pessimistic view of the age in which he lived.[12] Yet, as its title suggests, the poem is concerned with arguing a particular case: Jonson arranges the evidence regarding moral degradation at home in such a way that his friend Colby may be persuaded that his best recourse is to go off and fight, and if need be fall, in Europe. As in many another call for recruitment in many another age, certain ugly facts need to be highlighted, while certain other facts, equally ugly, need to be quietly suppressed. The case must seem persuasive and internally consistent; yet one should be cautious about concluding that it necessarily represents Jonson's own innermost and unchanging anxieties about the age in which he lived. Quite a different view of the state of society is presented in Jonson's poem to the Lord Chancellor, Thomas Egerton, in the 1616 folio:

> The *Virgin*, long-since fled from earth, I see,
> T'our times return'd, hath made her heaven in thee.
>
> (*Epigrams*, LXXIV. 9–10)

Like Jonson himself, the Virgin seems capable of being in several minds. *Fled . . . returned:* the words recur over and again throughout Jonson's writing, with significant alternations of meaning. Writing about Sir Thomas Overbury's arrival at court, Jonson declares that

> . . . since, what ignorance, what pride is fled!
> And letters, and humanitie in the stead!
>
> (*Epigrams*, CXIII. 7–8)

The poem was probably written about 1610. The following year, with the failure of *Catiline* on the public stage, the forces of darkness seemed to roll in again, and Jonson was to speak despondently in the folio dedication of that play to the Earl of Pembroke of "*so thick, and darke an ignorance, as now almost covers the age*." Such alternations of moral outlook are like the spectacular transformation scenes of the court masque, which often gave them physical expression. The effects are sudden, magical. Vices and virtues in turn flee, fly, vanish, are banished: as the characters in *Pan's Anniversary* are in a trice "in smoke, gone, vapour'd, vanish'd, blowne, and (as a man would say) in a word of two sillables, Nothing" (76–77). The moral victory may go this way or that. Sometimes a small textual change may be sufficient to suggest a significant wavering between degrees of moral optimism. *The Golden Age Restored*, for example, originally concluded with Pallas's ascent to heaven. While the 1616 folio was in the press, however, Jonson transposed the final sections of the masque, allowing it now to conclude with Astraea's declaration that she will stay on earth, transformed by the reign of King James.[13] In some ways, of course, Jonson's moral world is sharply polarized; yet it is also a world that admits of uncertainty and change. We find ourselves

> . . . in this strife
>   Of vice, and vertue; wherein all great life
> Almost, is exercis'd: and scarse one knowes,
>   To which, yet, of the sides himselfe he owes.
>
> ("To William, Earl of Pembroke":
> *Epigrams*, CII.5–8)

As in the poetry of Pope, the poet's darkest fears and most fervent hopes alternate sharply, creating in us less of a sense of moral certainty than of moral instability.

But even here it is necessary to speak with caution. Different occasions demand different voices, different views. A poet's skill is to be judged not simply in terms of his moral or logical consistency, but also by his alertness to the particular demands of particular occasions, and by his adroitness in convincing us that logically antagonistic attitudes and opinions may each have their

own peculiar attraction and force. Milton's twin poems cele-
brating the active and the retired lives are testimony to such
skill, a skill that we know was formally cultivated in the schools
of the day—such as St. Paul's—and at the Universities of Oxford
and Cambridge: we know, too, for example, that Milton in his
seventh Prolusion was prepared to argue not merely that "Learning Makes Men Happier Than Ignorance," but also for the
reverse of that proposition.[14] Jonson has something of the same
flexibility of mind. Consider, for example, what contrary views
of the military life are given in Jonson's "Epistle to a Friend, to
Persuade Him to the Wars," and in these lines from his poem
"To Sir Robert Wroth":

> Let others watch in guiltie armes, and stand
>   The furie of a rash command,
> Goe enter breaches, meet the cannons rage,
>   That they may sleepe with scarres in age.
> And shew their feathers shot, and cullors torne,
>   And brag, that they were therefore borne.
>
> *(The Forest,* III.67–72)[15]

Or consider, again, the diverse and at times contradictory maxims scattered throughout Jonson's poetry concerning the relative
values of the public and the private lives, or concerning the wisdom of tolerating, or opposing, the opinion of the crowd.[16]
Or compare the view expressed in Jonson's poem, "To the
World," that the world is "shrunke up, and old" (*The Forest,*
IV.14) with the firm statement to be found in *Discoveries,*
124–28:

> I cannot thinke *Nature* is so spent, and decay'd, that she can bring
> forth nothing worth her former yeares. She is alwayes the same, like
> her selfe: And when she collects her strength, is abler still. Men are
> decay'd, and *studies:* Shee is not.

Not even Jonson's attitude towards the power of poetry itself is
entirely constant. The view expressed in his "Epistle, to Elizabeth, Countess of Rutland," that "It is the *Muse,* alone, can raise

to heaven" (*The Forest*, XII.41) is quite different from the more humble and circumscribed view of the poet's role that is expressed in the great ode to Sir Lucius Cary and Sir Henry Morison (*The Underwood*, LXX).[17] Jonson seems at times concerned actually to highlight the variousness of his views, to draw attention to his readiness to be persuaded from one opinion to another. Consider the epigram "To a Friend":

> To put out the word, whore, thou do'st me woo,
> Throughout my booke. 'Troth put out woman too.
>
> (*Epigrams*, LXXXIII)

But the implication that all women are whores is at once neutralized by the affectionate epigram to Lucy, Countess of Bedford, that immediately follows this poem in the 1616 folio.[18] The juxtaposition serves to refute the first poem's implied generalization. To read Jonson's *Epigrams* from beginning to end is to experience a number of similar and significant juxtapositions, shifts, modifications, contradictions of moral opinion, to feel oneself in the company of a man who is passing through many moods and many attitudes. To read Jonson's work as a whole is to be made even more acutely aware of the dynamic, shifting, and various nature of his moral thought.

Even more striking than this variety, however, is Jonson's habit of humorously and gently questioning the propriety of being a moralist at all; his comic awareness of the many ways in which a moralist, in the midst of his denunciations, may appear excessive, misguided, or self-indulgent. The relationship between Jonson's dramatic and nondramatic verse is of particular interest here. The elder Knowell's laments about the degeneracy of his age in *Every Man in His Humour* are reminiscent at many points of Jonson's own similar laments in his nondramatic verse: in "A Speech According to Horace," for example, or "Let me be what I am . . ."[19] But Jonson brilliantly tips Knowell's speeches a little off-center, suggesting that his ethical vigor is misplaced and that his fears are largely groundless; Knowell's moralizing,

unrelieved by generosity or by humor, becomes itself the cause
of humor. Here is Knowell early in the play, reproaching his
slow but genial nephew, Stephen, who—among his many weak-
nesses—has expressed a simple wish to "show himself like a
gentleman":

> Nor, stand so much on your gentilitie,
> Which is an aërie, and meere borrow'd thing,
> From dead mens dust, and bones: and none of yours
> Except you make, or hold it.
>
> (1.1.86–89, Folio)

This is a sentiment that derives ultimately from Ulysses' speech
on virtue in Book XIII of the *Metamorphoses* and from Juvenal's
eighth satire; Jonson was fond enough of the sentiment to repeat
it in different ways in different parts of his work; in the eighth
section of his *Eupheme*, for example, where he addresses the
children of Kenelm and Venetia Digby:

> Boast not these Titles of your Ancestors;
>   (Brave Youths) th'are their possessions, none of yours:
> When your owne Vertues, equall'd have their Names,
>   'Twill be but faire, to leane upon their *Fames;*
> For they are strong Supporters: But, till then,
>   The greatest are but growing Gentlemen.
>
> (*The Underwood*, LXXXIV. 8.10–15)

And so on. But this is how Jonson allows events to continue in
Every Man in His Humour:

> *Enter servant*
> *Servant:* Save you, gentlemen.
> *Stephen:* Nay, we do' not stand much on our gentilitie, friend; yet, you
> are wel-come, and I assure you, mine uncle here is a man of a thousand
> a yeare, *Middlesex* land; hee has but one sonne in all the world, I am
> his next heire (at the common law), master Stephen, as simple as I
> stand here, if my cossen die (as there's hope he will) I have a prettie
> living o' mine own too, beside, hard-by here.
>
> (1.2.1–8)

Like Pompey and Lucio in *Measure for Measure*, Stephen is morally impervious, morally irrepressible, and despite—or because of—all this, curiously endearing at the same time. This dramatic moment, like the action of the comedy as a whole, reminds us that there are actions that may be at once reprehensible and diverting, just as there are other actions that may be morally blameless and yet emotionally uncompelling. In a delicate insight, Jonson suggests that human behavior is always more complex than the moral precepts that attempt to regulate it. While the moral precepts in themselves are not rendered ludicrous or invalid, they may nevertheless be given a decisively humorous inflection.

Here is another example of Jonson's playful but sensitive experiments in moral tone. In his "Epistle to Edward Sackville," Jonson writes about men who begin by borrowing money, and rapidly proceed from that point to demanding money by threats:

> But these men ever want: their very trade
> Is borrowing; that but stopt, they doe invade
> All as their prize, turne Pyrats here at Land,
> Ha' their *Bermudas*, and their streights i'th'*Strand*:
> Man out their Boates to th' Temple, and not shift
> Now, but command; make tribute, what was gift;
> And it is paid 'hem with a trembling zeale,
> And superstition I dare scarce reveale. . . .
>
> (*The Underwood*, XIII. 79–86)

The Bermudas and the straits in the Strand referred to here were a maze of alleyways and lanes near Covent Garden, just north of the Strand, which had a notorious reputation at this time. It is curious to remember that a few years earlier in *Bartholomew Fair*, Jonson had allowed Justice Overdo also to attack the iniquities to be found in this part of London:

> Looke into any Angle o' the towne (the Streights, or the *Bermuda's*) where the quarrelling lesson is read, and how doe they entertaine the time, but with bottle-ale, and tabacco? The Lecturer is o' one side, and

his Pupils o' the other; But the seconds are still bottle-ale, and tabacco, for which the Lecturer reads, and the Novices pay. Thirty pound a weeke in bottle-ale! forty in tabacco! and ten more in Ale againe. Then for a sute to drinke in, so much, and (that being slaver'd) so much for another sute, and then a third sute, and a fourth sute! and still the bottle-ale slavereth, and the tabacco stinketh!

(2.6.76–86)

Jonas Barish has pointed to the curious fact that several of Justice Overdo's other speeches in this play seem to parody speeches that Jonson had given to the morally exemplary Cicero in his previous play, *Catiline*, three years earlier:

> For Jonson to parody the admired Cicero in the crackbrained Overdo, and the conspiracy of Catiline in the "enormities" of Bartholomew Fair, was to turn the tables on himself with a vengeance, to acknowledge the suspicion that Cicero was a canting prig and Catiline a preposterous bogey, to affirm once again the truthfulness of appearances, and so, in a sense, to heap ridicule on his own lifelong stance as watchdog of public morality.[20]

The case is acutely and convincingly argued; but the interest of the parody is increased if we observe the echo and re-echo of one particular Ciceronian phrase, not merely in these two plays, but more extensively throughout Jonson's work. The famous lament of the historical Cicero, "O tempora! O mores!" (*In Catilinam*, 1.1.2) is (inevitably) repeated by Jonson's dramatic character, Cicero, in the tragedy of *Catiline* in 1611: "O age, and manners!" (4.190). Cicero is denouncing Catiline formally in the senate, inveighing against the corruption of his personal morals, and his plot to overthrow the state. The phrase is echoed (though Barish does not specifically note the fact) by Adam Overdo in *Bartholomew Fair* in 1614:

> O *Tempora! O mores!* I would not ha' lost my discovery of this one grievance, for my place, and worship o' the *Bench*, how is the poore subject abus'd here! . . .
> *Ursula:* What new Roarer is this?

(2.2.113–15, 123)

Overdo has discovered that Ursula the pig-woman is adulterating her tobacco, giving short measure on her bottle-ale, and over-charging for pork: the humor of the moment arises from the obvious disparity between the kinds of moral degeneracy re-called by Overdo's Ciceronian phrase and the altogether milder malpractices of the fair. And here is part of the same phrase again, with yet another inflection, in the revised version of *Every Man in His Humour*, published in the folio of 1616; the speaker is the younger Knowell:

> O, manners! that this age should bring forth such creatures! that Nature should bee at leisure to make 'hem!
>
> (4.7.146–48)

("O, manners!" replaces "O God!" in the earlier quarto version of the play.)

For Dessen, who is much concerned with the ethical values of Jonson's comedy, "the audience's reaction surely echoes" Knowell's (or Lorenzo's) reaction here: the phrase is nothing but an ethical pointer, a reminder of higher values that lie neglected.[21] Yet the moment is again essentially a comic one. Bobadill has just outlined to young Knowell his plan to save the nation, along with other handpicked and gentlemanly swords-men, in an extensive series of personal duels. He also uttered some ferocious threats as to the way in which he would treat George Downright, if only he could manage to encounter him. As ill chance would have it, Downright at this moment appears, disarms Bobadill, beats him thoroughly, and leaves him almost, but not entirely, speechless: ". . . sure I was strooke with a plannet thence, for I had no power to touch my weapon" (4.7.141–42). "O, manners!" The fantastic Bobadill is not really like Catiline, and both Knowell and the audience are fully aware of the fact; the humor of the moment, our delight in the ex-travagance of Bobadill's schemes and the abruptness of their deflation, temper in a significant way any kind of judgment that we might make at this point. The humor in *Bartholomew Fair* might be thought to be even broader and more obvious, but Dessen will not weaken to it. While conceding that Overdo's Ciceronian lament may be a little excessive in the circumstances, he nevertheless takes the moment solemnly, and remarks that the cry, "*O Tempora! O Mores!* provides an epigraph for *Bartholomew Fair* and indeed for Jonson's moral comedy in general."[22] Yet perhaps the most subtle and Christian of moral insights in this play is that it is exceedingly difficult for any man to pass moral judgment upon another. At the end of *Every Man in His Humour*, Justice Clement is thanked for his "humanity"; at the end of *Bartholomew Fair*, Justice Overdo is reminded of his: "remember you are but *Adam*, Flesh, and blood!" (5.6.96). One of the most central, delicate, and shifting problems in all Jonson's work is how to reconcile the need for moral judgment with the need to recognize tolerantly, realistically, and humorously the claims of common and fallible humanity. But the moral critics clamor for judgment. Dessen is distressed at Overdo's negligence in failing to exercise judgment at the end of the play: ". . . Overdo offers no hope for the future fulfillment of his particular role, and, in a violation of 'quality,' indiscriminately invites all those present home with him."[23] This seems to me very severe, both in its moral and in its social implications.

But the story does not stop there. Here is the Ciceronian phrase again, in "An Epistle to a Friend, to Persuade Him to the Wars," a poem that was probably written about 1620, six years after *Bartholomew Fair*. This time Jonson evidently wishes to restore to the phrase something of its original Ciceronian force:

> O times,
> Friend, flie from hence; and let these kindled rimes
> Light thee from hell on earth: where flatterers, spies,
> Informers, Masters both of Arts and lies;
> Lewd slanderers, soft whisperers that let blood

The life, and fame-vaynes (yet not understood
Of the poore sufferers) where the envious, proud,
Ambitious, factious, superstitious, lowd
Boasters, and perjur'd, with the infinite more
Praevaricators swarme.

(The Underwood, XV. 161–70)

Despite the rough energy and ingenuity of much of this—"Masters both of Arts and lies" is a characteristically felicitous linking, and a wry one if we remember that Jonson had just been granted (in 1619) the degree of Master of Arts from the University of Oxford—the passage sinks beneath the weight of its excessive and insufficiently differentiated nouns and adjectives; the final verb of the passage emerges exhaustedly and unexpectedly, like a drowning man surfacing for a fourth time. What is interesting is that Jonson should turn back to a mode of moral invective that he had already parodied in *Bartholomew Fair*, attempting, as it were, to rehabilitate the mode, but failing to take its full measure. It is not that Jonson outgrows an early period of moral satire, and moves decisively into a new, more relaxed, more tolerant period of writing; it is rather that he continues throughout his life to experiment with the comic and serious potentialities of moral invective. As late as 1629, with the distant thunder of Civil War already to be heard, Jonson adopts yet again the role of Cicero in his poem upon the anniversary of the accession of Charles I:

O Times! O Manners! Surfet bred of ease,
    The truly Epidemicall disease!
'Tis not alone the Merchant, but the Clowne,
    Is Banke-rupt turn'd! the Cassock, Cloake, and Gowne,
Are lost upon accompt! And none will know
    How much to heaven for thee, great Charles, they owe!

(The Underwood, LXIV. 17–22)

I have been concerned in this paper to look at those areas of Jonson's writing that are most explicitly moral, and that might also seem to be most open to the charge of repetitiveness. I have argued that while Jonson is obviously in some ways a writer who enjoys returning to familiar themes and formulae, he does so in a manner that is more various, more critical, than is generally recognized. I should want finally to suggest, however, that Jonson is not always at his happiest in his more hortatory and explicitly moral verse; when he is most determinedly ethical. I find it difficult to agree with John Broadbent's view that "An Epistle to a Friend to Persuade Him to the Wars" is Jonson's "greatest" poem, and I hesitate over his general advice as to how this and other poems of Jonson are to be read:

> Lean on the words until the colloquial idiom blurts through the metre; until the stuff that Jonson swells his lines with fills your mouth: and until you are dragged into agreement with the remorseless ethical emphasis.[24]

This sounds an unpleasant experience, which the reader might do well to resist. It is indeed precisely because of the remorselessness of the ethical emphasis, precisely because the reader is dragged, not delighted, into agreement, that the epistle cannot be ranked among Jonson's greatest poems. What a pleasure it is to turn from that epistle to a poem such as "Inviting a Friend to Supper," with its superb modulations of tone, from gravity to wit; with its steady and good-humored detailing of the way in which good friends may meet; with its relaxed confidence that allows values to be implied, rather than stated:

> Ile tell you of more, and lye, so you will come:
>   Of partrich, pheasant, wood-cock, of which some
> May yet be there; and godwit, if we can:
>   Knat, raile, and ruffe too. How so ere, my man
> Shall reade a piece of Virgil, Tacitus,
>   Livie, or of some better booke to us,
> Of which wee'll speake our minds, amidst our meate;
>   And Ile professe no verses to repeate:
> To this, if ought appeare, which I not know of,

That will the pastrie, not my paper, show of.
Digestive cheese, and fruit there sure will bee;
    But that, which most doth take my *Muse*, and mee,
Is a pure cup of rich *Canary*-wine,
    Which is the *Mermaids*, now, but shall be mine:
Of which had Horace, or Anacreon tasted,
    Their lives, as doe their lines, till now had lasted.

(Epigrams, CI. 17–32)

"Which is the *Mermaids*, now, but shall be mine": Leigh Hunt was delighted by this line, as an example of Jonson in his "entirely happy, familiar, unmisgiving, self-referential, and yet not self-loving" mood; "Why did he not write more such?"[25]

I believe that Jonson did write more such, and that his poems offer more than either he, or we, have often chosen to admit. Jonson is still the most seriously underestimated major poet of the seventeenth century, and perhaps of any period of our literature. But it is worth remembering a fact that Jonson himself at times forgot: serious underestimations are not always best countered by overserious estimations. In the last years of Jonson's life, a Gloucestershire clergyman named Nicholas Oldisworth saw the way things were tending; and wrote that, if Jonson and his admirers were to be taken at their word,

Some future Times will, by a grosse Mistake,
Johnson a Bishop, not a Poet make.[26]

We owe it to Jonson not to mistake too grossly the nature of his genius, to see that he was not merely a moralist, but something more.

NOTES

1. *Volpone*, "To the Two Most Noble and Most Equall Sisters," ll. 93–94. All quotations from *Ben Jonson*, ed. C. H. Herford and P. and E. Simpson, 11 vols. (Oxford, 1925–52): u/v and i/j are regularized; words in small capitals are given in upper and lower case.

2. A. C. Swinburne, *A Study of Ben Jonson* (London, 1889), p. 95.

3. *Epigrams*, XLIX.6. Cf. *Epigrams*, XVII.6; "Proludium," 1.6 (Herford & Simpson, 8: 108); and the concluding lines of Jonson's dedication of the *Epigrams*, to William, Earl of Pembroke.

4. E.g., *The Underwood*, LVIII.12.

5. W. Cartwright, "In the memory of the most Worthy Benjamin Johnson," l. 86; Lord Falkland, "An Eglogue on the Death of Ben Johnson . . ." ll. 113–16 (Herford & Simpson, 11: 457, 432).

6. Alan C. Dessen, *Jonson's Moral Comedy* (Evanston, 1971), p. 243.

7. Lord Byron, *Works: Letters and Journals*, ed. R. E. Prothero (London, 1901), 5.554.

8. G. A. E. Parfitt, "Ethical Thought and Ben Jonson's Poetry," *Studies in English Literature, 1500–1900* 9 (1969): 123–34 (quotation, pp. 128–29); Dessen, p. 243; Gabriele Bernhard Jackson, *Vision and Judgment in Ben Jonson's Drama*, Yale Studies in English 166 (New Haven & London, 1968): 1.

9. Parfitt, p. 133. Much the same view is developed in his article, "The Poetry of Ben Jonson," *Essays in Criticism* 18 (1968): 18–31.

10. For Knights's more recent views, however, see his "Ben Jonson: Public Attitudes and Social Poetry," in *A Celebration of Ben Jonson*, ed. W. Blissett, Julian Patrick, and R. W. Van Fossen (Toronto, 1973), pp. 167–87; esp. pp. 171–72.

11. "Ben Jonson," in *Selected Essays*, 3rd ed. (London, 1951), pp. 147–60: quotation, p. 148. (Originally published in *The Times Literary Supplement*, 13 November 1919.) For an attempt to look at Jonson's poetry in the context of his work as a whole, see Arthur F. Marotti, "All About Jonson's Poetry," *ELH* 39 (1972): 208–37.

12. Dessen, pp. 141–43.

13. Herford & Simpson, 7: 420. Cf. *Part of the King's Entertainment in Passing to his Coronation*, ll. 523–28.

14. D. L. Clark, *Milton at St. Paul's School* (New York, 1948); *Complete Prose Works of John Milton*, ed. Don M. Wolfe (New Haven and London, 1953), 1.290; E. M. W. Tillyard, *The Miltonic Setting* (Cambridge, 1938), p. 15.

15. Of the several classical models that may lie behind this passage, Tibullus 1.1 and 1.10 are of especial interest. It is curious, incidentally, to notice the recurrence in "An Epistle to a Friend, to Persuade Him to the Wars" of a phrase that Jonson had used many years before in his touching lines on the death of his son; the same phrase in its different contexts carries quite contrary charges of meaning: "This hath our ill-us'd

freedome, and soft peace / Brought on us, and will every houre increase" (*The Underwood*, XV. 121–22). "Rest in soft peace, and, ask'd, say here doth lye / Ben. Jonson his best piece of *poetrie*" (*Epigrams*, XLV. 9–10).

16. See, for example, *Epigrams*, CXIX.12, *The Forest*, XIII. 55–58, *The New Inn*, 4.4.213–15.

17. See my article, "Jonson's Ode to Sir Lucius Cary and Sir H. Morison," *Studies in the Literary Imagination* 6 (1973): 139–52.

18. Yet the Countess of Bedford is commended in *Epigrams*, LXXVI. 13 for possessing "a learned, and a manly soule." David Wykes discusses some aspects of the arrangement of poems throughout the *Epigrams* in "Ben Jonson's 'Chast Booke'—the *Epigrammes*," *Renaissance and Modern Studies* 13 (1969): 76–87.

19. Compare Knowell's opening speech in Act 2, scene 5 (folio) with *The Underwood* XV and XLIV; and Act 4, scene 2 with *The Underwood*, XLII.

20. Jonas A. Barish, *Ben Jonson and the Language of Prose Comedy* (Cambridge, Mass., 1960), p. 213.

21. Dessen, p. 45; quoting the quarto text.

22. Dessen, p. 162.

23. Dessen, p. 217.

24. John Broadbent, introduction to his *Poets of the 17th Century* (New York, Scarborough, Ontario, and London, 1974), 1.15.

25. "On Poems of Joyous Impulse" (15 March 1854), in *Leigh Hunt's Literary Criticism*, ed. L. H. and C. W. Houtchens (1956), pp. 543–44.

26. Bodleian MS. Don. c. 24; quoted Herford & Simpson, 1: 113, and there wrongly ascribed to Michael Oldisworth of Wotton-under-Edge. Nicholas Oldisworth may have had particular cause for thinking Jonson sensitive on questions of morality: as the nephew of Sir Thomas Overbury and author of *A Book touching Sir Thomas Overbury* (see *D.N.B.*, Giles Oldisworth), he may have remembered Jonson's indignation at being asked by Overbury to act as go-between in Overbury's suit of the Countess of Rutland (see *Conversations with Drummond*, 1: 170, 214–19).

Richard C. Newton

"Ben./Jonson"

THE POET IN THE POEMS

The attempt to "place" Jonson in a single space, to "define" him as a poet, and to enumerate his essential qualities, or perhaps even to list the brief but exquisite list of his real successes, has long played a dominant part in Jonson studies. There are few who have written much about Jonson's poetry who have not at one time or another tried it. In defense of all those others, and of myself, I would like to identify Jonson himself the original tempter to this enterprise. Jonson himself is the inviter of, the motivator of, "Ben Jonson's Poetry" (Clarke), "The Tone of Ben Jonson's Poetry" (Walton), "Ben Jonson's Poems" (Maclean), "The Masterpoet and the Multiple Tradition" (Skelton), "Ben Jonson and the Centered Self" (Greene), to name a few, and now I would include, if modesty permits, " 'Ben./Jonson': The Poet in the Poems."[1]

Implicit invitation to the critical spirit that encloses, defines, seeks the essences of things is, in my opinion, the most important underlying characteristic of Jonson's poetic oeuvre. In attempting to join the exclusive circle of Jonson's "understanders," we inevitably are entangled in the attempt to understand Ben Jonson himself. This is a problem for us. The name Ben Jonson pervades all of his poetry, and it sometimes emerges explicitly (and heroically), as in the famous enjambment in the Cary/Morison ode, to which I allude in my title. Yet it is peculiarly difficult for us to know in any detailed and useful way just who Ben Jonson is. *Our* problem, I think, is Jonson's, too. We perceive, we experience in Jonson's poetry a problem of Jonson's own. It is an elusive thing to grasp; Jonson himself is evasive about it. And in evading it, he evades his admiring readers as well.

165

We find in Jonson's poetry, I believe, a dual commitment to experience and to the art that renders it. We find two differing apprehensions of the texture of our life that (though ultimately not necessarily opposed) elicit from us—in our moment by moment experiences of life—responses, attitudes, and strategies of perception that *are* opposed and that threaten mutual cancellation. This dual commitment is reflected in Jonson's choice of two very different men as literary heroes: Francis Bacon and Sir Philip Sidney. One can hardly fault the choices. Each of them strongly influenced the English cultural scene. The writings of each, and their personalities as well, gather up as well as express quite different but equally major cultural trends of the English Renaissance. And Jonson admired each enormously. They together, I think, represent a significant part of Renaissance English culture and a significant part as well of what I believe to be the intellectual and emotional climate of Ben Jonson's mind.[2] I will treat first the Baconian side, as being perhaps the less familiar and the more difficult to define.

One of the most notable characteristics of Jonson's poetic personality—at times I am tempted to think of it as the major characteristic—is his peculiar habit of making negative statements and excluding possibilities and interpretations from his verse, when to all appearances he either is or ought to be making positive assertions and enriching their complexity and depth. Sometimes this habit is quite obvious; at other times and rather more continuously it is unobtrusively imbedded in the texture of the verse.

Among the more obvious instances we find the famous opening lines of "To Penshurst" (*The Forest* 2):

> Thou are not, PENSHURST, built to envious show,
>   Of touch, or marble; nor canst boast a row
> Of polish'd pillars, or a roofe of gold:
>   Thou hast no lantherne, whereof tales are told;

Or stayre, or courts; but stand'st an ancient pile. . . .³

(1-5)

In a series of assertions in the negative mode, the lines toss aside
all traditional and neoclassical marks of distinction, leaving
Penshurst with *no* physical characteristics of its own. It is
virtually a part of nature, "an ancient pile."

To be sure, Jonson does not entirely limit himself to negative
exclusions. Once he has reduced Penshurst to an elemental
naturalness, he then goes on to ornament it in a positive way
with its *natural* surroundings:

Thou joy'st in better markes, of soyle, of ayre,
    Of wood, of water. . . .

(7-8)

And, having safely excluded all of outside civilization from
the charmed estate, he may proceed in a quite literary and
positively assertive way to mythologize the surroundings with
"Thy *Mount*, to which the *Dryads* doe resort, / Where PAN, and
BACCHUS their high feasts have made . . ." (10-11). Notably,
however, each mention of intrusive civilization is accompanied
by an exclusion of negative possibilities. The mention of walls
generates the assurance that:

They'are rear'd with no mans ruine, no mans grone,
There's none, that dwell about them, wish them downe.

(46-47)

And when the surrounding population is acknowledged to exist,
a significant *part* of their existence is excluded: "But all come
in . . . *though they have no sute*" (48-50, italics mine). This
exclusion of negatives leaves only the overflowing of natural
positives:

Some bring a capon, some a rurall cake,
    Some nuts, some apples; some that thinke they make

> The better cheeses, bring 'hem; or else send
>> By their ripe daughters, whom they would commend
> This way to husbands; and whose baskets beare
>> An embleme of themselves, in plum, or peare.
>
> (51–56)

All this profusion of food introduces the civilized habit of hospitality, and another negative assurance. Penshurst's

> . . . liberall boord doth flowe,
>> With all, that hospitalitie doth know!
> Where comes no guest, but is allow'd to eate,
>> Withoute his feare, and of thy lords owne meate.
>
> (59–62)

> Here no man tells my cups; nor, standing by,
>> A waiter, doth my gluttony envy. . . .
>
> (67–68)

> Thy tables hoord not up for the next day,
>> Nor, when I take my lodging, need I pray
> For fire, or lights, or livorie: all is there.
>
> (71–73)

And, finally the fruition of the human family itself is hedged in by exclusions:

> Thy lady's noble, fruitfull, chaste withall.
> His children thy great lord may call his owne:
>> A fortune, in this age, but rarely knowne.
>
> (90–92)

In each of these instances, Jonson first encounters his subject negatively, and only after first excluding some negative potential does he unleash the positive affirmation that within it may seem to inhere.[4]

It is not hard to find similar explicit negations in the service of affirmation throughout his poems. An early poem (*The Forest* 11), printed in the 1601 *Phoenix and Turtle*, begins:

> Not to know vice at all, and keepe true state,
>   Is vertue, and not *Fate:*
> Next, to that vertue, is to know vice well,
>   And her blacke spight expell.

                                                                                    (1-4)

And a late dedicatory epistle to Michael Drayton in 1627 (*Ungathered Verse* 30), in a sort of orgy of negations, begins with the denial of a negative suspicion by acknowledging the *omission* upon which the suspicion was grounded:

> It hath beene question'd, MICHAEL, if I bee
> A Friend at all; or, if at all, to thee:
> Because, who make the question, have not seene
> Those ambling visits, passe in verse, betweene
> Thy *Muse*, and mine, as they expect. 'Tis true:
> You have not writ to me, nor I to you;
> And, though I now begin, 'tis not to rub
> Hanch against Hanch, or raise a riming *Club*
> About the towne. . . .

                                                                                    (1-9)

And in 1625, he denies the forms of epitaphs (*Ungathered Verse* 28):

> I could begin with that grave forme, *Here lies*,
> And pray thee *Reader*, bring thy weepinge Eyes
> To see (who'it is?)

                                                                                    (1-3)

> But every *Table* in this *Church* can say,
> A list of Epithites. . . .

                                                                                    (7-8)

> But, I would have, thee, to know something new,
> Not usual in a *Lady;* and yet true. . . .

                                                                                    (13-14)

More familiar, and from the earlier work again, is the famous "Inviting a friend to supper" (*Epigrams* 101):

> To night, grave sir, both my poore house, and I
>   Doe equally desire your companie:
> Not that we thinke us worthy such a ghest. . . .

(1–3)

After a plethora of luxurious promises of food, literature, and drink, the poem concludes on a negating and excluding note:

> And we will have no *Pooly'*, or *Parrot* by;
> Nor shall our cups make any guiltie men:
>   But, at our parting, we will be, as when
> We innocently met. No simple word,
>   That shall be utter'd at our mirthfull boord,
> Shall make us sad next morning: or affright
>   The libertie, that we'll enjoy tonight.

(36–42)

The love and liberty of symposium is assured by exclusion.

But even though Jonson's verse abounds in *but* and *yet, not* and *nor*, there are many poems, and of course the great majority of lines, in which these words and their equivalent meanings do not appear. I want to argue, though, that they are really there anyway, in the texture of the verse. These negations in the texture of the verse are the cause of the second major characteristic of Jonson's verse, at least of the great majority of it: its relative obscurity. Obscurity came to be regarded as a good thing in literature around the end of the sixteenth century, and we should not be surprised to find Jonson himself among the mob of gentlemen who wrote with difficulty. But there are a lot of different ways of being obscure, and Jonson's is probably unique. It accounts, more than anything else, I think, for the peculiar difficulty we so often find in thinking up anything interesting to *say* about the texture of Jonson's verse. The witty difficulty of Donne's verse is far different, and the energetic leaps and decisions we must make to understand Donne's verse are very much a part of our conscious or at least semiconscious understanding of it. We *always* about must and about must go, and we *know* that this about-going is part of the meaning of what we are reading. Donne, as often as not, says so.

Jonson does not. We have to go about and about with his verse, too, rereading, looking ahead, changing our minds about the syntax, figuring out the meter, and so on. But about all this mental activity and juggling of the diverse resources of the poetry, Jonson has nothing to say. He acts *as if* he were not going on at all. And unlike Donne, unlike Chapman, Hall, Marston, and the rest, he pretends that what he says—most of it anyway—is clear, perspicuous, and easily arrived at by any right-thinking person. I should note, too, that the obscurity of Jonson's verse is not a mere fad of the 1590s out of which he grew in later years. It is in fact more characteristic of the verse written after the *Epigrams* (1612) than that written before. But it appears throughout. Here are the opening lines of a poem from 1600 (*The Forest* 12):

MADAME,
Whil'st that, for which, all vertue now is sold,
    And almost every vice, almightie gold,
That which, to boote with hell, is thought worth heaven,
    And, for it, life, conscience, yea, soules are given,
Toyles, by grave custome, up and downe the court,
    To every squire, or groome, that will report
Well, or ill, onely, all the following yeere,
    Just to the waight their this dayes-presents beare;
While it makes huishers serviceable men,
    And some one apteth to be trusted, then,
Though never after; whiles it gaynes the voyce
    Of some grand peere, whose ayre doth make rejoyce
The foole that gave it; who will want, and weepe,
    When his proud patrons favours are asleepe;
While thus it buyes great grace, and hunts poore fame;
    Runs betweene man, and man; 'tweene dame, and dame;
Solders crackt friendship; makes love last a day;
    Or perhaps lesse: whil'st gold beares all this sway,
I, that have none (to send you) send you verse.

                           (1–19)

These lines are exceptionally obscure to be sure, but not untypically so. And they typify the difficulties we face in reading Jonson's lines, difficulties we face *every time we read* them, whether to ourselves or to another.

First note that Jonson nowhere suggests that the lines are difficult. The lucid conclusion of the passage offers an uncluttered meaning for "gold" and "sway." Their meanings are not problematical. They are clear, and they are clearly rejected: "whil'st gold beares all this sway, / I, that have none (to send you) send you verse." So part of what we have to do as readers is to *overcome* Jonson's seeming poise, to overcome his repression of the strenuous difficulty of his verse.

And how do we do this? Perhaps most important, we do syntactic analysis, and at a rather high level of conscious awareness. There is simply no other way to understand the verse. The main thing Jonson forces the reader to do with his syntax is reanalyze it. Again and again, you are led to *feel* that a syntactic unit has reached closure, has formed a completed unit, only to discover in the next phrase that it has not. So you have to "reopen" that seemingly concluded unit, sometimes only to put in something else, sometimes to reinterpret it completely and perceive an entirely new closure.

Small examples of this abound. The first of the lines in the passage above begins with a coincidence of metrical line and syntactic unit; a noun phrase containing a relative clause apparently ends at the end of the line: "Whil'st that, for which, all vertue now is sold." We naturally interpret the noun phrase as a subject and thus expect the predicate (of the clause introduced by *Whil'st*) to follow. Instead we get a half-line addition to the relative clause, "And almost every vice," that forces us to discard our previous feeling of closure and to reopen the syntactic unit to put in the new element. With the addition of the new element comes an even stronger sense of closure, precipitated by the stumbling thump of the half-line unit and the parallelism of *vertue* with *vice*. Once again, we are wrong, and the relative clause is extended once again, with the appositive "almightie gold." *Now* we have closure, surely. The end of the couplet, the end (the third end) of the relative clause, and the rime of *gold* with *sold* all surely tell us so. *Now* the predicate of the *whilst*-clause will follow.

It does not. Instead, a most unlikely second appositive is added: "That which, to boote with hell, is thought worth heaven." I say "most unlikely" because this is an appositive to the whole *noun phrase;* we might by now have come to expect additions to the relative clause. It takes a minute to figure out what has happened. To be sure, this is very close to anaphora. Jonson could have made it into anaphora and we would have no problems: "*Whilst* that which, t'boote with hell, is thought worth heaven." The meter is possible for Jonson, and the added *whilst* would tell us immediately where we are in the sentence and would obviate all need for the sort of analysis that its lack imposes upon us.

Under the pressure of this continuing demand for analysis, I am always stunned for a second when I reach the main verb of the *whilst*-clause: "*Toyles*, by grave custome, up and downe the court." I guess the main reason I am so struck is that in the previous line Jonson has abandoned the relative pronoun altogether: "And, for it [not *which*], life, conscience, yea, soules are given." So far behind has that introductory *whilst* been left, that I suspect Jonson could have put a period right here, and it would be a long time before most readers would catch the grammatical error. So it takes a pretty massive analytical effort to connect *toyles* of line five with *Whilst that* of line one. You have to overcome all the successful closures reached and re-reached in the previous lines, and you especially have to dismiss the grammatically false closure prompted by the immediately preceding abandonment of the relative mode.

My point is—and I will not carry this analysis any further to make it—that Jonson *habitually* writes this way. His consistent mode is to *encourage* his readers to arrive at closure along the way at many points of the sometimes torturous route of his syntax and then to force us to *discard* the analysis, idea, or feeling that has enabled that closure.

The stylistic devices that he uses to effect this trickery are of course extremely varied; you can find new ones every time you read. But the principal ones are the ones that Jonas Barish has found to be characteristic of Jonson's prose, devices that take potentially symmetrical effects of language and twist them into asymmetrical shapes: disturbing the word order by adding unexpected elements or putting expected elements in unexpected places, aborting rhythm by destroying parallelism, varying the length and shape of successive clauses.[5] The style is founded upon symmetry and parallelism; we are usually given enough sense of artificial form to make (usually unconscious) predictions about the conclusion of a phrase or clause. But much of the time we are wrong. We are "stung" again and again.

I am sometimes amazed that despite so much experiential evidence that we will be wrong, we go on trying to predict. It is my experience, however, that we do. It is our consistent mode of reading in Jonson's poetry continually to affirm interpretations of the syntax, only to have them refuted by further reading. This process continues through the reading of a meaningful unit, which is usually, though not always, a sentence.

When the refutations are at an end (usually, when we get to the end of the sentence), we "know" what Jonson "means." By that I mean we are left with the *feeling* that Jonson has spoken with perfect clarity. There are no lingering ambiguities, no hidden suggestive corners to be illuminated:

> Brave Infant of *Saguntum*, cleare
> Thy comming forth in that great yeare,

When the Prodigious *Hannibal* did crowne
His rage, with razing your immortall Towne.

(The Underwood 70.1–4)

I think that any careful reading of these opening lines of the
Cary/Morison ode (1629) will show that the infant's "coming
forth" is not "cleare" at all, though to us now it is certainly
"famous." But despite the awkward mystery of the lines—a
mystery that is the source of considerable disagreement among
critics of the poem—the lines themselves refuse to suggest that
there is mystery or ambiguity at all. The meaning of *cleare* is at
first potentially ambiguous, but typically, the ambiguous meaning is "cleared up" by the lines as we read: *brave, great, prodigious, immortal* tell us that *cleare* is a literal translation of
Latin *clarus*. The brave infant of Saguntum is famous. It happens that this elucidation of meaning provides Jonson's usual
illusion of clarity and thus reincorporates the rejected English
meaning of *clear* in a compressed pun. Fundamentally, though,
the impression of clarity is achieved by the *rejection* of the
English meaning in favor of the Latin.

Jonson's verse, then, tends to be obscure, but it denies its own
obscurity. It represses all knowledge of its difficulty and claims
instead to be perfectly lucid. It achieves the impression of
lucidity by requiring continual decisions of the reader that call
for exclusions of possible meanings and interpretations in favor
of a single (or at least apparently single) one. In a great many of
his explicit statements in the verse and in the continuous texture of the verse itself, Jonson excludes, denies, refutes, and
rejects, in order ultimately to affirm.

Now exclusion in the service of affirmation is a familiar
phenomenon of seventeenth-century literature. The fad of
obscurity of the 1590s amounted largely to an explicit rejection
of "sugared" sixteenth-century style, a rejection of "ornament"
for "truth," of "words" for "things." A great deal of seventeenth-

century prose defines itself in terms of what it *rejects*. Again
and again, prose writers set out to clear the field of error. Sir
Thomas Browne, anxious to affirm many things, writes *Pseudo-
doxia Epidemica*, with a first book on the causes of errors.
Thomas Hobbes writes an early essay that is later incorporated
into *Leviathan* as "Of Darkness from Vain Philosophy and
Fabulous Traditions." Milton's first major prose tract, *Of
Reformation*, has for its proposition the refutational aim
of inquiring "what, and how many the cheife causes have
been, that have still hindred" the fulfillment of reformation
in England. The catalogue of early seventeenth-century literature, which is marked or defined by exclusion, rejection, or
denial, could grow quite large before we even touch on Francis
Bacon, who is the greatest denier, rejector, and excluder of
them all.

The particular book of Bacon's that Jonson in the *Discoveries*
singles out for highest praise is the *New Organon*, for "it really
openeth," he says, "all defects of Learning, whatsoever."[6] The
New Organon in particular displays the fundamental role that
the process of exclusion plays in Bacon's thought. Exclusion
dominates not only his approach to learning and the divisions
thereof but also his understanding of the perception of reality
itself.

In this latter respect Bacon is differentiated, as is well known,
from most other thinkers of his time.[7] For most—while participating in the general urge to expose past errors and purge the
garden of knowledge of its rank medieval needs—generally
subscribed to the notion that affirmation, not negation, is the
greatest strength of the human mind. There *are* some rational
or mathematical models for the positive construction and organization of the knowable and known, as Descartes and
Hobbes believed. Or our faith may direct us to proper per-
cepts, or our inner selves, as Browne and Burton and Milton
knew. Or some perceived empirical data reveal the structure of

other phenomena, as Gilbert and Kepler thought. But Bacon held:

> . . . To god, truly, the Giver and Architect of Forms, and it may be to the angels and higher intelligences, it belongs to have an affirmative knowledge of forms immediately, and from the first contemplation. But this assuredly is more than man can do, to whom it is granted only to proceed at first by negatives, and at last to end in affirmatives after exclusion has been exhausted.
>
> We must make, therefore, a complete solution and separation of nature, not indeed by fire, but by the mind, which is a kind of divine fire. The first work, therefore, of true induction (as far as regards the discovery of forms) is the rejection or exclusion of the several natures which are [found to be irrelevant to the given nature]. Then indeed after the rejection and exclusion has been duly made, there will remain at the bottom, all light opinions vanishing into smoke, a form affirmative, solid, and true and well defined. . . . (*New Organon* 2.15–16)[8]

"This is quickly said," he adds, "but the way to come at it is winding and intricate." Admittedly, Bacon does not really insist on the pure induction. He does allow the researchers, at a certain point, "to make an essay of the Interpretation of Nature in the affirmative way," which he calls "*Indulgence of the Understanding*, or the *Commencement of Interpretation*, or the *First Vintage*" (*New Organon* 2.20). He does allow, that is to say, hypotheses. But he tightly hedges them around with reminders that they are not "true," that they are merely indulgences of human frailty, and that *real* truth will only emerge —almost magically—after the fire of the human mind has done its work of dissolution and rejection. We can take two and two apart, but we cannot be trusted to put two and two together.

Bacon's stupendously incorrect notion of the complexity of the physical universe and his disastrously wrongheaded distrust of mathematics are familiar themes in the history of science. But their reasons are clear. Mathematics is a method of moving entirely by affirmatives, anathema to Bacon, and it was also tied up with the mystique of individual genius and with systems of universal (and affirmatively explanatory) cosmological analogies against which Bacon fought. As for the complexity of the universe, who could have guessed it? Moreover, Bacon was entirely disposed to believe in a knowable universe—really his system requires it—and he argued urgently against those "Skeptics and Academics" who "denied any certainty of knowledge or comprehension; and held opinion that the knowledge of man extended only to appearances and probabilities" (*Advancement of Learning* 2.13.4).[9]

Bacon's legacy to his successors through the nineteenth century was a conviction of a knowable universe and a theory of experimental induction. Fortunately the theory was bent to a practice more accepting of hypothesis, and mathematics was accepted. The implications of these two changes did not become apparent until this century, when the universe dissolved before the eyes of physicists and astronomers. In the meantime, science was blessed with a sort of "myth of certainty" in the pursuit of its endeavors.

I digress to this Baconian myth of scientific certainty because I want to suggest that what lies behind it—the theory of nonaffirmative and hence nonpersonal emergence of truth through the process of exclusion—is available to other forms of discourse besides the scientific. It is available as well (properly transformed) to poetry, and in particular to the poetry of Ben Jonson.

Jonson, we know, aspired to the status of dictator of letters and morals. It is a peculiar dictatorship that he sought, however. When we examine his work for positive dictates, it is astounding how little we find that is both specific and his own. The great exception to this would seem to be the *Discoveries*, but I think we should remember that work is a series of distillations rather than of concoctions. It is the residue of Jonson's reading, not the synthesis. More strikingly, in the poems, again and again what seems to be solid dissolves before our eyes, and we are left to construct the statement for ourselves.[10] But as I have said, the verse itself makes no admission that such acts of "construction" are going on. Hence, the meaning of the statement seems to emerge on its own. Another way of putting this is to say that in reading Jonson's verse we have the experience of *seeming* to know what he is going to say before he says it, or at least *as* he says it. Through the explicit rejections of the statements and the implicit rejections involved in the reading process, irrelevant meanings are discarded—impersonally and without acknowledged individual effort.

It is a peculiar way of writing poetry. Take, for example, Jonson's poem to the painter Burlase (*The Underwood* 52), which Wesley Trimpi selects as his "most moving poem on friendship, and one of his most disarming."[11] Jonson begins by complaining with the humor of "My Picture left in Scotland," about the superficial accuracy with which Burlase has portrayed his mountain belly and stooped back, concluding:

> But whilst you curious were to have it be
> An *Archetype*, for all the world to see,
> You made it a brave piece, but not like me.
>
> (13-15)

Having rejected the painting of mere "superficies," he moves to a more revelatory, explanatory, and creative notion of representation:

> O, had I now your manner, maistry, might,
> Your Power of handling shadow, ayre, and spright,
> How I would draw, and take hold and delight.
>
> (16-18)

But of course, these ideas are entirely counter to the Baconian ideal of impersonal discovery by dissolution and exclusion. And they are rejected, are in fact expelled from *verbal* art altogether:

> But, you are he can paint; I can but write:
> A Poet hath no more but black and white,
> Ne knowes he flatt'ring Colours, or false light.
>
> (19-21)

If we examine this closely, we find that what Jonson has really done is appropriate to his own art the plainness and direct revelatory power of which he complains in Burlase's art at the beginning. But the process of rejecting first the superficial and then the "flattering" has transmuted the meaning of "plain." Burlase's superficial plainness, which is after all still personal and creative art, is appropriated to another art defined almost entirely by lacks, exclusions, and limitations.

At the end, this appropriated plainness is returned to Burlase, now fully transformed into Jonson's own language, as a generous compliment:

> Yet when of friendship I would draw the face,
> A letter'd mind, and a large heart would place
> To all posteritie; I will write *Burlase*.

(22–24)

A mean spirit might drive us to ask where this "friendship" comes from, whence this "letter'd mind" and "large heart." I say "mean spirit" because the poem does not permit a challenge of these bountiful endowments. The processes by which they are generated—excluding irrelevancies to reveal the real—are concealed. They go on nonetheless, and I believe we experience them as we read. Hence, the statements of truth that Jonson delivers, though curiously undefined and unargued, carry their own "myth of certainty," like the scientific knowledge Bacon hoped for. It *is* a disarming way of writing poetry, for its own sources of affirmation are concealed, and it thus deprives us of the comfort of our own. Through it we gain new knowledge or renew old gains, but it denies us knowledge of these gainings.

Naturally, I do not wish to claim that Jonson "derived" this method of writing from Bacon, and certainly not from the rather late *New Organon*. The two men participated with many others in what was a general trend of the age, but these particular two men seem especially close in spirit. I imagine that Jonson was "influenced" by Bacon in the sense that he intuited in Bacon's writing and thought a great similarity to his own. This would naturally lead him to admire Bacon. And for such generous narcissism who can be severely blamed? It would also, I should think, tend to confirm him in his own way of writing and of perceiving.

Jonson shared another intellectual trait with Bacon. Or perhaps I should say that the intellectual sympathy between them had another common manifestation. This is a tendency toward fragmentation. Bacon's distrust of individual genius, a priori systems, and rhetorical schemata manifested itself in a tendency to write in aphorisms, a tendency that is entirely explicit in the *New Organon* and easy to see even in the earliest essays. Though disinclined to allow it any particular conceptual significance, Brian Vickers argues that division—the habit of breaking discourse into even smaller units—is Bacon's "major structural method."[12] The smallest unit of division is aphorism. In the *New Organon*, as much as anywhere else, you can see Bacon trying to make fullest use of tradition of knowledge by aphorisms, to avoid the imposition upon the mind that the fraudulent completeness of what he calls "methodical" writing forces. (See esp. *New Organon* 1.86.) But even as early as the *Advancement* his reasons for preferring aphorisms for the tradition of knowledge, as opposed to "methods," are explicit and decisive. Since illustrations, examples, sequences and consequences, and "descriptions of practice" are all "cut off," "there remaineth nothing to fill the Aphorisms but some good quantity of observation." Aphorisms suit better the dispersed and discrete nature of particulars. Also, "representing a knowledge broken," they "do invite men to inquire further." Methods, on the contrary, "are more fit to win consent or belief . . . for they carry a kind of demonstration in orb or circle, one part illuminating another, and therefore satisfy." Needless to say, since methods do carry this artificial illusion of self-completeness, "carrying the show of a total, they do secure men, as if they were at farthest" in the path of scientific inquiry.[13] The aphorism, for Bacon, represents our most honest, direct, and useful means for rendering accurate knowledge of particulars and observations of experience.

In Jonson, I believe, we find exactly the same belief. It appears with almost boring clarity, of course, in the kind of poems he chooses to write and the valuation he sets upon them. His *Epigrams*, we inevitably recall, were "the ripest of his studies." I suppose everybody interested in Jonson has a slightly different interpretation of what exactly this phrase means. But we can probably all agree that it indicates in some way that the *Epigrams* are very important, more so than at least some others of the *Workes* published in 1616, and are deserving of "study" in return. Notable, too, is the fact that the *Epigrams* are dedicated to the Earl of Pembroke, to whom also is dedicated *Catiline*, the most arrogantly "studied" of Jonson's plays. Moreover, *Catiline* and the *Epigrams* together form a kind of centering keystone in the actual physical arrangement of the *Workes*. The plays Jonson chose to save for posterity are presented in chronological order, capped by *Catiline* and the *Epigrams*, both dedicated to Pembroke, followed by the briefer, more miscellaneous and undedicated *Forest* and then the masques. We note as well that while there is talk in various places of long works and heroic studies, none appear. I do not believe that the 1623 library fire was entirely responsible for the fact that the longest nontranslated poem we have from Jonson is the mocking "Voyage It Selfe," the scatological concluding poem of the *Epigrams*. And surely it is not merely an accident, too, that the two expository prose works, the *English Grammar* and the *Discoveries*, are essentially aphoristic— organized not to present comprehensive theories or syntheses but rather to present observations of limited scope, "discoveries," and aperçus.[14]

An epigram is very much like an aphorism. They share the common intent of seizing the imagination of their readers and focusing on a rather narrow fragment of experience. They want to convince their readers of the truth of what they say about the narrow fragment they treat of. And the limitation of their scope is their principal persuasive device. They may imply but they do not explicitly require a reader's subscription to arguments and facts beyond what they present. And by this exclusion, when successful, they become "facts" themselves, as in "To Foole, or Knave" (*Epigrams* 61):

> Thy praise, or dispraise is to me alike,
>> One doth not stroke me, nor the other strike.

We may recall Jonson's odes to himself, apologies, addresses to the reader, and so forth, for the arguments that lie behind this epigram, but it does not insist that we do so. Its success as a rhetorical act makes it a fact.

There is, to be sure, a certain ambiguity in the meaning of both aphorism and epigram. One meaning of aphorism is *maxim* or *axiom*, a concise summation of received information.[15] The epigram, and especially the English epigram before Jonson, appropriates this meaning. One of Jonson's that is closest to it is "Of Death" (*Epigrams* 34):

> He that feares death, or mournes it, in the just,
>> Shewes of the resurrection little trust.

The Baconian aphorism and the typical Jonsonian epigram certainly strive for a similar authority. But they seek the authority while performing the multiple tasks of rejecting received and external authority, offering a new and personal observation of empirical reality, and attempting to establish a sense of authority that is not merely personal:

> Who can consider thy right courses run,
>> With what thy vertue on the times hath won,

And not thy fortune; who can cleerely see
    The judgement of the king so shine in thee;
And that thou seek'st reward of thy each act,
    Not from the publike voyce, but private fact;
Who can behold all envie so declin'd
    By constant suffring of thy equall mind;
And can to these be silent, *Salisburie*,
    Without his, thine, and all times injurie?
Curst be his *Muse*, that could lye dumbe, or hid
    To so true worth, though thou thy selfe forbid.

                             (*Epigrams* 63)

The praise of Robert, Earl of Salisbury rejects traditional symbols (fortune, public voice), claims empirical observations (virtue, equal mind), and distracts from too close a scrutiny of these claims by diverting the concern of the poem to the *right* of the poet to praise. That finally Jonson writes the poem over the *objections* of his subject—thus converting private fact to public fact—proves the truth of the argument.

To this picture of Jonson I have been drawing—a Jonson inclined to fragments more than to wholes and to denials more than to affirmations, committed to a Baconian narrowing of empirical observation—there is a serious objection. He is not entirely the Jonson we *feel* when we read. Oh yes, he is something like that. We remember his verse breaking pretty much into couplets or smaller parts. We recall his reputation for saying the negative thing before the positive. He does seem crabbed and halting at times. But what we remember about him most of all is his profound, at times thrilling, and unwavering commitment to a world of grand and even heroic humanistic values. We remember his apparent self-assurance and assertiveness. And we remember him, perhaps with greatest pleasure, as the creator of some of the most exquisite lyrics in English poetry, lyrics that one thinks could not be further from the negating Baconian empiricist I have been presenting.

It does indeed seem true that in those few poems of his where
he succeeds in creating a golden nature rather than a brazen
one, Jonson has somehow broken free from one kind of poetry
into another, more preferable kind, a paradisal kind, an ameliora-
tive and fictive kind of poetry. The same is true, I think, of
those poems and parts of poems where he breaks into affirmation of a heroic vein and indeed virtually of a returned golden
age. "UV'DALE, thou piece of the first times," he begins one
poem (*Epigrams* 125). And to Benjamin Rudyard, "If I would
wish . . . / The aged SATURNE'S age, and rites to know; / If I
would strive to bring back times, and trie / The world's pure
gold," I would "studie thee" (*Epigrams* 122).

Jonson's lyric impulse moves quite opposite to his Baconian
tendencies toward negation and fragmentation. It tends not to
posit a Baconian world stripped to its merely brazen facts and
broken into discrete pieces but rather directly to affirm instead
a special world, a golden, coherent, and ornamental one.

> Kisse, and score up wealthy summes
> On my lips, thus hardly sundred,
> While you breath. First give a hundred,
> Then a thousand, then another
> Hundred, then unto the tother
> Adde a thousand, and so more:
> Till you equall with the store,
> All the grasse that *Rumney* yeelds,
> Or the sands in *Chelsey* fields,
> Or the drops in silver *Thames*,
> Or the starres, that guild his streames,
> In the silent sommer-nights,
> When youths ply their stolne delights.

(*The Forest* 6.6–18)

The borrowed kisses from Catullus themselves create a golden
scene, which in turn generates yet more kisses (or at least
"stolne delights"). Recall, too, the mythological bounty of the
Sidney estate Penshurst, where Jonson sees Dryads dancing and

fish that fling themselves into your net. Indeed, if Bacon is the patron of Jonson's nonlyric genius, Sidney is the genius of his lyric. More than any other name, the Sidney name brings its own, *inherited* authority into Jonson's verse. One of the Sidneys he praises, for instance, is Mary, Lady Wroth, who in one poem is described as a kind of lyrical poem of the golden age herself:

> MADAME, had all antiquitie beene lost,
>   All historie seal'd up, and fables crost;
> That we had left us, nor by time, nor place,
>   Least mention of a *Nymph*, a *Muse*, a *Grace*,
> But even their names were to be made a-new,
>   Who could not but create them all, from you?
>
> *(Epigrams* 105.1-6)

She is "*Natures Index*" (19) and does restore, in herself, "all treasure lost of th'age before" (20). Another poem for her (*Epigrams* 103) has a simpler way of praising. She would easily be known "a SYDNEY, though un-nam'd" (4), "And, being nam'd, how little doth that name / Need any *Muses* praise to give it fame?" (5-6).

Of Jonson's admiration for Sidney we have ample testimony. For a poet's hero, Sidney is of course an excellent choice, both for his criticism and art and for his social station and personal style. Sidney the artist merges, in retrospect at least, with Sidney the man in a single image, which unites life with art, epitomizing a world that *is* coherent, complete, and golden. As an aristocrat, he seems to fulfill the responsibilities of his station with completeness, magnanimity, and style, of which his art is only a natural extension. And his art thus seems, as John Danby has said, "an aspect of his own magnanimity, a self-dedication, a free gift."[16] In every way, he could be taken as the finest expression of English culture and a fulfillment, even a justification, of its social structure. Were every man a Sidney, the world (for men at least) would be golden indeed.

Behind much of Jonson's praises of people in the world lies the idea of Sidney as a man. I do not mean, of course, that Jonson "derives" his terms of praise from Sidney any more than he derives his nonlyric writing from Bacon, but Sidney, or the myth of Sidney, is "in resonance" as it were with Jonson's lyric genius, and Sidney's social and poetic aura is continually present as a dim image of the world as Jonson would wish it.

The world, alas, was *not* as Jonson wished it. Sidney was long dead, and if the family continued, it is unhappily true that Jonson's one poem to the inheritor of the family name is to the wayward son of Sir Robert Sidney, a long and strained ode urging the boy not to rest on his family name but to strive to deserve it (*The Forest* 14). He did not. The rest of the social structure, too, was in extraordinary flux, as new titles were created out of thin air, and old families declined and new ones rose with a disturbing rapidity.[17] And the monarch lacked the dictatorial brilliance and command of public metaphor to maintain at least an illusion of coherence and stability, as Elizabeth for so much of her reign was able to do. In the momentary brilliance of a masque, Jonson may have been able to place the monarch at the center of a numinous and stable court,[18] but the realities that invade his poems and his commitment however painful to empirical facts prohibits such indulgences.

Some readers of this paper may have noted that in the poem to Salisbury that I quoted earlier I failed to comment on the lines, "who can cleerly see / The judgement of the king so shine in thee." I avoided the lines because in this instance Jonson *does* appeal to a myth outside the epigram and either invokes the authority of the king to validate his subject, or uses his subject to validate the king. In either case, it overloads the epigram, as do similar lines from the next epigram, also to Salisbury (*Epigrams* 64):

When so wise a king
Contends t'have worth enjoy, from his regard,
    As her owne conscience, still, the same reward.

(12–14)

I think it is probably no accident that Jonson followed his
overextended poems to Salisbury with an argument with his
muse ("To My Muse," *Epigrams* 65):

Away, and leave me, thou thing most abhord,
    That hast betray'd me to a worthlesse lord.

(1–2)

It is always a danger that an epigram may not be true, but the
danger is especially fierce when the poet is so self-indulgent as
to allow himself to appeal to external sources of authority.
Significantly, in the *Epigrams*, after this outburst, Jonson never
again appeals to the authority of the king. More and more he
appeals to an authority that resides almost entirely in himself,
the poet. "That *Poets* are far rarer births then kings," he writes
to Philip Sidney's daughter Elizabeth, "Your noblest father
prov'd" (*Epigrams* 79).

Jonson does possess the impulse to fulfill the Sidnean vision
of the poet, to give poetry to the world purely as a generous
and heroic free gift of the extended self, to give poetry to the
world as a priest, and to give the world, through poetry, a better
and more beautiful thing than it has or is. And he *does* sometimes, in some brief lyrics and lyric passages and in the grand
praises of heroic magnanimity in men and women.

But from consistently or habitually fulfilling the Sidnean role
as poet he is blocked. Socially, he is not Sidney; his poetry
cannot really and merely express his own magnanimity. Even
had he been Sidney, the late Tudor and the Stuart social, political, and economic scene was too very different from what, to a
poet looking back, that of Sidney at least *seemed* to have
been. Jonson's own London world would seem only capable of

supporting what we find everywhere in the best poetry of the time, the exploration of individual perceptions, consciousness, and authority. Moreover, Jonson's own strong Baconian predispositions would seem a harsh and immovable roadblock in themselves to a poetry of golden worlds and scenes for completed heroic actions.

Some compromise is called for. Sidney's and Bacon's impulses are similar in that both aspire to reveal or discover what is, in a radical sense, true. But their basic motions are radically opposed. To put it starkly, the latter negates, the former affirms. We feel both actions in Jonson, expressed as a kind of blocked and endlessly questioned poetic vision. Jonson could never have written, I believe, the *Arcadia, The Faerie Queene, The Tempest*. But that should not lead us to believe, I think, that he did not aspire to.

But the manner in which he aspired was distinctive. If Jonson wrote, or tried to write, an epic, that epic is his *Workes*. I have always been struck by Jon Enck's observation that Jonson had "a penchant for completeness."[19] Though he tended to produce in fragments, he aspired to the creation of wholes. His best way of doing this was to bring his fragmentary creations together in collections. Significantly, the *Epigrams* are called "Book 1." He apparently expected to collect more later. And we know that in the case both of the plays and of the poems he was careful to suppress work he felt inappropriate to the collection. Through careful editing (or exclusion) he sought to create a whole.[20]

It is at this point that I may return to my initial observation, that Jonson himself is the tempter of us all to take him all in all and understand.

> Pray thee, take care, that tak'st my booke in hand,
>   To reade it well: that is, to understand.
>
> (Epigrams 1)

How rich and challenging this flat sounding couplet becomes as we enter ever more deeply into the texture of Jonson's poetic oeuvre. Can we ever be really *included* enough in Jonson's verse truly to claim that, yes, Ben, we do understand? And did Ben in fact himself believe we ever could?

For at least moments at a time, I think, surely the answer to the latter question is yes. After all, the implicitly promised second book of *Epigrams* never came forth. And it does seem true that the much looser collection of *The Underwood*, though not fully edited by Jonson, does in general reflect his intentions: he apparently no longer deemed it necessary to construct tight collections of a single genre like the *Epigrams* or very small carefully selected and constructed collections like *The Forest*. He still wanted his poems, his fragments of experience, to "help" each other in a collection; but a miscellany was help enough. Perhaps as well, though this speculation depends on the degree of his own editorship, he was less *exclusive* in his choices, and was more willing to let whatever he had written stand or fall as it would in the collection.

More worth our note is the rather large number of longer poems, epistles, really, though not always so named, in which Jonson addresses a specific person who at least at the moment of the writing is *known* to understand, to understand completely. The number of statements that may be extracted from such poems that exemplify the ideals of the plain style, the Horatian epistolary style, are legion.[21] After over a hundred lines of lecture on friendship and true generosity, he declares to Edward Sackville, Earl of Dorset, "And you, Sir, know it well to whom I write" (*The Underwood* 13.109). To John Seldon: "I know to whom I write. Here, I am sure, / Though I am short, I cannot be obscure" (*The Underwood* 14.1–2). More metaphysically, he addresses a friend,

> . . . which name your selfe receave,
> And which you (being the worthier) gave me leave
> In letters, that mix spirits, thus to weave.
>
> (*The Underwood* 37.10–12)

The receivers of these addresses "understand," on a basis that is mutual and unquestioned, and in a curious way unstated though often much talked *about*.[22]

But what of us, can we "understand" as well? To this I must give, and I believe Jonson gives as well, conflicting answers. We may fairly bring to mind here, I think, what Jonson confided to Drummond of Hawthornden: "His Impresa was a Compass with one foot in Center, the other Broken, the word. Deest quod duceret orbem" (*Conversations* 578–79, Herford & Simpson, 1: 148). To the completion of the circle, to the total inclusion of his perfect or perfectible readers in the charmed circle of his perfective world, he aspired; but in his own estimation some vital part, which would complete that circle, was missing. So one answer is no, he did not succeed; we finally cannot understand him.

But another answer is yes, he does succeed. At least, as I have said, at moments. Ultimately it is *Ben Jonson* we must understand. We must match our understandings with his as we twist our way through his verse, trying to keep pace with his unacknowledged Baconian exclusions, revisions, rejections, reassessments. And we must match our understanding with his as he relinquishes the supports of an external world of unreliable and increasingly tawdry public metaphor and turns more and more to reliance on his own perceptions as a poet and on the public personality that in his Works he strives to shape. When these understandings coalesce, the experience is, for me, one of the great experiences of English poetry:

Call, noble *Lucius*, then for Wine,
And let thy lookes with gladnesse shine:
Accept this garland, plant it on thy head,
And thinke, nay know, thy *Morison's* not dead.
Hee leap'd the present age,
Possest with holy rage,
To see that bright eternall Day:

Of which we *Priests*, and *Poets* say
Such truths, as we expect for happy men,
And there he lives with memorie; and *Ben.*

Jonson, who sung this of him, e're he went
Himselfe to rest. . . .

(The Underwood 70.75–86)

The famous enjambment of Ben Jonson's name in the Cary /
Morison ode is such an experience.[23]

In the stanza that begins, "Call, noble *Lucius*, then for Wine,"
Jonson appropriates to himself, allows unto himself, an affirmative power, a Horatian and a Sidnean "holy rage" of his own,
through which he becomes the poet-priest and maker of truths.
Almost simultaneously in the same stanza, he reduces his claims
to those of the simple perceiving poet-friend: "And there he
lives with memorie: and *Ben.*" We are at once affirmatively to
know of things perfect and eternal, and also to know that these
very things are of one man, our Ben. But not *only* Ben, after
all. Our felt resolution of the clause now is in the next stanza
undone, and in one of his most generous extensions of himself,
Ben gives us a *new* person, who includes Ben but is more than
him, who is the public personality Ben Jonson, author of works,
dictator of letters, master of studies.

An intuitive knowledge of this public personality, I think, is
necessary for our reading of this poem, as it is for the great
majority of Ben Jonson's others. That is why he assembled his
collections. That is why he strove to shape his oeuvre in editions
and in works. *There*, if anywhere, the circle is complete.

While one of the greatest of our poets, Jonson is the author of
remarkably few of those poems that make up our anthologies.
The Bacon in him seems to balance too evenly with the Sidney
for single poems of his to stand comfortably alone. Hence our
efforts, perhaps ever to be repeated, to *complete* the circle and
to strike its center for the riches we know are there. Is the

circle *really* complete? Can we the center find? I myself in the long run doubt it. I find in Jonson's poetry an irresolvable tension between its conflicting aims and at the same time, or really as a part of that tension, an incredibly fierce repression of all knowledge of the conflict's being. There seems no way to succeed in the taking of the whole, the *parts* are so insistent. At the same time, obviously, I cannot resist the temptation that Ben Jonson through his fierce repression offers us, to try again, and again to try, to complete the circle nonetheless, to know the sum and find the center. It is in the *action* of succumbing to that temptation, I believe, in the struggle of *know* what seems so knowable, that we do indeed come closest to knowledge of the figure who invites us to the knowing, Ben Jonson, the poet in the poems.

NOTES

1. Egerton Clarke, *Dublin Review* 201 (July–Oct. 1937): 325–38. Geoffrey Walton, *From Metaphysical to Augustan* (London, 1955). Hugh Maclean, in *Essays in English Literature . . . Presented to A. S. P. Woodhouse*, ed. Millar MacLure and F. W. Watts (Toronto: University of Toronto Press, 1964). Robin Skelton, *Style* 1 (1967):225–46. Thomas M. Greene, *SEL* 10 (1970): 326–48. This list is of course arbitrarily selected and could be extended by many titles.

2. A similar dualistic approach is that of Arthur F. Marotti, who adopts as basic terms Dionysian and Apollonian, in "All About Jonson's Poetry," *ELH* 39 (1972): 208–37. Our essays will bear comparison at many points, though we finally reach nearly opposite conclusions about Jonson's essential poetic personality. In "'A More Secret Cause': The Wit of Jonson's Poetry," in *A Celebration of Ben Jonson*, ed. William Blisset, Julian Patrick, and R. W. Van Fossen (Toronto: University of Toronto Press, 1973), Hugh Maclean sees in Jonson a commitment at once to "reasoned judgment" and to "a deeply imagined and very Elizabethan pleasure in the perception of resemblance and analogy" (p. 139), and argues, as I do not, for the dominance of the latter commitment in the poems, the former in the plays.

3. The text I use is that in vol. 8 of *Ben Jonson*, ed. C. H. Herford and Percy and Evelyn Simpson (Oxford: Oxford University Press, 1925–1952). All other citations are from this volume.

4. Raymond Williams has noted Jonson's "exclusive" tendency in this poem in *The Country and the City* (Oxford: Oxford University Press, 1973), p. 28. Arthur Marotti notes Jonson's tendency to define things by saying what they are not (225); G. A. E. Parfitt regards Jonson's exclusions as a narrowing of world view that makes his other strengths possible, in "Ethical Thought in Ben Jonson's Poetry," *SEL* 9 (1969), esp. pp. 132–33.

5. Jonas A. Barish, *Ben Jonson and the Language of Prose Comedy* (Cambridge, Mass.: Harvard University Press, 1960), pp. 69–77.

6. *Discoveries*, 935–36, Herford & Simpson, 8: 592. It is just possible that Jonson intends to include in his praise the entire *De Augmentiis Scientiarum*. The praise itself and the negative form that it takes nonetheless indicate the peculiar sympathy of mind between the two men.

7. Marjorie Hope Nicolson repeatedly and casually cites Bacon as being an exception to the general rule of his time, in *The Breaking of the Circle*, rev. ed. (New York: Columbia University Press, 1960).

8. *The New Organon and Related Writings*, ed. Fulton H. Anderson (Indianapolis and New York: Bobbs-Merrill, 1960).

9. *The Advancement of Learning*, ed. G. W. Kitchin (New York: Everyman's Library, 1869).

10. This somewhat extreme statement runs counter to most overall impressions of Jonson. I believe it to be true, however, that *construction*, rather than an easier and more simple *perception*, is necessary to make any kind of detailed sense out of Jonson's ethical and literary pronouncements. This difficulty is noted in passing by Greene in "Centered Self" (330). See also James D. Redwine, Jr., *Ben Jonson's Literary Criticism* (Loncoln: University of Nebraska Press, 1970), p. xii.

11. *Ben Jonson's Poems: A Study of the Plain Style* (Stanford: Stanford University Press, 1962), p. 156.

12. *Francis Bacon and Renaissance Prose* (Cambridge: Cambridge University Press, 1968), p. 58.

13. *Advancement of Learning* 2.17.7. See Paolo Rossi's "Logic, Rhetoric, and Method," in *Francis Bacon: From Magic to Science*, trans. Sacha Rabinovitch (London: Routledge & Kegan Paul, 1968), pp. 135–51.

14. There was a possible change towards the end of his career that might have made possible larger works. See the conclusion of this paper and the remarks of Greene, "Centered Self" (347–48).

15. Vickers, p. 63.

16. John Danby, *Eliabethan and Jacobean Poets* (London: Faber and Faber, n.d.), p. 31.

17. See Lawrence Stone, *The Crisis of the Aristocracy, 1558–1641*, abridged ed. (New York: Oxford University Press, 1967), pp. 36–95.

18. Stephen Orgel, *The Jonsonian Masque* (Cambridge, Mass.: Harvard University Press, 1965), pp. 61–80.

19. John J. Enck, *Jonson and the Comic Truth* (Madison: University of Wisconsin Press, 1966), p. 15.

20. Perhaps it is unfair to think of the task of the editor as the negative one of excluding error rather than as the positive one of creating truth and beauty. But in many cases, including Jonson's, surely the negative conception is in large part correct.

21. See Trimpi, *Ben Jonson's Poems*, esp. pp. 136–59.

22. It is notable that the plain style, which is supposed to support and convey these understandings, is itself largely defined by what it is not rather than by what it is. See Trimpi, *Ben Jonson's Poems*, pp. 3–75.

23. Curiously, Herford & Simpson omit the folio period after *Ben*, thus insisting on and making inevitable the enjambment. Just the opposite would be more in accord with Jonson's usual practice, hence my restoration of it.

The English Institute, 1976

In Memoriam: William K. Wimsatt
1907–1975

All of us know how the very absence of a person can be a living presence. When Professor Garber spoke of the labyrinth as "icon of human society" and when Professor Barber prefaced his talk by a distinction between Shakespeare's personality and the "achieved winning of art," we were continuing a conversation with W. K. Wimsatt. Scholars are not only students of the past; our experience at the English Institute demonstrates that we are also students of one another. A great teacher and critic, like a great poet, remains constantly with us.

One of W. K. Wimsatt's strengths as a teacher and critic was his intellectual rigor. Even when he marked a paper "Excellent!" his student would find the pages completely interlineated with questions, stylistic improvements, and pointed comments on ambiguities, circular arguments, or elegant variations. Wimsatt insisted both on the logic and economy that he prized so much in chess problems and on grace and vividness. In response to one draft of my dissertation on Jean Paul, he said, "You have been reading too many Germans." Always forthright about his opinions, he was driven to speak by principles even larger than himself. At times his pursuit of truth through mental combat forced him to take both sides of a debate, as in his essays on the poem as organic form and as battered object. That mental balance, the humanity and spirit of generosity made him a fit heir to Coleridge.

If he was a hard-liner, "frankly polemical," in his construction of contraries, he lured us into the realm of his concerns by his imagination and warmth. When you walked into his office, lined with books, Pope portraits, journals, and rocks, he would push toward you his latest project in order to elicit your opinion and provoke a response. To make a point about Plato he might pull an old Pogo strip from his wallet or refer you to an example of op art. His hobbies and his critical theses were not hobby horses, because they had to be of interest to some other person. As he said in his Christmas Book on chess, "There is no human passion or concern which can flourish except as a transaction between persons."

All his passions were interrelated, as readers of that Christmas Book know. He showed and presented rocks to his students with that same thoughtful scrutiny and cherishing delight of participation that made him a great critic. I think he was especially fond of geodes, "the charmed closure of the whole," whose beauty is revealed when open.

Teaching was one of Wimsatt's passions, and as a teacher Wimsatt gave himself to his students. The last night of his life, lying uncomfortably in the hospital, he graded the papers for his undergraduate course. Those undergraduates set up in his memory a chess table inscribed with these lines:

> The generous critic fanned the poet's fire,
> And taught the world with reason to admire.

Margaret R. Higonnet
The University of Connecticut

The Program

Friday, September 3, through Monday, September 6, 1976

I. Marlowe

Directed by Alvin B. Kernan, Princeton University

Fri. 1:45 P.M. "Infinite Riches in a Little Room": Closure and Enclosure in Marlowe
Marjorie Garber, Yale University

Sat. 9:30 A.M. Marlowe and Renaisance Self-Fashioning
Stephen J. Greenblatt, The University of California, Berkeley

Sat. 11:00 A.M. Marlowe and the Histrionics of Ravishment
Michael Goldman, Princeton University

II. Psychoanalysis and Criticism

Directed by Richard Onorato, Brandeis University

Fri. 3:15 P.M. The Family in Shakespeare's Development: The Tragedy of the Sacred
Cesar Lombardi Barber, The University of California, Santa Cruz

Sat. 1:45 P.M. Scientific Art and *The Interpretation of Dreams*
Paul Schwaber, Wesleyan University

Sat. 3:15 P.M. Psychoanalysis: The French Connection
Geoffrey Hartman, Yale University

III. Reading

Directed by Stanley Fish, The Johns Hopkins University

Sun. 9:30 A.M. One Reader Reading
Norman Holland, The State University of New York, Buffalo

Sun. 11:00 A.M. Reading in the Performance of Writing
Richard Poirier, Rutgers University

Mon. 9:30 A.M. The Unobserved and All Observers
Stephen Booth, The University of California, Berkeley

Mon. 11:00 A.M. Prolegomena to a Theory of Reading
Jonathan Culler, Brasenose College, Oxford

IV. The Postwar American Novel
    Directed by Morris Dickstein, Queens College, City University of New York

Sun. 1:45 P.M.	Contemporary American Fiction: An Overview *Richard Locke, The New York Times Book Review*
Sun. 3:15 P.M.	History, Paranoia, and the Novel *Leo Braudy, Columbia University*
Mon. 1:45 P.M.	Kafka Logic *Leonard Michaels, The University of California, Berkeley*
Mon. 3:15 P.M.	Other People: Social Texture in the Postwar Novel *Philip Stevick, Temple University*

Registrants, 1976

Michael Vannoy Adams, Brandeis University; Ruth M. Adams, Dartmouth College; Paul Alpers, University of California, Berkeley; Svetlana Alpers, University of California, Berkeley; Valborg Anderson, Brooklyn College, CUNY; Jonathan Arac, Princeton University; Alberta Arthurs, Harvard University; Nina Auerbach, University of Pennsylvania

George W. Bahlke, Kirkland College; C. L. Barber, University of California, Santa Cruz; James E. Barcus, Houghton College; J. Robert Barth, University of Missouri-Columbia; John E. Becker, Fairleigh Dickinson University; Lawrence Benaquist, Keene State College; John B. Bender, Stanford University; Todd K. Bender, University of Wisconsin; Carole Berger, Dartmouth College; David Berndt, Boston University; Warner Berthoff, Harvard University; Lawrence Besserman, Harvard; Murray Biggs, MIT; Haskell M. Block, SUNY-Binghampton; Morton W. Bloomfield, Harvard; Charles Blyth, Cambridge, MA; Sally Boland, Plymouth State College; Stephen Booth, University of California-Berkeley; Paul Bové, Columbia University; Robert Boyers, Skidmore College; John D. Boyd, Fordham University; Leo Braudy, Columbia University; Susan H. Brisman, Vassar College; Marianne Brock, Mount Holyoke College; Leonora Leet Brodwin, St. John's University; Christine Brooke-Rose, Wellfleet, MA; Elizabeth Bergen Brophy, College of New Rochelle; James D. Brophy, Iona College; Barbara Brothers, Youngstown State University; Maurice F. Brown, Oakland University; Nicholas K. Browne, Harvard University; Elizabeth Bruss, Amherst College; Daniel Burke, La Salle College; Richard A. Burt, SUNY-Buffalo; Andrew Busza, University of British Columbia; Mervin Butovsky, Concordia University

Terry P. Caesar, Clarion State College; John Cameron, Amherst College; Ruth A. Cameron, Eastern Nazarene College; Margaret Canavan, College of New Rochelle; Virginia M. Carr, Clark University; William C. Carroll, Boston University; David Cavitch, Tufts University; Thomas H. Chalfant, Alabama State University; Cynthia Chase, Yale University; Ralph A. Ciancio, Skidmore College; Dietmar Claas, SUNY-Buffalo; James L. Clifford, Columbia University; Paul Clogan, North Texas State University; Richard Cody, Amherst College; M. Donald Coleman, NY Psychoanalytic Institute;

Arthur N. Collins, SUNY-Albany; Margaret Comstock, New York University; Frederick W. Conner, University of Alabama; John A. Costello, Marymount Manhattan College; Patricia Craddock, Boston University; G. Armour Craig, Amherst College; Martha Craig, Wellesley College; Robert Crosman, Providence, RI; Jonathan Culler, Brasenose College, Oxford

Emily K. Dalgarno, Boston University; Ruth Danon, University of Connecticut; Winifred M. Davis, Columbia University; Robert Adams Day, CUNY; Raymond M. Deck, Jr., Brandeis; Robert DeMaria, Vassar College; Joanne T. Dempsey, Harvard University; Morris Dickstein, Queens College, CUNY; Joanne Feit Diehl, Kenyon College; Evelyn C. Dodge, Framingham State College; Stephen Donadio, Columbia University; E. Talbot Donaldson, Indiana University; Sister Rose Bernard Donna, The College of Saint Rose; John H. Dorenkamp, Holy Cross College; Charles T. Dougherty, University of Missouri; Anne Doyle, Mount Holyoke College; Georgia Dunbar, Hofstra University; Norma E. Dunn, University of Maryland

Delbert L. Earisman, Upsala College; Doris L. Eder, University of Rochester; Dwight Eddins, University of Alabama; John C. Elder, Middlebury College; Robert C. Elliott, University of California, San Diego; David A. Ellis, Tufts University; Monroe Engel, Harvard; Edward Engelberg, Brandeis University; Martha W. England, Queens College-CUNY; David Erdman, SUNY-Stony Brook; Peter Erickson, Williams College; Sister Marie Eugénie, Immaculata College

George Fayen, New Haven, CT; Susan Feinberg, Purdue University; Arthur Fenner, Wayne County Community College; Jean Fenner, Wayne County Community College; Anne Lathrop Fessenden, Willow, NY; Philip J. Finkelpearl, University of Massachusetts; Stanley Fish, Johns Hopkins University; Philip Fisher, Brandeis University; Angus Fletcher, CUNY; Edward G. Fletcher, The University of Texas; Jeanne Flood, Wayne State University; Dean Flower, Smith College; Ephim Fogel, Cornell University; Leslie D. Foster, Northern Michigan University; Sheila Casey Flynn, J. Sargeant Reynolds Community College; Richard Lee Francis, Western Washington State College; Michael Frank, University of Chicago; Warren G. French, Indiana University; Michael Fried, Johns Hopkins University; Albert B. Friedman, Claremont Graduate School; William Frost, University of California-Santa Barbara; Northrop Frye, Massey College, University of Toronto; Margaretta Fulton, Harvard University Press

Susan L. Galleck, Connecticut College; Marjorie Garber, Yale University; Burdett Gardner, Monmouth College; Blanche H. Gelfant, Dartmouth College; Jessie A. Gilmer, Staten Island Community College; Michael T. Gilmore, Brandeis University; Lorrie Goldensohn, Goddard College; Michael Goldman, Princeton University; Herbert Goldstone, University of Connecticut; George Goodin, Southern Illinois University; David J. Gordon, CUNY Graduate Center; Michael T. Gosman, The Catholic University of America; Joseph Graham, SUNY-Binghampton; Vernon Gras, George Mason University; Lawrence Graver, Williams College; James Gray, Dalhousie University; Stephen J. Greenblatt, University of California, Berkeley; Robert A. Greene, University of Toronto; Allen R. Grossban, Brandeis; Allen Guttmann, Amherst College; Stanley T. Gutman, University of Vermont

Claire Hahn, Fordham University; Mason Harris, Simon Fraser University; Victor Harris, Brandeis; Joan E. Hartman, Staten Island Community College, CUNY; Geoffrey Hartman, Yale University; Richard Haven, University of Massachusetts; Michael Hays, Columbia University; Ray L. Heffner, Jr., The University of Iowa; Margaret R. Higonnet, University of Connecticut; William B. Hill, University of Scranton; C. Fenno Hoffman, Jr., Rhode Island School of Design; Daniel Hoffman, University of Pennsylvania; Norman N. Holland, SUNY-Buffalo; Alan M. Hollingsworth, Michigan State University; Laurence B. Holland, Johns Hopkins University; Benjamin Hoover, Brandeis; Suzanne R. Hoover, Sudbury, MA; Vivian C. Hopkins, SUNY-Albany; Bernard Horn, Northern Essex Community College; Frederick D. Horn, Westminster College; Susan R. Horton, University of Massachusetts; Chaviva Hošek, University of Toronto; Clifford C. Huffman, SUNY-Stony Brook

Gabriele Bernhard Jackson, Temple University; Katherine R. Jackson, Bowdoin College; Lee A. Jacobus, University of Connecticut; Daniel Javitch, Columbia University; Nora Crow Jaffe, Smith College; Edward Jayne, University of Massachusetts; Claudia D. Johnson, University of Alabama; Richard A. Johnson, Mt. Holyoke College; Judith L. Johnston, Columbia University; Michael P. Jones, Canton, MA

Ethel R. Kaplan, Harvard; Judith A. Kates, Harvard; Carol McGinnis Kay, University of Alabama; Marjorie Kaufman, Mt. Holyoke College; Patrick J. Keane, Skidmore College; Winifred G. Keaney, George Mason University;

Helen Kensick, University of Massachusetts; Alvin B. Kernan, Princeton University; Rudolf Kirk, Rutgers University; Theodora J. Koob, Shippensburg State College; Michael Kowal, Queens College; Lawrence Kramer, University of Pennsylvania; Victor A. Kramer, Georgia State University; Karl Kroeber, Columbia University; Maire T. Kurrik, Barnard College

J. Craig La Driere, Harvard; G. P. Lair, Delbarton School; Roy Lamson, Massachusetts Institute of Technology; Jon Lanham, Northeastern University; John Lauber, University of Alberta; Penelope Laurans, Yale University; Lyman L. Leathers, Ohio Wesleyan University; Nancy Leonard, University of Pennsylvania; David Levin, University of Virginia; Alan Levitan, Brandeis; Thomas S. H. Lewis, Skidmore College; Ely M. Liebow, Northeastern Ill. University; Lawrence Lipking, Princeton University; A. Walton Litz, Princeton University; Richard Locke, The New York Times Book Review; Joanne Long, Rutgers University; Joseph P. Lovering, Canisius College; Sister Alice Lubin, College of St. Elizabeth

Isabel G. MacCaffrey, Harvard University; Richard C. McCoy, College of New Rochelle; Bernard MacDonald, Eastern Connecticut State College; Warren J. MacIsaac, Catholic University; Daniel Marder, University of Tulsa; Paul Mariani, University of Mass.; James E. Marlow, SE Mass. University; Arthur F. Marotti, Wayne State University; Walter Bland Mathis, The Citadel; Howard Mayer, University of Connecticut; Heather McClave, Harvard University; Stuart Y. McDougal, University of Michigan; Bernard McElroy, Loyola University of Chicago; Margaret R. McGavran, U. Mass-Boston; Terence J. McKenzie, U.S. Coast Guard Academy; Donald C. Mell, Jr., University of Delaware; Leonard Michaels, University of California, Berkeley; John H. Middendorf, Columbia University; Alice Miskimin, Yale University; Robert T. Mundhenk, Fordham University; Rosemary J. Mundhenk, Lehigh University

Rae Ann Nager, Harvard University; Jack Nelson, Agnes Scott College; John Nesselhof, Wells College; Alicia K. Nitecki, Somerville, MA; Donald R. Noble, University of Alabama; Barbara Nolan, Washington University; Gerda Norvig, Ben Gurion University

John S. O'Connor, George Mason University; James Olney, North Carolina Central University; Richard Onorato, Brandeis University; Stephen Orgel, Johns Hopkins University; James M. Osborn, Yale University; Charles A. Owen, Jr., University of Connecticut

Morton D. Paley, Boston University; Stephen Maxfield Parrish, Cornell University; Coleman O. Parsons, CUNY; Robert L. Patten, Rice University; John Patrick Pattinson, New Jersey Institute of Technology; Emily H. Patterson, San Diego State University; Felix L. Paul, West Virginia State College; Richard Pearce, Wheaton College; Alan D. Perlis, University of Alabama; Patricia Petsch, Brandeis University; Burton Pike, Queens College, CUNY; N. S. Poburko, Dalhousie University; Richard Poirier, Rutgers University; Jonathan F. S. Post, Yale University; Robert O. Preyer, Brandeis; John W. Price, The Middlesex School; Carmine Prioli, Tufts University; Matthew N. Proser, University of Connecticut; Max Putzel, University of Connecticut

Shaista Rahman, Brooklyn College-CUNY; Gideon Rappaport, Brandeis; Joan E. Reardon, Barat College; Donald H. Reiman, The Carl H. Pforzheimer Library; Louis A. Renza, Dartmouth College; Amy K. Richards, Wayne State University; Eleanor N. Richwine, Western Maryland College; Keith N. Richwine, Western Maryland College; Harriet Ritvo, American Academy of Arts and Sciences; Susannah Robbins, Vassar College; Adrianne Roberts-Baytop, Douglass College, Rutgers University; Phyllis Rose, Wesleyan University; Rebecca D. Ruggles, CUNY, Brooklyn College; Richard Ruland, Washington University; Roberta Russell, University of Connecticut; Lorraine Ryan, University of Rhode Island

Elaine B. Safer, University of Delaware; Nancy K. Salter, Eastern Connecticut State College; Thomas N. Salter, Eastern Connecticut State College; Dorothy Ione J. Samuel, Tennessee State University; Paul S. Schiffer, University of California at Santa Cruz; Ben Schlerfer, Chestnut Hill College; Helene B. M. Schnabel, New York, NY; Joseph L. Schneider, Curry College; H. T. Schultz, Dartmouth; Paul Schwaber, Wesleyan University; L. F. Sells, Westminster College; Joan R. Sherman, Rutgers University; Susan Shwartz, Harvard; Deborah Ayer Sitter, University of Massachusetts; Patricia L. Skarda, Smith College; Jennie Skerl, Utica College of Syracuse University; Janet Levarie Smarr, University of Boston; Alex Smith, University of Connecticut; Carol Smith, Douglass College, Rutgers University; Jane Smith, Northwestern University; Paul Smith, Trinity College; Sarah W. R. Smith, Tufts University; Mark Spilka, Brown University; Robert Spiller, University of Pennsylvania; Robert Sprich, Bentley College; Thomas F. Staley, University of Tulsa; Jeremiah P. Starling, University of Louisville; Susan Staves, Brandeis University; A. Wilber Stevens, University of Nevada; Holly Stevens, Yale University;

John W. Stevenson, Converse College; Ruth MacDonald Stevenson, Union College; Philip Stevick, Temple University; Fred E. Stockholder, University of British Columbia; Albert Stone, Jr., Hellenic College; Rudolf F. Storch, Tufts University; Bruce Stovel, Dalhousie University; Jean Sudrann, Mount Holyoke College; Maureen Sullivan, Marquette University; William Sullivan, Keene State College; Stanley Sultan, Clark University; Donald R. Swanson, Wright State University; Peter Swiggart, Brandeis University

Ann M. Taylor, Salem State College; Ruth Z. Temple, CUNY; Elizabeth B. Tenenbaum, Herbert Lehman College, CUNY; Leonard Tennenhouse, Wayne State University; Robert D. Thornton, SUNY-New Paltz; David Tomlinson, U.S. Naval Academy; Robert Towers, Queens College, CUNY; Henry S. Traeger, Columbia University; C. J. Trotman, Lincoln University; Lewis A. Turlish, Bates College; Molly B. Turlish, Bates College; Ralph M. Tutt, Jr., Narragansett, RI

Robert W. Uphaus, Michigan State University

Richard Velen, Wittenburg University; Helen Vendler, Boston University; Howard P. Vincent, Romona College

Willis Wager, Boston University; Eugene M. Waith, Yale University; Andrews Wanning, Bard College; Emily M. Wallace, Philadelphia, PA; Aileen Ward, New York University; Herbert S. Weil, Jr., University of Connecticut; Judith R. Weil, Storrs, CT; Sister Mary Anthony Weinig, Rosemont College; Philip J. West, Skidmore College; Laura J. Wexler, Columbia University; Lawrence Wharton, University of Alabama; Robert Ogden White, Massachusetts College of Pharmacy; Ruth Whitman, Radcliffe Institute; Roger E. Wiehe, University of Lowell; Epi Wiese, Harvard University; Joseph Weisenfarth, University of Wisconsin; Maud E. Wilcox, Harvard University; Marilyn L. Williamson, Wayne State University; Mrs. W. K. Wimsatt, New Haven, CT; Joan D. Winslow, College of the Holy Cross; Nancy Wolcott, New York University; Thomas J. Wolfe, Brandeis University; Michael Wood, Columbia University, Linda L. Woods, Agnes Scott College

Library of Congress Cataloging in Publication Data

English Institute.
    Two Renaissance mythmakers, Christopher Marlowe and
Ben Jonson.

    (Selected papers from the English Institute ; 1975-76,
new ser. 1)

    1. Marlowe, Christopher, 1564-1593—Criticism and
interpretation—Addresses, essays, lectures. 2. Jonson, Ben,
1573?-1637—Criticism and interpretation—Addresses, essays,
lectures. I. Kernan, Alvin B. II. Title. III. Series: English
Institute. Selected papers from the English Institute ; new
ser. 1.
PR2674.E5 1977   822'.3'09   77-3518
ISBN 0-8018-1971-7